First published in 2019 by Barrallier Books Pty Ltd,
trading as Echo Books

Registered Office: 35—37 Gordon Avenue, West Geelong, Victoria 3220, Australia.

www.echobooks.com.au

Copyright ©Allan Hawke

Creator: Hawke, Allan: Author.

Title: Calamity and Conquest: A chronicle of the convict Joseph Blundell and his consort Susan Osborne

ISBN: 9780648554059 Paperback

NATIONAL LIBRARY OF AUSTRALIA

A catalogue record for this book is available from the National Library of Australia

Book layout and design by Peter Gamble, Canberra.
Set in Garamond Premier Pro Display, 12/17 and Garamond Premier Pro Semibold Display

www.echobooks.com.au

Calamity
and
Conquest

A chronicle of the convict Joseph Blundell
and his consort Susan Osborne

Blundells' Cottage, Canberra

David Flannery 2017

Allan Hawke

Contents

Diagrams and Pictures

Dedication

I have had the great fortune to be married to Maria Michele Senti for 42 years. A book about her Italian/Sicilian family history is nearing completion.

We have been blessed with a daughter who is a PhD in Clinical Psychology, a son-in-law with Ernst and Young, a two-year old fun-filled grand-daughter and a newly born grandson.

This work—which is dedicated to them—shows how they are descended from my maternal grandmother's lines and the associated family history.

My favourite singer-songwriter-troubadour Harry Chapin, was posthumously awarded the Congressional Gold Medal in 1987—the highest civilian award in the USA. It will be up to Rosa and Harry to stoke the flames of that passion and inspiration to keep his legacy alive.

The Gold Medal Collection includes a few vignettes of Harry reflecting on the meaning of life and the causes/issues he was involved with during his time, pointing to the sense of the personal and the necessity of situating whatever you do in the context of the larger picture—the social and political dimensions—and the inherent difficulties of integrating those competing forces. He sums it up by quoting a Pete Seeger aphorism:

> 'I can tell you one thing, that involvement with these issues means you are involved with the good people, the people with the live hearts, the live eyes and the live heads.'

Consider the people you associate with—your friends and the people you keep coming back to—the people who make your life worthwhile—it's usually those that are committed to something.

In the final analysis, commitment in and of itself irrespective of whether you win is truly something that will make your life worthwhile. If you care enough you can have an impact. We can maximise the brief flicker of time we have on this planet by being hungry for experience and meaning. You can be very effective if you want to be.

Allan Hawke
14 June 2019

Foreword

Fortuitously, 14 June 2019 will be remembered for the Memorial Service of the Honourable Robert James Lee Hawke AC at the Opera House. We were acquaintances and served on the Committee for the Economic Development of Australia Board of Governors together. The Penzance-Truro area of Cornwall is where we originate from, although I haven't yet found the link between our ancestral lines. Bob was Labor's longest serving Prime Minister—from 11 March 1983 until 20 December 1991—when he was deposed by Paul Keating.

At that time, I was the Deputy Secretary of Strategy and Intelligence in the Department of Defence and we were having a holiday at Maria's parent's Orchard Farm at Wamoon near Leeton. I was immediately recalled to duty to brief the new Prime Minister on the USA Alliance and our broader intelligence relationships. Thinking this would be a reasonably short briefing I turned up at the Parliament House Office to find it was just me and the new Prime Minister who took copious notes in a Stenographer's Handbook as he interrogated me up hill and down dale for some two hours. I had occasional interactions with him after that including a discussion that led to the acquisition of additional FIIIs.

To my surprise, I became Paul's Chief of Staff (having declined an offer to be Opposition Leader John Howard's Chief of Staff in the late 80s) from August 1993 until March 1994. That brief period is filled with defining moments in Australian history—to be the subject of a separate book. An *amuse-bouche* includes:

- establishing the APEC Leader's Forum and the associated recalcitrant remark about Prime Minister Mahathir of Malaysia;
- the MABO legislation, which the Opposition disagreed with and fought every step along the way;
- reform of the Commonwealth Heads of Government Meeting;
- meetings with the Queen at Balmoral and Limassol;
- winning the Sydney 2000 Olympic Games at Monte Carlo in Monaco;
- conclusion of the Uruguay Round of the Multilateral Trade Negotiations;
- the Republic issue; and
- the State Visit to Ireland where Paul addressed the Dail Eireann and visited the village of his ancestors.

We were present for the exhumation from Adelaide War Cemetery outside Villers Bretonneux of the Unknown Australia Soldier. The Reinterment Ceremony on Remembrance Day 1993 at the Australian War Memorial was accompanied by the best speech ever given by any Australian in my view. It sits proudly on the left-hand side column at the entrance to the Hall of Memory.

Keating had an extraordinary vision for Australia and its place in the World and especially—in and with Asia. Every initiative was tested to see whether and how it fitted into that picture before proceeding. Successive Prime Ministers since then have eschewed 'the vision thing '—to our detriment as a nation.

Acknowledgements

L et me first acknowledge David Flannery for the frontispiece illustration.

The National Capital Authority restored this workman's Cottage on the eastern shores of Lake Burley Griffin in Canberra's Parliamentary Triangle and re-opened it towards the end of 2018. It is named after Joseph and Susan Blundell's third child George who lived there for over 50 years.

In these days of dedicated genealogy software, the Internet, on-line records, personal computers and search engines much of my correspondence about our Blundell ancestry with Dorothea Teague and hired specialists in England in the 1980s and 1990s was *via* air mail and sometimes 'snail mail'.

Exchanges of letters, telephone calls and visits to people and places in Australia and Britain also constitute an important input, especially our trips to England in 2016 and 2018 to complete the research for what follows. That said, a work of this kind is never finished as other details and lines of enquiry inevitably arise.

Mrs Teague's 90 pages about *Shadrach Blundell His Family and Property 1580-1880* was published in 1985. She then completed a significantly revised edition called *Shadrach Blundell His Family and Property 1580 to Modern Times* of some 220 pages. Published in 2003, this version also deals with some other Australian Blundell lines and their derivation—it's still in print and obtainable from www.synjonbooks.co.uk

I recommend readers get a copy to enjoy the twists and turns of the Blundell Family's Lost Inheritance together with the characters involved and our ancestral background, as an adjunct to my synopsis and the further detail provided herein.

Borrowing a maxim quoted by Mrs Teague explains why we share an obsession with delving into our roots:

> 'A lively desire of knowing and of recording our ancestors so generally prevails, that it must depend on the influence of some common principle in the minds of men. We seem to have lived in the person of our forefathers. Our imagination is always active to enlarge the narrow circle in which nature has confined us. Fifty or 100 years may be allotted to an individual; but we step forward beyond death with such hopes as religion and philosophy suggest; and we fill up the silent vacancy that precedes our birth by associating ourselves to the authors of our existence.'[1]

Dorothea's son Tony has shared some critical information about Chapters Three and Four and suggested other lines of enquiry. I was fortunate to meet Tony and his wife Rebecca in August 2018.

Pam Glover, who is descended from Thomas Blundell (the brother of Joseph the convict's Father) contacted me out of the blue in the latter half of 2017. Our exchanges about Wills, analyses of their content and implications and her painstaking forensic work on dates, names and places has significantly benefitted Chapters Three and Four. We met up in Paris in 2018 to discuss our mutual interests—while our spouses feigned interest.

I am grateful for Pam's ongoing efforts and assistance as we try to verify and document the lines of descent prior to the known record which starts with John of Bletchingley in Chapter Three.

Patricia Evans drew my attention to an 1842 newspaper clipping which solved the problem of 'Susan Osborne's' real name. William Good's article

---

1   *Memoirs of My Life and Writings* Introduction Edward Gibbon.

about that discovery is drawn on in Chapter Seven. Pam Elliott reviewed the penultimate draft of that Chapter and mentioned William Good's—*A Forest of Blanches–the Story of the Blanch Family 1838-1988.*

Many Blundell relatives and other people have also helped with this story and I have tried to recognise significant contributions in the text or as a footnote in the Chapters that follow.

I also want to thank my son-in-law Matthew Whittaker and nephew David Heness for their assistance with research and sorting out various technical matters and computer issues.

Although this work might not always meet the exacting standards of a professional historian, considerable effort has been expended to ensure the accuracy of dates, places and other details cited.

As we will see, history is usually dictated through the lens of the participants, being presented in a polished and laundered manner to conceal and/or varnish the truth.

Some inclusions border on self-indulgence, but they provide a quite different take than the usually accepted view. They also serve as a backdrop to the picture of our ancestry as well as being of intrinsic interest.

About the Author

D r Allan Hawke AC, FAICD, FIML[1], FIPAA is a great great grandson of Joseph Blundell and 'Susan Osborne' through the 10th of their 11 children—Rosanna Meech (née Blundell).

Born at Royal Canberra Hospital on 18 February 1948, Allan moved to the family home at 13 Bruce Street Queanbeyan three days later, attending Harris Park Pre-school, Isabella Street Infants and Primary, and Queanbeyan High where he was School Captain, completing the Leaving Certificate in 1965.

Probably the first of his extended family to finish High School, he went on to The Australian National University—graduating with a First Class Honours Bachelor of Science degree (1970) and Doctor of Philosophy (1976).

Allan joined the Commonwealth Public Service in 1974 through the selective Administrative Trainee Scheme with the Public Service Board, rising through the ranks to Deputy Secretary Strategy and Intelligence in Defence in 1991 and Deputy Secretary in the Department of the Prime Minister and Cabinet in 1994.

He was Chief of Staff to Prime Minister Paul Keating in 1993-1994; Secretary of Veterans' Affairs from 1994-1996; Secretary of Transport and Regional Services from 1996-1999 and Secretary of Defence from 1999-2002.

---

1   Formerly the Australian Institute of Management.

His final posting was High Commissioner to New Zealand after which he *retired* to become The Australian National University's 10th Chancellor on 28 February 2006—the only graduate of his *alma mater* to hold that prestigious position.

In a similar vein, Allan is the only Secretary of Defence to receive a Farewell Parade with full military honours—in October 2002—presided over by then Chief of the Defence Force General Peter Cosgrove AC MC who went on to be knighted as Governor General of Australia. *Inter alia*, General Cosgrove said:

> '... For today this great Department, 80000 servicemen and women of the ADF and the men and women of the public service farewell one of their finest: a man who has served his profession, his colleagues and his country with the greatest distinction.'

Dr Hawke became a Fellow of the Australian Institute of Public Administration in 1998[2] and Fellow of the Institute of Management and Leaders in 1999 in recognition of his outstanding contribution to public service. He was awarded Fellow of the Australian Institute of Company Directors in 2001, the same year that *The Australian Financial Review*'s 'Boss' Magazine named him as one of Australia's top 30 true leaders in its inaugural list.

In 2003, he was a Centenary Medal recipient—only the third specific Australian Commemorative award. Created to mark Australia's 100 years of Federation, it was bestowed on people considered to have contributed to Australian society or government and laid solid foundations for the nation's future.

Dr Hawke received Australia's highest civilian honour when appointed a Companion in the General Division of the Order of Australia in the 2010 Queen's Birthday List for eminent service to public administration, particularly through the formulation and implementation of policy in

---

2   He was subsequently made a National Fellow and Lifetime Member of the ACT Division in recognition of his outstanding contribution to the study and practice of public administration.

the areas of defence, transport and education, and strengthening bilateral relations with New Zealand.

When conferring the honour, Governor General Quentin Bryce commended:

> '... his prolific and sustained contribution to public service over many years, dedication to serving the Australian public and reputation for boundless energy, exemplary leadership and management skills. During his diverse range of national and international appointments, he has been at the forefront of public policy reform, development and implementation that will be of lasting benefit to our nation.'

Allan represented Queanbeyan High School in athletics, rugby union and swimming at the ACT District level, and the ACT in the latter two pursuits at NSW championships. He was one of 60 inductees at the launch of Queanbeyan's Sporting Gallery in 1993 as the 1965 NSW Royal Lifesaving Society's 'Iron Man' Champion (having come third in 1964 and second in 1966). He was also one of Queanbeyan's 22 most notable citizens who had a plaque recognising their achievements unveiled when the Queanbeyan Honour Walk was established in Crawford Street on 28 September 2012.

Genevieve Jacobs, host of the ABC's 666 Morning Program called Allan 'The Last of the Great Mandarins' when commenting on his appointment as Chairman of the Southern NSW Local Health District Board in August 2017.

Allan is one of 25 eminent Australians on the Committee for the Economic Development of Australia Leadership Council. His other current appointments include Non-Executive Director of Lockheed Martin Australia; Chairman of the Canberra Raiders and Chairman of the Canberra University Campus Development Joint Venture. He is Patron of Respite Care Queanbeyan and until recently was ACT Cricket Patron, Chairman of Trusted Systems and Solutions and President of Barnardos ACT.

From 2006 to 2016, he undertook 21 independent enquiries on an eclectic range of subjects for the Federal, ACT, NSW, NT and Victorian Governments.

Allan struggles with golf and writes about family history and Australian leadership as well as coaching, mentoring and speechifying on the latter subject.

One
Introduction

The inspiration for this work arose from various sources. First, my elder brother John's persistence in pursuing the Hawke genealogy. Second, Australia's Bicentennial and the Centenary of Canberra. And third, reading such books as Marcus Clarke's *For the Term of His Natural Life*, Robert Hughes' *The Fatal Shore* and Samuel Shumack's *Tales and Legends of Canberra's Pioneers* which mentions Joseph Blundell as one of the true pioneers of what is now the national capital.

As Hughes points out, until the end of the 1970s Australia was affected by collective amnesia—a national pact of silence about convict ancestry—a stain on history which contributed mightily to our well-known cultural cringe. Little was written on the experiences and lives of such men and women.

Family history research revolves around answering four basic questions:

- where did they come from?
- why did they come to Australia?
- how did they get here?
- when did they arrive and subsequent developments?

My discovery that Joseph Blundell was a convict stimulated efforts to find out more about his antecedents and the fate of his 11 children, having completed the study of my great grandmother Rosanna (the 10th child).

Joseph's 'wife' remained a mystery until relatively recently when it turned out that—like Joseph—her declared *history* was fictitious and that she had created the 'Susan Osborne' pseudonym to conceal her real identity and background.

This then, is the story of Joseph Blundell and 'Susan Osborne' as well as their origins, feats and family.

A separate publication dealing with Joseph and Susan's 11 children, 75 grandchildren, over 270 great grandchildren and the associated genealogical record is intended to be completed towards the end of 2021.

Origins of the Blundell name

Most sources attribute the Blundell name as deriving from the Old French word 'Blondel' meaning a blond man—fair of hair or complexion. 'Blundr' was an old Norse personal name derived from 'dozing' or 'slumber.[1]

Noted in both Normandy[2] and Breton[3] from the early 10th Century, the first recorded military enterprise involving the Blundell name was in the Holy Wars in Southern Spain against the Moors.[4] Natives of the Barbary States,[5] the Moors were Moslem conquerors of Southern Spain in the 8th Century.

Although there were Crusades[6] against these people in the 9th Century, it was the 10th Century Wars that ousted the Moors from Spain. These battles are considered to be the bloodiest and most uncompromising in history—even in a period when no quarter was asked for and none was given was the norm.

---

1   *The Origin of English Surnames* P H Reaney published by Routledge and Kegan Paul London 1967. 'British Family Names their Origin and Meaning' Reverend Henry Barber Baltimore Genealogical Publishing Company 1968. 'A Dictionary of British Surnames' P H Reaney published by Routledge and Kegan Paul London and Boston 1976.

2   A northern France Province on the English Channel named after the Scandinavians who invaded and settled there in the 10th Century.

3   The Brittany Province on the English Channel in France arising from the celtic language associated with Irish and Welsh invasion and settlement there.

4   Muslim people of mixed Arabian and Berber descent often referred to as 'Saracens'.

5   A coalition of North African States.

6   A series of Papal Holy Wars to defend the Catholic Church and Christians from Islam.

In researching the Blundell name, spelling variations can be problematic. The two 'll's' on the end are sometimes confused for an 'n' (Blunden, Blonden, Blundon) or recorded as only one 'l' (Blundel, Blundle) and in some cases as Blendell, Blondell or Blundall.

The Domesday Book and Chancery Oblata/Fines[7] records from 1066 to 1641 show various versions of the Blundell name, their given names (Henricus, Johan, Jordanus, Radulphus, Sein *etc*) and the places they lived.

Some claim that our family name descends from Blundell de Nesle—a Norman Knight who came to England to fight with William the Conqueror in 1066 and was rewarded with lands in Lancashire. From him stem two venerable families:

- the Ince-Blundells of Blundellsands; and
- the Blundells of Crosby Hall.

No link between our line and theirs has ever been proven, although many have tried to claim the 1620 English Blundell clan Coat of Arms, pointing out the family name on the Roll of Honour of Norman Knights hanging in Battle Church in Sussex—stemming from William Blondell or Henry Blundell who are mentioned in the Roll of Honour.

Joseph was by no means the only Blundell forebear to come to Australia. No Blundells came out on the First Fleet, but convict shipments lists include Frances, Henry, two John's, two Joseph's, Sophia, Stephen and two Thomas's.

If you know or think you might be a descendant of Joseph Blundell or Susan Osborne, please feel free to contact Allan.Hawke@raiders.com.au

Offers and/or suggestions about additional material or corrections to the information contained in this book will be gratefully received.

---

7   Records of payments/offerings to the Crown to facilitate transactions of an administrative or judicial nature.

Two
British History

In the Preface to his remarkable *Gwynne's Kings and Queens* sub-titled *The Indispensable History of England and Her Monarchs*, Gwynne[1] says:

> 'The reality is that our country's history is a fundamental part of what we actually are.'

He observes that teaching history has been downgraded from a mainstream subject in our schools; religion is no longer the centrepiece of people's lives and the British Monarchy is nearing the end of its hold over other Commonwealth nations. Indeed, I hope to live long enough to see Australia become a Republic.

Nowadays many Australians know little about British History and often what they do is an idealistic and carefully whitewashed presentation.

This short summary might tempt readers to read Gwynne's 323-page treatise in its entirety. For those inclined to think some of what follows is fanciful, far-fetched or non-factual—read Gwynne's book and analysis of the sources and judge for yourselves.

Kings, Queens and Royal families seem to have existed since time immemorial with their divine right to rule and reign. In earlier times, some were regarded as Gods themselves and all were expected to marry others of Royal blood.

---

1   *Gwynne's Kings and Queens* by N M Gwynne Ebury Press London 2018.

Gwynne fills the void from Brutus (hence Brittania) the first King of the Britons 957-945BC back to his great grandfather Aeneas[2]—a Prince of Troy from 1104-1081BC and then forward showing the lines of descent and how the various Monarchs are related to each other.

After Brutus conquered Aquitaine—along the Atlantic Ocean of France with the Pyrenees Mountain Range in the south bordering Spain—he set sail for the island called Albion[3] coming ashore near Exeter, subsequently founding a city named New Troy on what came to be called the River Thames.

When Brutus died in 945BC, his co-leader Corineus[4] remained in Cornwall and Brutus' three sons inherited 'England' (Locrinus—called Loegria after him), Scotland (Albanactus—hence Albanian) and Wales (Kamber—hence Cambrian)—explaining how those four parts of Great Britain originated.

King Lud 73-58BC rebuilt the walls of New Troy and fortified the city with many towers. On his death, he was buried at the entrance to the city—Ludgate—which was renamed Kaerlud (the city of Lud) thence Kaerlundein which the Romans took up as Londinium and finally London—one of the world's greatest cities with Paris and New York.

Julius Caeser[5] invaded Britain in 55 and 54BC. It's passing strange that most lists of English Kings start some 900 years later in the AD800s.

Emperor Claudius invaded Britain in 43AD and was defeated by King Arvirargus 43-57 who was succeeded by his son King Marius 57-97.

---

2   The hero of Virgil's *Aeneid* and related to King Priam of Troy.

3   Which was inhabited by a small number of giants who retreated to their caves. The 'perfidious Albion' term denotes acts of deception, duplicity and betrayal in international relations by UK Governments/Monarchs. Albion probably originates from the White Cliffs of Dover.

4   A separate Trojan group leader that joined forces with Brutus—Brutus becoming King of all of them.

5   Gwynne argues that from the time of Caeser's invasions of Britain until the Norman conquest in 1066, the history is largely agreed, but is contestable before and after that.

During Marius' reign, Suetonius Paulinus was Roman Governor. Queen Boudica[6] of the Iceni rebelled in 61 invading Londinium and Verulamium (St Albans) massacring 70000 Romans but eventually being defeated with 80000 Britons being killed. Emporer Nero recalled Suetonius and it wasn't until 78 that Emporer Julius Agricola completed the conquest of Britain.

Emporer Hadrian's period in Britain 119-122 saw the 73-mile stone wall built from Carlisle to Newcastle to restrain the Caledonians (*aka* Picts—painted men) who were constantly invading Britain from Scotland north of the Wall.

After King Lucius 137-186 wrote to the Pope in 156 seeking to become a Christian, two learned men were despatched to do the honours and it was not long before paganism came to an end on the island.

Emperor Severus arrived in 208 and his many attempts to subdue the Caledonians all failed.

The Briton Asclepiodotus defeated the Romans in 296 and became King. In 303 Emporer Diocletian retaliated and sent General Maximanius Herculius to restore Roman rule—he knocked down all the churches, burnt all copies of the holy scriptures and butchered all the priests, side-by-side.

As Rome weakened in the 3rd Century, the Caledonians and Scots[7] invaded Britain's western shores while the eastern coast was harassed by the Angles/Saxons from Germany.

King Constantine I 312-337 went to Rome in 312 to rescue it from the despotic rule of his brother-in-law Maxentius, who had seized dictatorial power, and became the legendary Emporer Constantine legalising Christianity after Rome had persecuted it for the previous three Centuries. He encouraged his Mother Helen (who was subsequently canonised) to

---

6   Queen of a British Iron Age Celtic tribe from Norfolk and East Suffolk—*aka* Boedicea.

7   The tattooed men who conquered Northern Ireland and then invaded Britain's western shores.

undertake a pilgrimage to Jerusalem which had been destroyed and was being rebuilt where she is thought to have discovered the cross on which Jesus Christ had been crucified.

King Gracianus 375-389 seized the throne without any legitimate claim, setting new standards in tyranny to the extent that a group of his subjects assassinated him. That led the Danes, Huns, Picts, Norwegians and Scots to invade and ravage England. Rome came to the rescue and then left England for good around 410 to defend Rome which was under attack.

Vortigen murdered King Constans in 437 and invited the Jutes from Denmark to fight off the Picts and Scots which they did and then replaced him in 455 with their warlords Hengist and Horsa as rulers.

King Vortigen's duplicity and wickedness must be read to be believed, including his measures to obliterate Christianity. During his second reign 460-480 Merlin[8] the prophet/magician appears on the scene and his prophecies assumed an important place in the scheme of things.

King Aurelius Ambrosius 480-501 returned to England from Brittany— burnt Vortigen alive, forced the Saxons to retreat to Albany (Scotland), successfully led the Christians to defeat the pagans and then beheaded their leader Hengist.

Aurelius sought to perpetuate the memory of Hengist's Saxon 'Treachery of the Long Knives' and honour the victims of the massacre of Britain's leading nobles. Merlin was called on for advice and accompanied by Aurelius' brother Uther and an Army of 15000 sailed to Ireland, marched to Mount Killarus and defeated the Irish King Gillomanus, before removing the stones which had been brought from Africa by the giants of old, transporting them back to Stonehenge where Merlin had them erected exactly as they had been on Killarus thus ensuring they would stand forever. Aurelius 'retired' to London where he ruled wisely and justly until poisoned by a Saxon acting on behalf of Vortigen's youngest son.

---

8   Merlin's Mother was the daughter of a King and she claimed that Merlin's Father didn't exist other than in some ghostly form.

Uther Pendragon 501-521 succeeded his brother and led the Britons to rout the Saxons. While travelling to London to be crowned King he became captivated by Ygerna—the wife of Gorlois—Duke of Cornwall. Merlin offered Uther drugs that transformed him into Gorlois' doppelganger and he deceived the Duchess into committing adultery without her realising it—leading to the conception of Arthur, who became King at the age of 15, ruling from 521-542.

As well as establishing the Round Table, Arthur conquered the Irish, Picts, Saxons, Scots, most of Europe and the Roman Legions he encountered. On his way to attack Rome, word reached him that his nephew Mordred had become a treacherous tyrant and was living in adultery with Queen Guinevere. Arthur returned to Britain immediately and in the last of several battles was fatally wounded and Mordred was killed. After handing the Crown to his cousin Constantine, Arthur was carried to the Isle of Avalon where he died in 542.

Most historians dispute Arthur's existence and achievements, but Gwynne cites some leading scholars of that period whose evidence argues convincingly that Arthur and his accomplishments were real.

From 555-616, King Keredic and three successors suffered invasions from King Gormund[9] the leader of 160000 Africans who devastated the entire country, the surviving Britons seeking refuge in Brittany, Cornwall and Wales.

In 597, Pope St Gregory the Great sent Augustine the monk to England where he converted King Ethelbert of Kent and the rest of the Anglo Saxons, founding seven bishoprics and becoming Archbishop of Canterbury.[10]

645 saw Civil War followed by severe famine and plague—reducing the population to such an extent that they were unable to withstand the return of hordes of Saxons[11] who conquered the country. 80 years of skirmishes by a dwindling number of Britons proved futile against the dominant Saxons.

---

9   King of the Africans.

10   The Principal Bishopric.

11   The Angles, Jutes and Saxons.

Offa of Mercia 757-796 is generally cited as the first modern King of England.

King Alfred the Great 871-899, a wonderful man of so many parts and accomplishments who deserves greater recognition. Again, Gwynne sets the record straight. Alfred's son Edward 899-924 and grandson Ethelstan 925-939 put the finishing touches to Alfred's work, unifying Britain. Ethelstan adopted a new title *Rex Anglorum*—King of the English—giving England its name.

King St Edward the Confessor 1042-1066 is largely ignored as one of England's most important and long lastingly effective Kings as well as the first to take a non-Royal wife.

William the Conqueror led the Norman invasion of England in 1066, won the Battle of Hastings, put down a series of insurrections, established the feudal[12] system, allowed Jewish settlement in England for the first time, conducted the famous Domesday Book land-holding survey and ruled until 1087.

Henry II[13] 1154-1189 appointed Thomas a Becket as Chancellor[14] in 1155 and Archbishop of Canterbury in 1164. He clashed with the King over the Church being superior to the Monarchy on religious matters, leading the latter to say, 'Will no one rid me of this turbulent priest?' prompting four of his Knights to travel to Canterbury and hack the Archbishop to pieces as he was praying at the High Altar in the Cathedral. Martyred, canonised and venerated, a Becket's shrine[15] is still visited by pilgrimages from around the world by Catholics and Protestants.

Henry IIs heroic penance at what had happened to his friend involved fasting, walking barefoot in nothing but a woollen shirt to the new shrine and allowing himself to be publicly scourged by every Bishop, Abbott and Monk—laying all night and the next day on the cold stones.

---

12   William confiscated the lands from the Saxons and allocated it to his family members and Norman Lords in return for taxes and the provision of Knights and soldiers when required.

13   The first of the Plantagenet dynasty which finished with the death of King Richard III.

14   The King's right-hand man. Unusually, Becket was a commoner.

15   The destination of The Pilgrims' Way in England.

Gwynne's coverage of King John 1199-1216, King Henry III 1216-1272 and Henry VI 1422-1461 and 1470-1471 is a remarkable expose of how and why history has wrongly treated three such extraordinary Monarchs and their deeds.

1348 to 1350 visited the Black Death[16] on England.

Henry Vs 1413-1422 reign is widely acclaimed by historians, but Gwynne depicts him in an entirely different light as an unspeakably malevolent person who deployed mass slaughter, arson and rape as weapons of war. His wife—Catherine of Valois—had an illegitimate child (Edmund Tudor) with the Keeper of her Wardrobe Owen Tudor—the Earl of Richmond.

Henry VIs periods at the helm featured Joan of Arc, the end of the 100 Years War with the English driven out of France and the War of the Roses.[17]

King Richard III 1483-1485 turns out to be a much-maligned figure in Shakespeare's play of the same name, the truth warranting better treatment of his time on the Throne, its events and matters of special interest.

A slightly more eclectic account of happenings that marked our ancestors' lives from 1485 onwards—as per the sequence below—follows:

- Henry VII   1485–1509;

House of Tudor;

- Henry VIII   1509–1547;
- Edward VI   1547–1553;
- Mary I   1553–1558;
- Elizabeth I   1558–1603;
- James I   1603–1625;

---

16   A bubonic plague pandemic from rodents transmitted to humans by fleas which killed about a third of the population.

17   A series of Civil Wars from 1455 to 1487 for the Throne between the Plantagenet Royal Houses descending from Edward III—involving the House of York (white rose) and the House of Lancaster (red rose).

House of Stuart;

- Charles I   1625–1649;
- The Interregnum   1649–1659;
- Charles II   1660–1685;
- James II   1685–1688;
- William III[18] and Mary II   1688–1702;
- Anne   1702–1714;
- George I   1714–1727;

House of Hanover;

- George II   1727–1760;
- George III   1760–1820; and,
- George IV   1820–1830.

Edmund Tudor's son Henry was forced to flee to Brittany when 14. He later married Princess Elizabeth of York, a daughter of King Edward IV and niece of King Richard III who was his third cousin, thus uniting the Royal Houses of York and Lancaster—the protagonists in the War of the Roses from 1455-1487.

Henry Tudor defeated King Richard III 1483-1485 at the Battle of Bosworth Field in 1485. His supporters took Richard's Crown from his corpse and gave it to Henry. While he had no entitlement by Royal descent/bloodlines, Henry VII usurped the Crown by right of conquest—a medieval way of becoming King.[19]

His outrageous wickedness, which knew no bounds, is seldom commented on, but after fraudulently declaring himself King he used legal manoeuvres, wholesale murder and other means to eliminate contenders for the Crown including the two Princes in the Tower of London.[20] He restored the Star Chamber,[21] levied extraordinary taxes which made him 'a colossal personal fortune' and created a personal bodyguard— 'The Yeoman of the Guard'.

---

18   Who went insane.

19   In Henry VII's case, a definitional impossibility.

20   His wife's brothers.

21   A Court which sat at the Royal Palace of Westminster, comprising Judges and Privy Councillors that grew out of the medieval King's Court as a supplement to the regular justice of the common-law Courts.

The Catholic Church and Pope were central to people's lives. Many prayed the Liturgy of the Hours with three main and four minor prayers every day. Sex was prohibited during Advent, Feast and Fast Days, Lent and on Sunday, Saturday and Wednesday. One third of women died from childbirth during Tudor times.

Henry VII had seven legitimate children, betrothing his eldest son Arthur to Catherine of Aragon when she was three years of age and marrying his daughter Princess Margaret to King James IV of Scotland.

As if Gwynne's observations about King Henry VII weren't revealing enough in themselves, his analysis and treatment of some of the following Monarchs differ markedly from most historical portrayals.

The following paragraphs describe people and events that occurred from the time of what seems to be our earliest known ancestor—John Blundell the Elder who was born and died in Worth from 1510 to 1587.

King Henry VIII 1509-1547 became King because his brother Arthur died of sweating sickness[22] five months after his marriage to Catherine of Aragon on 14 November 1501 when they were both 15 old.

As King, Henry VIII adopted a practice of going on progression with the Court from May to October each year to avoid the smell of London's open sewers and the associated danger of the sweat and plague, sleeping in a different house each night. His maternal grandmother[23] had also died from the plague which occurred in five epidemics across England between 1485 and 1551.[24]

At that time Bletchingley was on a crossroads between the Channel Ports and London and The Pilgrims' Way for the Cathedral cities of Canterbury and Winchester. The Redbrick Old Hextails Lodge at Bletchingley is thought to have been a stopping point for one of Henry's hunting routes. The house at the entrance to nearby Place Farm was

---

22   Thought to have been anthrax or a virus spread by rats.

23   Elizabeth Woodville, known as the White Queen, wife of Edward IV and Mother of Edward V.

24   Kaya Burgess in *The Times* London April 2019.

the Gatehouse[25] to Bletchingley Palace, a great Tudor house which Ann of Cleves used as her primary residence for some seven years after her marriage to Henry VIII was annulled.

Arthur was raised to be King while Henry was indulged and 'spoiled rotten.' That might explain his gargantuan appetite for food, sport and women in a seemingly endless quest for a male heir and a spare or two.

Henry petitioned Pope Alexander VI in August 1503 for annulment of his brother's marriage on the unlikely basis that it hadn't been consummated. Although Arthur's widow, Catherine of Aragon, testified to that effect, Canon Law forbade Henry marrying his brother's widow. The Pope responded to Henry saying that he needed more time to consider the matter. Pope Julius II granted the dispensation in October 1504 and the marriage took place on 11 June 1509 seven years after Arthur died and six years after their betrothal—he was 18 and she was 23.

They were married for 25 years, but Catherine's six pregnancies had produced only one living child—Princess Mary. Catherine now approaching 40 seemed unlikely to deliver the male heir he so desperately wanted. Henry believed this was nothing to do with him, his Courtiers flattering him that he was perfect in every way. After all, he had produced a son with Bessie Blount named Henry FitzRoy who he made a Duke—theoretically a bastard having no rights in law.

Henry set eyes on Mary Boleyn when she married William Carey[26] in 1520 and their affair started soon after—he fathered her children Catherine and Henry[27] and had at least four more illegitimate children with other women. Around March 1526 Henry turned his attention to Mary's sister Anne.

---

25   The only trace of the Palace still standing.

26   Henry bestowed significant benefits on William Carey who had no children with Mary and died of the sweat in 1528.

27   Catherine married Sir Francis Knollys and founded a great Elizabethan dynasty while Henry became an Adviser and Courtier to Queen Elizabeth who made him Viscount/Baron Hunsdon.

Henry then had a convenient revelation that he should never have been permitted to marry Catherine.[28] Knowing the Catholic Church didn't approve of divorce, he petitioned Pope Clement VII in 1527 to annul the marriage. Clement refused and this led to the schism with the Catholic Church known as The English Reformation.

Henry VIII declared himself Head of a new Church of England, destroying convents and monasteries—leading to his excommunication by Pope Clement VII and Pope Paul III. This triggered a great uprising of 40000 men in the north determined to defend the church and the holy houses. Henry offered them a pardon and a Parliament. They accepted and as soon as their Army was disbanded, he ended the disturbance by beheading 200 of their leaders.

Anne Boleyn was determined that the only way Henry would have her was through marriage which occurred seven years after their courtship began. It seems unlikely that Henry remained chaste during that time and Anne eventually relented. She got pregnant and they married in a private ceremony on 25 January 1533 while he was still married to Queen Catherine. There are disputed claims that Anne's Mother Countess Elizabeth Wiltshire told Henry that he couldn't possibly marry Anne as he must know that she was their daughter—that didn't dissuade him either![29]

Elizabeth was born on 17 September followed by three miscarriages including a stillborn son on 29 January 1536.[30]

Henry's fancy turned to Jane Seymour and he asked Thomas Cromwell to free him from the marriage to Anne. Allegations of conspiracy and witchcraft were levelled against Anne who was charged with multiple treasonous

---

28 Claiming the Pope didn't have authority to set aside Leviticus 20:21 forbidding marriage to a brother's wife.

29 Gwynne points to Dr Bayley's *Life of Bishop Fisher*, Cardinal Gasquet's investigation and Cobbett's *History of the Protestant Reformation*. See also the Jesuit Nicholas Sander's report quoted by the authors Elizabeth Warren and Kelly Hart *The Mistresses of Henry VIII* which address this issue.

30 Expediently attributed by Anne to her shock over Henry having fallen from his horse in a jousting accident—although he was not injured—six days earlier.

adulteries and incest with her brother George—all five male suspects were beheaded on 17 May 1536 followed by Anne two days later. Arguments about whether the charges were real or manufactured continue, but adultery by the wife of a King was technically treason. The incest with her brother charge seems highly unlikely as, although married, he may have been of the other persuasion.

Meanwhile, Mary Boleyn/Carey had secretly married William Stafford in 1534. When it was discovered in 1535 that she was pregnant they were banished from Court. She died seven years later leaving two further children—Edward and Anne—neither of whom survived infanthood.

Henry VIII married Jane Seymour on 30 May 1536 eleven days after Anne Boleyn's execution. She died twelve days after delivering Edward, the King's only legitimate son. This put paid to the alternative plans being put in place to have Henry FitzRoy recognised as his legitimate heir and successor as King. In the event, these measures would not have borne fruit as Henry Fitzroy died on 22 July 1536 of consumption (tuberculosis).

On 24 June 1536 in a jousting event at Greenwich, Henry fell off his horse, which crashed on him and almost killed him. His health deteriorated, a leg was infected, ulcerated and continually reinfected for the rest of his life causing a very bad odour. Racked by constant pain, his personality changed—becoming brutal, capricious, depressed, with an explosive temper, insecure with bouts of paranoia, prone to volatile mood swings, unreasonable, tormentive and vindictive. He became morbidly obese, his girth expanding to 52 inches (20 more than when he became King) and increasingly impotent.

Anne of Cleves a German Princess was his next bride. He chose her based on a portrait by his artist Hans Holbein but was repulsed by Anne's physical appearance when they met. Nevertheless, they married on 6 January 1540.

Aged 48, Henry became attracted to the 16-year-old Catherine Howard and some five months later obtained yet another annulment arguing that Anne of Cleves had a pre-marriage contract in place at the time she married him.

Anne agreed and testified that the marriage had never been consummated; she didn't arouse Henry. In return, she received considerable property including Hever Castle[31] Penshurst and Richmond Palaces, maintaining a friendly relationship with Henry for the rest of his life as 'The King's Beloved Sister.'

Henry married Catherine Howard on 28 June 1540. Her illicit sexual liaisons before the marriage and adultery with Thomas Culpepper afterwards led to her execution on 13 February 1542.

Last, he married Katherine Parr on 12 July 1543—who had already been married four times. She proved very adept as a loving wife and Queen, ignoring the stench and nursing Henry, a first-class step-Mother who *inter alia* returned his daughters Mary and Elizabeth to favour at Court and protected his son Edward from undue influence until Henry VIII died on 28 January 1547.

She then secretly married the dishonourable, unscrupulous and ruthlessly ambitious Thomas Seymour (Queen Jane and Edward Seymour's brother) later in 1547 having wanted to do so before her marriage to Henry VIII.

Katherine died on 5 September 1548 soon after giving birth to a still-born daughter amidst claims Thomas Seymour had poisoned her because Katherine discovered he had seduced the 14-year old Elizabeth who was living with them! We do know that Thomas Seymour had asked Elizabeth to marry him as soon as her Father died, ignoring the fact that he was already married to Katherine Parr the Queen Dowager at the time.

In January 1549, Thomas Seymour, who was plotting to forcibly take the Lord Protector[32] role from his brother Edward—the Duke of Somerset—was charged with treason—leaving Edward no option other than to have his brother executed.

---

31   Anne Boleyn's childhood home.
32   Edward Seymour was Lord Protector to Edward VI at that time.

Henry VIII used treason and heresy to quell dissent or dispose of those standing in his way, often executing those accused without trial—may be 72000 men—whose only crime was to disagree with him or practice the Papist faith. Some of his Chief Ministers[33] suffered this fate or were banished from Court.

Death for High Treason involved being hung, drawn and quartered:

'That the offender be drawn[34] to the gallows, on the ground or the pavement: That he be hanged by the neck, and then cut down alive: That his entrails be taken out and burned while he is still alive: That his head be cut off: That his body be divided into four parts: And that his head and quarters be at the King's disposal.'

Women were only to be drawn and hanged.[35]

Inconceivable today, Henry's egocentric monstrosity led him to introduce laws where being unemployed was punishable with death or sentenced to slavery.

It's worth recording here that many liaisons and marriages were often surreptitiously planned to bolster the family's position at Court and benefit the women's male relatives who ruled their wives and children with an iron hand. Fortunes, favours and honours rose or fell depending on the women's capacity to satisfy the King. Licentiousness, debauchery and promiscuity were commonplace at Court and among the Courtiers.

Henry VIIIs son—King Edward VI 1547-1553 came to the throne aged nine.

Improbably, his six-year reign was marked by a greater number of executions than occurred during his Father's 48 years as King. He presided over the next stage of The English Reformation begun by his Father—replacing Catholicism with Protestantism and its ecclesiastical practices—the nine-year old Edward also being declared Pope of England when he was crowned King.

---

33   Thomas Wolsey, Thomas More, Thomas Cromwell, Richard Rich and Thomas Cranmer as well as Cardinal John Fisher.

34   Dragged on a wooden frame to the place of public execution.

35   *The Story of the Convicts* Charles White Free Press Office George Street Sydney 1889.

While his Father plundered Catholic church lands and other property, Edward confiscated the possessions of schools, colleges and Guilds,[36] conferring the proceeds on the Privy Councillors[37] thus creating a new class of super rich for the first time in England. Education was virtually abolished, except for the children of the rich, for some 50 years.

Edward died from tuberculosis on 6 July 1553, bequeathing the Throne to the pious scholarly Lady Jane Grey[38] who was 16 years of age—excluding his half-sisters, the Princesses Mary and Elizabeth on the grounds of their previously declared illegitimacy by his Father Henry VIII. Four days after Edward's death, Jane was proclaimed Queen by her father-in-law—she lasted nine days.

The people who had never heard of Lady Jane objected, preferring Princess Mary who marched on London and was crowned Queen Mary 1553-1558.

Jane was imprisoned in the Tower of London which was one of the Royal Palaces at the time, with the White Tower used as a prison from 1100. The King's Protector (John Dudley) and his son Lord Guildford Dudley who was Jane's husband were executed. From her prison cell, Jane who was a committed Protestant kept writing letters opposing restoration of the Catholic religion by Queen Mary, eventually leading to her beheading on 12 February 1554.

The Dudleys and Seymours come back into our story later.

---

36   Confraternities of tradesmen in a city for each trade which grew into associations of artisans and merchants to oversee the practice of their craft.

37   Originally the King's Council from William the Conqueror's time, the word Privy meant hidden, an advisory body to the King like a Cabinet today. The King/Queen appointed the Councillors, usually Noblemen, Clergy and Officers of the Crown.

38   On the instruction of the King's Protector, John Dudley—the Duke of Northumberland. Jane was married to his youngest son Guildford and was also Henry VIIIs younger sister Mary's granddaughter. The whole Dudley family was attainted and condemned to death but only the Duke and Guildford were subsequently executed with the other brothers including Robert Dudley (on page 21) subsequently released from custody.

As the oldest surviving child of Henry VIII by Catherine of Aragon, Mary immediately annulled Edward VIs statutes relating to religious matters. Papal delegate Cardinal Pole[39] returned to England as Archbishop of Canterbury and set about restoring Catholicism which was widely accepted by the people. Far from being the 'Bloody Mary' portrayed in history books, she was a just and merciful Queen, kind to the poor, courageous and resourceful in defeating a Protestant rebellion against her reign and governed with good intentions.

Mary maintained her devotion to the Catholic religion all her life. When she died on 17 November 1558, her half-sister Elizabeth succeeded to the throne.

Queen Elizabeth I 1558-1603 changed from Catholic to Protestant then to Catholic and then back to Protestant again! She solemnly swore an oath to adhere to and defend the Catholic faith when crowned. Six weeks later she set about the third stage of The English Reformation—thousands were butchered, hung up, cut down alive, their bowels ripped out and their bodies chopped into quarters—all because they were Catholics.

Far from being revered and delivering peace and reconciliation, she developed the autocratic processes of her Father and brother to an art form. Declarations of treason, confessions through torture followed by the Scaffold or burning at the stake were commonplace as part of her Advisor William Cecil's grand plan to protect England from Papists, the Spanish and the Queen of Scots—Mary Stuart—who inherited the throne from her Father James V of Scotland when she was only six days old. Elizabeth had Mary Queen of Scots detained for 19 years and eventually beheaded for treason aged 35.

Elizabeth resisted all entreaties by her Advisers to marry and rejected all the many suitors for her hand, preferring to rule unfettered by a husband. It was her failure to marry that led to her being called 'The Virgin Queen', because she was far from deserving of that appellation.

---

39   A son of the Countess of Salisbury executed by King Henry VIII.

She had a long-term intimate relationship with the infamous Robert Dudley[40] who wanted to marry her so that he could 'share' the Throne. His wife Lettice Knollys[41] 'fell' down the stairs of their family home and died, together with the associated disbelief that it was an accident extinguished that plan.

The romanticised depictions of Henry VIII, Edward VI and Elizabeth I are at best naïve—the reality of their reigns is that they were manifestly evil.

Ironically, on Elizabeth's death, James I 1603-1625 (the only son of Mary Queen of Scots and who was also King Henry VIIs great great grandson) inherited the Crowns of England, Scotland and Ireland, having refrained from any comment whatsoever on his Mother's death at Elizabeth's hands. He faced growing discontent from Protestants known as Puritans (a characteristic of our Blundell family) and the many closet Catholics in England.

Charles I 1625-1649 second son of James I succeeded him, his elder brother Prince Henry having died of typhoid fever at the age of 18.

Resistance of successive Parliaments led Charles I to rule through the Star Chamber. He suffered some unpopularity with the power brokers because of the need to raise money through means that had never been used before. In 1642, the impasse between the King and the Parliament led to Civil War between the Roundheads (supporters of the Parliament) and the Cavaliers who believed Charles was King by God given right.

Parliamentary Commander in Chief Sir Thomas Fairfax defeated the Royalist Forces in 1645—England was then proclaimed a Commonwealth and free state with Fairfax becoming the military ruler of the Republic in the same year.

Fairfax was overshadowed by his Deputy, Lieutenant General Oliver Cromwell—who was more politically adept and radical in his actions and measures against Charles I—which Fairfax didn't support.

---

40   The same Robert Dudley mentioned in footnote 38.

41   See footnote 27.

Cromwell replaced him in 1657 ruling as Lord Protector (and absolute 'Monarch') until he died on 3 September 1658.

Charles I was very popular with the people who objected to his trial and execution in 1649. Leaving aside the legal and other problems with the High Court conducting such a trial—orchestrated by Cromwell—the whole saga was really about a grab for power by a tiny minority.

Three other points:

- in 1652 the English Army's conquest of Ireland was accompanied by horrific atrocities;
- the expulsion of Jews from England enacted by King Edward I on 18 July 1290 has never been repealed; and
- Oliver Cromwell organised for his son Richard to be declared Lord Protector after his death (shades of a despot and nepotism).

Richard Cromwell abdicated in 1659 and retired to private life.

Fearful of Oliver Cromwell's extremism, including his expectation and exhortations that Christ's return was imminent, the new English Parliament invited Charles II 1660-1665 to be King on 1 May 1660, aided and abetted by Fairfax's role in that restoration.

From May to September 1665, the Great Plague passed from the Continent to London killing between 60000 to 100000 people out of the 300000 who lived there. In September 1666, the Great Fire broke out near London Bridge reducing two thirds of the city to ashes over three days.

Although Charles II 1660-1685 had no children with his wife, Gwynne notes that there are today more descendants of his mistresses than legitimate Royal descendants of all the Monarchs who have reigned since. Charles IIs wife—Catherine of Braganza—was infertile, but he had at least nine mistresses and accepted 12 children as his—there were probably 15 or more.

One of his offspring with the scandalous Barbara Palmer[42] was Henry FitzRoy the first Duke of Grafton whose descendants include Diana Princess

---

42   The Duchess of Cleveland/Countess of Castlemaine who had six children, five of whom were recognized by Charles II as his.

of Wales and Sir Charles Augustus FitzRoy the 10ᵗʰ and last Governor of the
NSW Colony—a real piece of work, as we shall see in Chapter Five.

For 300 or 400 years arbitrary and illegal punishments had been handed
out with impunity. Charles II introduced the Habeas Corpus Act to stop this
practice. His reign was dominated by an anti-Puritan reaction, culminating
in his brother—a Catholic convert—becoming King James II 1685-1668,
unleashing turmoil.

Protestants plotted to declare the Duke of Monmouth heir while the
Papists wanted the Duke of York who had been banished. Monmouth with
6000 followers was defeated on 5 July 1685 and beheaded. Pillaging and
other atrocities were committed by the troops while Chief Justice Jeffries
executed 240 political offenders in one sitting, boasting that he had hanged
more traitors than all his predecessors since the Norman Conquest.

Jeffries and the other judges were ordered to convict as many as possible
so that they could be bestowed as rewards on the Catholic Courtiers. 841
Protestant martyrs were handed over to be sold as slaves, 20% of whom died
and were flung overboard before they reached their destination.

Gwynne corrects the record of much-maligned King James II 1685-
1688, arguing that he was one of the greatest men in world history.

James IIs attempts to suspend the laws against both non-Catholics and
Nonconformist Protestants were resisted by many Bishops. He sent them to
trial for rebellion against the King's authority. Although a straightforward
case, the Jury inexplicably acquitted them. Parliament deposed James II in
1688 ceasing 150 years of instability.

The Church of England—dominated by centrists and conformists—
was established by law—excluding Catholics and Puritans (*ie* our Blundells
again).

James IIs daughter Queen Anne 1702-1714 the last House of Stuart
Monarch had at least 17 children, all of whom died from miscarriages, still-
births or post-birth illnesses. The place of Sarah Jennings and Abigail Hill in
Queen Anne's life features in the recent film called *The Favourite*.

Gwynne explains

'... With shameless dishonesty, the legally established laws of succession were overridden in order to manipulate on to the Throne a distantly related German princeling ...' (King George I 1714-1727) when candidates with greater claims to the Throne—James III and his son Charles Edward (Bonnie Prince Charlie)—were available.

George I's son George II reigned from 1727-1760, during which the infamous Battle of Culloden occurred. Gwynne cites the only reasonable explanation about why Bonnie Prince Charlie abandoned his march on London at the very time he was likely to succeed and restore the House of Stuart to the Throne.

King George III 1760-1820 presided over a series of significant events until his first bout of insanity in 1810. His eldest son George became Prince Regent from 5 February 1811 until his Father's death and inauguration. King George IV reigned from 1820-1830, his only legitimate child Princess Charlotte predeceasing him.

1826 marks Joseph Blundell's transportation for life from Sheerness to the NSW Penal Colony.

George IV was succeeded by his brother William IV 1830-1837 and the sequence of successors in the table below:

- Victoria   1837–1901;
- Edward VII   1901–1910;

House of Windsor;

- George V[43]   1910–1936;
- Edward VIII   1936;
- George VI   1936–1952; and
- Elizabeth II   1952–

Hilary Mantel's *Wolf Hall and Bring Up the Bodies*, *The Queen's Agent* by John Cooper, together with Alison Weir's and Philippa Gregory's series

---

43   King George V issued a Proclamation changing the Royal Family's name from Saxe-Coburg and Gotha to Windsor because of anti-German sentiment throughout the British Empire during World War One.

about the events and people during the reigns of Henry the 8ᵗʰ, the Catholic Queen Mary I and the return to Protestantism under Queen Elizabeth I provide a fascinating backdrop to our story—including the possibility of Henry VIII having a genetic condition which led to so many of his son's deaths. These books provide wonderful insights into those times, particularly the lot of women.

On 5 June 1975, Britain voted to join the Common Market—the precursor to the European Union—affecting Australia's trade access to Britain and other aspects such as the Heathrow arrival 'experience'.

When in Paris on 23 June 2016 we watched the Brexit Referendum. The events since then and parallel with the Tudor dynasty and English Reformation and its rejection of Europe which took 150 years to resolve is inescapable.

Three
Blundell English Ancestry

Dorothea Teague's books focus on our Blundell name and genealogical descent from the Worth Parish Registers that record many of our ancestors' baptisms, marriages and burials. We owe her a great debt of gratitude for her assiduous pursuit of the work that led to *Shadrach Blundell—His Family and Property 1580 to Modern Times*—a more substantive version of the 1985 edition.

This and the following Chapter would not have been possible without drawing on Dorothea's material and I am very grateful for permission to include the extracts which are denoted with an* in the text.

Indeed, the skeleton derives directly from her work as does some of the clothing to fill out the related stories. Exchanges of correspondence with Dorothea in the 1980s and 1990s and additional investigations by the author—especially aided and abetted by Pam Glover—have also contributed to the end-product.

While in the UK in 2016, I bought a few books, thinking they might come in handy and inform some parts of this exposition. I got in touch with Synjon Books in an endeavour to contact Mrs Teague's daughter Helen Allinson for permission to quote from two of her publications.

Chapter Seven on 'Susan Osborne' draws on material from Helen's books about Life in the Workhouse[1] and Assisted Emigration from Kent.[2]

In what proved to be a case of serendipity if not divine intervention, Dorothea's son Tony replied to my email enquiry. I knew that he had computerised his Mother's records and maintained an associated comprehensive website for some time which was no longer accessible.

Imagine my surprise when I found out Dorothea and her husband John were still with us—in their 90s. I tried to find them prior to our visits to no avail, wanting to call on them in person, but such was not to be.

What an extraordinary contribution this family enterprise has made to record our Blundell English ancestry and history.

The maps which follow provide further perspective.

At the time John Speed did his work in the late 1590s and early 1600s England's population was only four million, mostly in scattered nucleated villages. Extraordinarily, the experts believed the country was full to bursting and couldn't sustain any further increase. Towns were struggling to cope with ribbon development beyond their medieval walls. London's population of 200000 was ten times larger than any other city at the time.

Travellers on horseback from London could reach Chester, Exeter or York within four days and coach services were introduced in 1637.

By 1700 England's population had reached about five and a half million, in 1801=8331434, 1811=9538271, 1821=11261437 and 1831=13089338.

Christopher Saxton drew the first engraved maps of Britain's Counties under the Privy Council's authority from 1574 to 1578. John Norden improved Saxton's work around 1593. John Speed's atlas was originally conceived as part of a History of Great Britain from the Roman conquest to the accession of King James I in 1603. His map of the Saxon Heptarchy shows Surrey and Sussex under the South Saxons Kingdom.

---

1   *Life in the Workhouse: The Story of Milton Union, Kent* Helen Allinson Synjon Books 2005.

2   *Farewell to Kent: Assisted Emigration from Kent in the 19th Century* Helen Allinson Synjon Books 2008.

England's 40 Counties stem from the Anglo-Saxon era, many being mentioned in history before extinction of the Heptarchy—which meant a shire or division governed by a Shire Reeve or Sheriff—a Chief Officer of the King. The Hundreds[3] were also of Anglo-Saxon origin based on population size. The Parish of the early Britons was synonymous with a Diocese—the District which submitted to a Bishop's authority.

The Surrey and Sussex maps—of particular interest to us—derive from the earlier versions by Saxton and Norden, but it isn't known how Speed dealt with the difficulty of a 'mile' differing in length from County to County until the statute mile of eight furlongs—1760 yards—was established by Parliament in 1593. Old miles fluctuated from 1925 to 2728 yards in Saxton's maps.

Thomas Moule's topographic work created during King William IVs reign 1830-1837 coincided with the 1832 Great Reform Act,[4] a communications and industry revolution and the first period of railway mania, including the depiction on the Surrey-Sussex map at page 35. In effect, Moule produced a Victorian era version of *The Domesday Book*. Unlike Speed, Moule included the principal roads and canals and a rendering of relief and hills.

From 1510, our ancestors were witnesses and/or participants in the times and tides of English history like the Civil War, the Commonwealth, the Restoration, The English Reformation, Bletchingley Secret Conventicles, Plagues and London's Great Fire outlined in Chapter Two.

The fundamental place of religion and the church in people's lives meant that more prominence was given to the date of baptism than birth and burial date rather than when someone died.

---

3   A Hundred was a medieval local government administrative and taxation area that was geographically part of a larger region.

4   Protests about the unfair electoral system which consisted of constituencies where only a handful of voters could elect two Members of Parliament led to reform. Although new constituencies were created of differing size, only men who owned property worth £10 or more could vote, cutting out the working class. The 'reform' didn't go far enough to stifle ongoing protests.

Readers might be surprised by the age of some from the distaff side when they married and the elapsed time between that and the birth of their first child.

Pre-nuptial pregnancies seem to have been an accepted occurrence among the Yeoman and higher classes. This was attributed to the desire to know that the intended bride was fertile before the marriage. Surprising to us now, it wasn't unusual among Royalty and the upper classes at this time for the parties to be betrothed before they entered their teens and to be married as soon as the woman reached puberty around 12 years of age.

The age of consent in the 16th Century was 14, up to 40% of women were pregnant at the time of their marriage, men tended to marry in their mid to late twenties while women generally married earlier.[5]

In the 17th Century, 13% of infants died before their first birthday and the average life span was around 40 years of age. Of course, many lived to their 50s and 60s and life expectancy increased significantly over succeeding centuries.

Primogeniture—a feudal rule by which the whole estate passed to the eldest son became the principle, law and custom of inheritance and succession by the paternally acknowledged first born son to the Father's entire Estate in preference to daughters or illegitimate sons. The motivation to keep the Estate whole and intact was followed particularly by agricultural land owners. With the important exceptions of William Blundell IIs and John of Bletchingley's Wills, this practice was largely followed by the Blundells although other family members also benefitted as will become apparent in what follows.[6]

---

5   Pam Glover from Bill Bryson's *Shakespeare*.

6   *The Macquarie Dictionary*. Under the feudal system, all land belonged to the Sovereign who divided it into fiefs which he distributed to his nobles to be held by them (not owned) subject to certain obligations. The nobles sub-let their land to their own vassals which were called mesne tenants as were their sub-tenants. The nobles undertook to supply the Sovereign with provisions and men for the Army when the King wanted to go to war—Gwynne *op cit*.

Worth

The village and civil Parish of Worth—probably the birthplace of our ancestry—is in the Crawley Borough of the mid-Sussex District of West Sussex. Worth Village had Saxon origins, appearing in *The Domesday Book*[7] as 'Orde', St Nicholas' church retaining its Saxon floor plan. St Nicholas—which was built around 950-1050 AD—was known to accommodate worship by dissenters.[8]

The East Crawley of 1841, which has been inhabited since the Stone Age, derives from the Saxon 'Crow's Leah' meaning a crow-infested clearing or Crow's Wood. It developed slowly as a market town from the 13th Century onwards serving the surrounding villages in the weald.

Weald was an old English name for woodland; the great Andreds Weald Forest, 120 miles long and 30 miles wide, deriving from the Saxons of 900AD as part of the Andredsweal—contiguous with Anderitum the Roman Fort at Pevensey, which was refurbished by William the Conqueror when the Normans invaded England in 1066. The weald of Kent, Surrey and Sussex encompasses the Lancaster Great Park formed in 1372, renamed as Ashdown Forest in 1672. A wealden iron industry flourished there in the 17th and 18th centuries and the railway of 1855 brought more employment to the area before it closed in 1967.

Worth's geographical position guarded it from the depredations that the rest of Sussex suffered after the Battle of Hastings in 1066, the County being divided into six equally sized 'Rapes' as a protective measure—each of which was sub-divided in to 'Hundreds'—Worth being in Pevensey Rape.

In 1861, Worth St Nicholas ranked as one of the largest Parishes in England, containing 2988 souls. It was formerly a Parish in the poor law union of East Grinstead, Buttinghill Hundred, Rape of Lewes in the

---

7   *The Domesday Book* included nearby Ifield, but not Crawley.

8   Derived from the Latin, meaning one who disagrees in opinion/beliefs— particularly religious matters; a feature of many of our Blundell ancestors which will be to the fore as we shall see.

East Division of Sussex two miles South East of Crawley. Later ecclesiastical creations divided the ancient Parish into seven different jurisdictions.

When Crawley New Town was created in 1947, Worth Village became part of the 'Pound Hill' Ward which was changed in 2004 to the 'Pound Hill South and Worth' Ward in keeping with the residents' wishes to preserve the Worth name. The 2001 Census recorded 9888 people, the 2011 Census 10378 and there were 14716 in the Pound Hill South and Worth Ward in 2017.

Three Bridges Station on the London to Brighton and South Coast Railway is near the greater part of Worth Village which is situated about three quarters of a mile east of the station while St Nicholas is half a mile south of Pound Hill.

Sussex

When John Speed created his map, Sussex was about 76 miles wide and 20 miles in breadth. The absence of good roads going north into Surrey and Kent meant that despite its geographical closeness to London, Sussex remained a somewhat isolated and introverted County well into the early 17th Century. It's no real surprise then that Roman Catholic and Puritan adherents resisted enforcement of the Church of England form of Protestantism.

As mentioned, the difficulties posed by the nature of the coast didn't safeguard Sussex from invasions. 1066 was followed by raids, landings and wholesale destruction such as the burning of Brighton in 1543 and successive wars between England and France after William the Conqueror's conquest.

John Speed's 1610 Map of Surrey and part of Sussex[9] (facing page) amended Saxton's and Norden's prior versions based on personal enquiry and observation. It shows Worth and Worth Forest positioned between Crawley to the west, Bletchinligh to the north, Burstow (Burftow) and East Grinstead to the north-east and Balcombe to the south.

---

9   From *Britain's Tudor Maps County by County* Pavilion Books Company Ltd London 2016.

Surrey

In the early days of our ancestry, Surrey was something of a paradox, close to both the capital and the Court but decidedly remote from London— due to the physical barrier of the Thames River which was bridged only at Chertsey, Kingston, Southwark and Staines—and by the marshiness of

Extract of John Speed's 1610 Surrey and Sussex Map

the land south of the Thames and London which until the 19th Century prevented development there beyond Southwark.

Southwark at the southern end of London Bridge was a London suburb with its inns and taverns, palaces and prisons, leather trade and other crafts, brothels and Roman style theatres designed so that audiences could get a good view of the action where the plays of Kyd, Marlowe and Shakespeare debuted.

A haven for undesirables, political and religious refugees, the approach to London Bridge from Southwark was renowned for its gruesome display of an array of beheaded human heads on pikes including a former favourite of Queen Elizabeth I—Robert Devereux, the Earl of Sussex—who she executed in 1601 for treason.

Plentiful game particularly deer made the area around Southwark attractive to Monarchs and Courtiers. Henry VII built a large Gothic Palace at Richmond which became Elizabeth I's fancied residence.

Surrey was not a prosperous County. In 1600, no town had more than a couple of thousand inhabitants. An extract from Thomas Moule's[10] 1830 Map of Surrey is on the facing page.

Bletchingley, Burstow, Chaldon, Godstone and Horne in the Tandridge Hundreds[11] are easily identified. Horley and Reigate are in the neighbouring Reigate Hundreds. One of the six castles of the earlier Lords stood on Blechingley Hill which commanded an extensive view of the surroundings.

Two of the then 14 Surrey Members of Parliament were from Blechingley, nine and a half miles from Worth and about 20 miles from Deptford/London.

The Domesday Book recorded this ancestral home as Blachingelei.

As was usual among families then—and will soon become obvious— generation after generation named their children in honour of grandparents, parents or other close relatives.

---

10   From *Victorian Maps of England: The County and City Maps of Thomas Moule* republished in 2018 by Pavilion Books London.

11   Denoted by the 11 on the map.

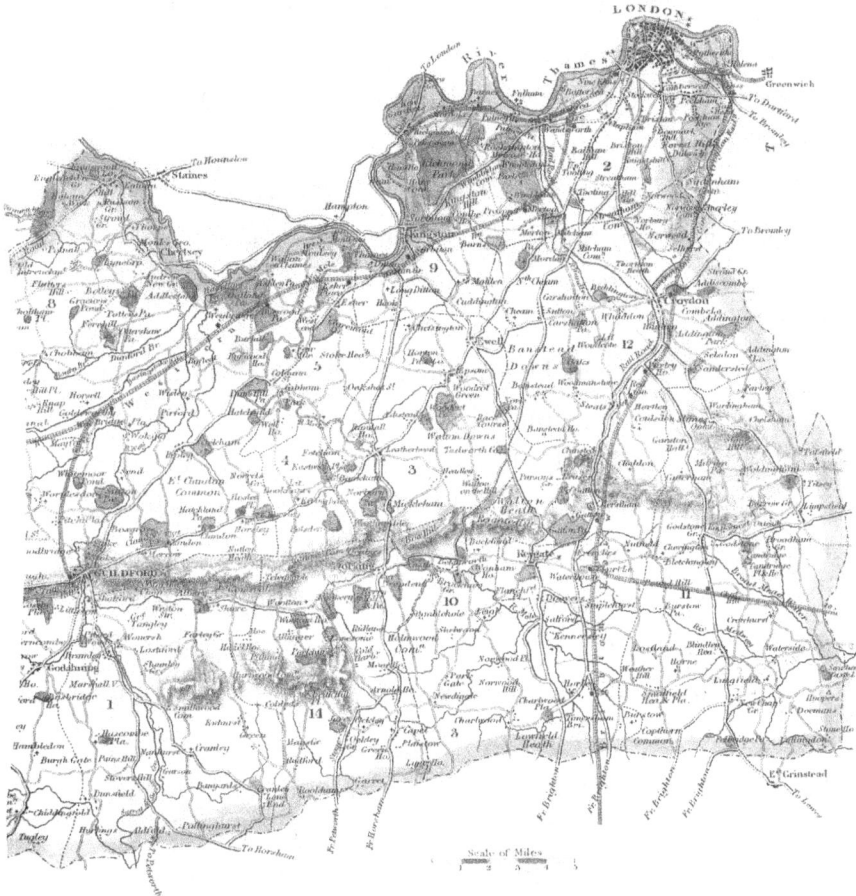

Extract of Thomas Moule's 1830 Surrey Map

The similar christian names have confounded efforts to distinguish which parent had which child *etc* prior to the known record, starting with John of Bletchingley on page 43.

Background

C J Sansom's *Tombland*[12] provides some great insights into the different classes in English Society and the 1549 Rebellions by the peasantry in various Counties; like previous large-scale peasant uprisings

---

12   Published in 2018 by Pan Macmillan London. This background section draws on Sansom's Historical Essay—a factual account of the events and people that Tombland is based on—which is at the end of his book.

such as the 1381 Peasant's Revolt and Cade's Rebellion of 1450, the State put down the latest effort.

At this time, Society was divided into two—the 2000 or so people in the gentleman class and everyone else. Those 2000 were further divided into gentlemen, Knights and the various levels of aristocracy who were visibly identifiable by the 'sumptuary laws' that defined what the various ranks could wear. These societal divisions were believed to have been ordained by God.

Henry VIII had left England in a mess. His wars with France and Scotland had proved enormously costly; he emptied the State coffers, levied heavy taxation and sold as much of the former monastic land as he could. His religious policy oscillated between semi-Protestantism and conservative Catholicism without the Pope, creating religious division and uncertainty among the populace. The result was high inflation, previously unknown in England; by 1549 prices were fifty per cent higher than in 1540 and they increased by 11% in 1549 alone. The poor were the worst affected as their wages remained static, while the purchasing power of semi-skilled workmen fell by a third in less than a decade causing widespread impoverishment.

Most commentators attributed this outcome to agrarian factors such as high rents, marketing problems and the replacement of food producing agriculture by sheep farming. There's no doubt that the Upper Classes systematic approach to the enclosure of what had previously been Common land had a huge impact. Until then, the lower classes had access to such land to grow crops and keep a few animals to supplement their meagre income and eke out a living. While this caused major social problems and injustices, it was debasement of the coinage that really caused the economic setback and triggered the 1549 Rebellions.

Proud, tactless and obstinate, Lord Protector Edward Seymour—the Duke of Somerset—was obsessed with and resolutely pursued the war he launched against Scotland in 1547, oblivious to its military failure and disastrous economic effects. He epitomised Laurence Peter's 'Peter Principle', having been promoted to a more senior level where he lacked the required skills and reached his level of incompetence.

As well as war, inflation and the rebellions Somerset presided over significant religious changes during 1547-1549. This included dissolution of the chantries where masses were said for the dead; Government appropriation of Catholic lands and property; removal of stained-glass windows, ornamentation and images from the churches; and introduction of the first Prayer Book in English.

The Earl of Warwick—John Dudley—commanded the forces which put down Kett's insurrection in Scotland, becoming the First Duke of Northumberland. On the Earl's return to London, Somerset surrendered the King to the Council, the Protectorate was abolished, and Dudley became the acknowledged Leader of the Council. His Father Edmund Dudley had been executed for high treason by Henry VIII as a scapegoat for his Father Henry VIIs unpopular financial policies. As we saw in Chapter Two, John Dudley suffered the same fate.

Our earliest known ancestors made their way in life against this backdrop. As Yeomen they prospered as part of the new rural gentry class that arose from the foregoing. The ruling classes of the 1540s were greatly concerned about the Anabaptists, a radical German Protestant group who believed in egalitarianism. We'll come to the Blundell Baptist beliefs.

Sansom cites Andy Wood[13] as having argued that 1549 was decisive in shifting the loyalties of the Yeoman class towards aspiration and gentleman status, valuing literacy for their children and becoming stalwarts of the Elizabethan State as the poor became even poorer. That summation applies to our Blundell forbears, but we turn now the hypothesis of our earliest ancestors, prior to the proven John of Bletchingley, the bold type signifying our direct line.

---

13   *The 1549 Rebellions and the Making of Early Modern England* Andy Wood Cambridge
Press NY 2007.

John Blundell the Elder 1510–1587[14]

Born/baptised 1510 in Worth and buried on 19 October 1587 in Worth, John married Johan/Joane Meadhurst c1515–13 December 1595 East Grinstead in Worth around ? and produced:

- **John the Younger c1535–1595**;
- William c1539–9.6.1607;
- Robert c1550 Worth–?;
- Roger[15] c1555 Sussex–12.1.1615 Worth West Sussex;
- George c1558 Worth–;
- Elizabeth c1559 Worth–;
- Margaret c1560 Worth–;
- Mary[16] 6.10.1561 Worth–; and
- Thomas ?–31.5.1573 Worth.

As there is some uncertainty about these children, they will be dealt with in Book Two. The 15-year gap between John the Younger and Robert looks odd—that may be because Johan wasn't John the Younger's Mother? Pam Glover suggested the addition of William in the table above, but the spacing between the first five children compared with the last four is peculiar. Collateral information suggests Roger (who married Margarett Warde) Mary and Thomas are correct—the latter two probably died without issue.

John Blundell the Younger 1535–1595

This John, thought to have been baptised around 1535 in Worth and buried on 27 September 1595 in Worth or 12 September 1596 East Grinstead, married Johan/Joane/Joan Swan/Swane 1540–5 March 1574 Worth at Worth on 18 February 1559, producing:

---

14   Occupation 'Clothier' John lived at Westminster in Southwark in 1538.

15   Pam Glover's alternative hypothesis to the one postulated here is that John of Bletchingley is this Roger's son. Pam has also helped me here with a few corrections and suggestions.

16   Alternatively, she was John the Younger's daughter.

- John 1559–14.12.1573 Worth;
- Johan 31.1.1560 Worth–5.3.1573 Worth;
- Mary 6.10.1561–?;
- Edward[17] 13.11.1566 Worth–c1633;
- William I 20.2.1568 Worth–22.7.1569 or 28.7.1576? Worth; and
- Roger 21 March 1571 Worth–1615?

Johan/Joane/Joan Swan/Swane was buried on 5 March 1574 in Worth. John the Younger then remarried Agnes Dovell (7.3.1558–1559 Worth? daughter of Peter Devill and Joane ?) at Worth on 13 June 1575, producing:

- William II c1576 Worth–4.2.1608 Worth;
- Martha c1577–4.6.1578 Worth; and
- Peter 11.2.1582 East Grinstead–25.1.1585 Worth.

Edward, a Bellows Maker, married Katherine Aburley 25.10.1562 Worth–28.9.1595 Worth at Worth on 9 September 1588, producing:

- Anne 1589–? who married John Staplehurst;
- Joseph(e) 1590–1634; and
- John 1592–1595.

Joseph(e) first married Mary, producing Edward 1622–? and then ? producing Berthia 1625–1626.

William II wed Agnes Aimas at Buckland on 23 November 1601, producing:

- Joahne 1.3.1606 Worth–5.5.1607 Worth; and
- Elizabeth 20.2.1604 Worth–27.3.1631 Balcombe.

John the Younger[18] lived at Lower Gibbs which was purchased from John and Ursula Dallett on 12 June 1564.

John the Younger evoked the inheritance custom of Borough English whereby the youngest son—*ie* William II—inherited Little/Lower Gibbs a Ven otherwise known as Fennes in Worth comprising a Cottage, four

---

17   Edward left a Will as did his son Joseph(e) and half-brother William II.

18   This next part is sourced from the Felbridge and District History Group. Felbridge straddles the Surrey-Sussex border some one and a half miles north-west of East Grinstead on the London Road.

acres of land, three acres of meadow, six acres of pasture and one acre of wood. John the Younger then enfeoffed[19] the property to be held in trust for William II.

In April 1600—John Gage, Lord of the Hedgecourt Manor—sued William II Blundell for trespass, claiming that the property was his, not William IIs—the Court found that it did belong to William II.

The papers associated with this property seem to offer a solution to the quandary of John of Bletchingley's forbears.

Now known as Michaelmas Farm, it is located on the southern side of Copthorne Road in Felbridge, wholly in Sussex, abutting the County boundary with Surrey. Adding to the difficulty of tracking freehold property in Manorial records in this case, there was confusion between the three local Manors about which Manor the various property holdings belonged to. Of interest to us here is that the holdings which today constitute Michaelmas Farm were amalgamated under the ownership of Sir Robert Clayton of Marden who held the Manor of Bletchingley in the mid-18th Century.

Some of the land belonged to the atte Fenn (Fenner) family who had connections with Worth from at least the 1300s when Gilbert atte Fenn gave his name to Gibbes affen which later came to be known as Lower Gibs a Ven and little Gibs a ven (aka Fennes in Worth).

Agnes Blundell (née Aimas) was her husband's Sole Executor. William II gave his lands in Horne and Worth to his half-brother Roger, including the house Roger was living in (Felcot Farmhouse) for the remainder of his life and on his death it was to pass on to Roger's son George and his heirs.

William II willed his house that he was living in and his lands in Worth (Little/Lower Gibbshaven) in trust to John Blundell (brother of George) and then to pass to John's heirs, although Agnes and Elizabeth were to remain in occupation until Elizabeth reached 18 or married whichever was sooner. Elizabeth was to be allowed to live in the property for the rest of her life

---

19   A method of avoiding restrictions on the passage of land title where the landowner gives the land to one person for the use of another person.

if she so desired when the property would become John's. When Elizabeth subsequently married John Faulconer at East Grinstead on 4 October 1624, the property became John Blundell's.

A codicil to the Will instructed that in the event of certain happenings such as Elizabeth dying before she reached 16, then his nephew George was to pay £4 to each of his siblings Thomasyn, Dorothye, Ursula, Margerie and **John** raised from the possession of the land that he had inherited from him.

Let's now look at William IIs half-brother Roger.

Roger Blundell son of John the Younger 1572–1615

Roger is thought to have been baptised on 21 March 1572 Worth and buried around 1615, marrying Margaret Agnes? at ? and producing:

- **John 3 August 1595 East Grinstead**;
- Thomasyn ?–?;
- George 1601–1659;
- Dorothye 1603–1587 East Grinstead–?;
- Ursula ?–?; and
- Margerie/Margerye/Margarett) 1605–?.

If the John above is our John of Bletchingley—Roger's son and the nephew of Edward and William II, then he would be Edward's son Josephe's first cousin and first cousin once removed to Josephe's son Edward. John's son Edmund would accordingly be the latter Edward's second cousin.

Pam Glover notes that 'cousin' was used differently in those days than now. Indeed, 'cousin' features in Chapter Four about the Blundell Lost Inheritance. Families consisted of parents, siblings and children with other relatives referred to as cousins, making it difficult to discern precise relationships.

Dorothea Teague has John born around 1580-1851 because of Chancery records, but no details of the precise date or where he was born are to hand. If her 1580-1581 date is true, then the whole scenario above falls apart.

Dorothea thought that John of Bletchingley was the son/brother of a Roger. In the case above, he is Roger's son.

The John above baptised in 1595 doesn't fit with the 1580 Chancery date. He can't be Roger's brother in this analysis as he would have been born after William II and inherited John the Younger's Estate as the youngest son instead of William II. William II makes no mention of having a brother John in his Will, but he does refer to his brother Roger and his sons George and John.

It may also be that John of Bletchingley is not descended from John the Elder.

They are the conundrums to be explored for Book Two.

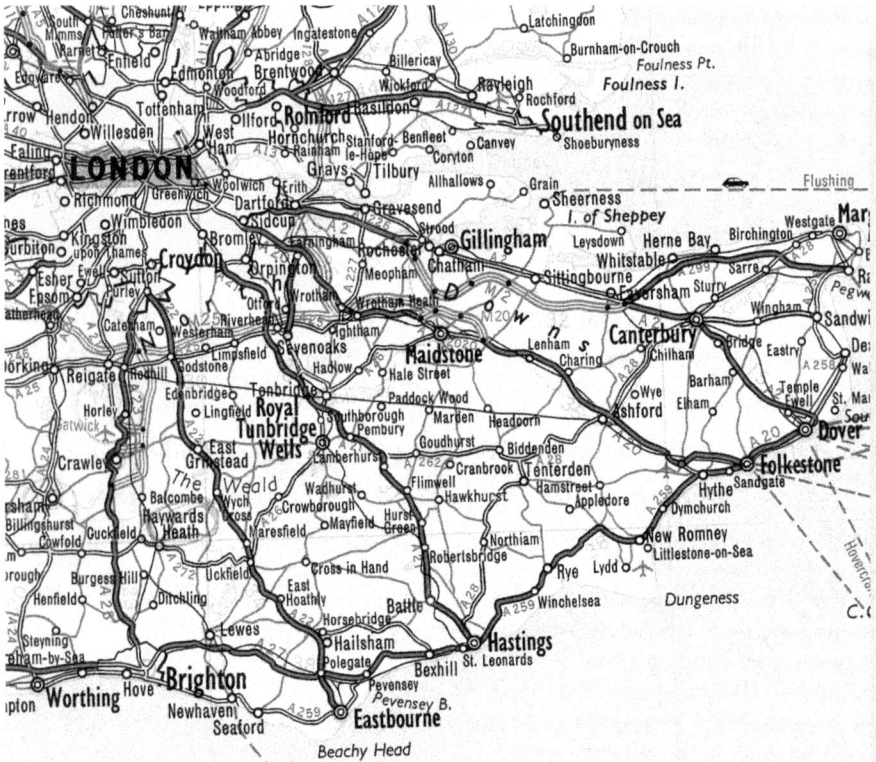

Extract of Road Atlas Map Showing Places of Interest.[20]

20   *Road Atlas Europe* John Bartholomew & Son Ltd Edinburgh..

Most of the following and the places mentioned can be found on the maps of the previous pages—occurring in London and three of the 'home counties' (*ie* Kent, Surrey and Sussex). Although the medieval village of Bletchingley is not shown on the next page, it lies between Redhill and Godstone on the A23 with Outwood on the road south to Horley.

The rest of this Chapter proceeds through John of Blehingly's proven line of descent from John of Bletchingley to our Joseph's Father, also named Joseph.

The Proven Record

John Blundell of Blechinglye 1580–1642

(now known as Bletchingley which has been adopted in the text)

John (born c1580[21]), a Yeoman, was buried on 17 June 1642 at Bletchingley.

The 1630s heralded a period of great social stress, leading to the Civil War between Royalists and the Parliament in England from 1642 to 1660. Families also split by their allegiance to the established church or radical puritanism.

A Yeoman was a small farmer who cultivated his own land, specifically one belonging to a category of freeholders ranking below the gentry[22] and formally qualified by owning property worth 40 shillings a year to enjoy certain legal privileges such as jury duty; a member of the most respected rank of the ordinary people and one of the highest class not entitled to heraldic arms.[23] *

The family lived in 'The Great House' in Hughes Fields Deptford in Kent at some stage and at least one of the children—Edmund—was born and lived there.

---

21 Based on John having been born/baptised in 1580 according to Mrs Teague's derivation from Chancery records that I haven't seen.

22 From the Old French *gentil* meaning Upper Class people who are well born, genteel and well-bred; specifically, the people just below the nobility in position and birth, being entitled to a Coat of Arms, especially those owning large tracts of land.

23 *The English Yeoman* by Mildred Campbell Merlin Press London 1983.

In the 'History of Dissenting Churches' published in 1884, Wilson writes that a Church of General Baptists existed at Deptford since Charles I.[24]

The History of Deptford Parish on the Thames River, about four miles from London in the north-west corner of Kent and partly in Surrey, was documented by Nathan Dews.[25] Kent is unquestionably the only County of Celtic[26] origin, the others deriving from Teutonic sources.[27]

Known as the village of West Greenwich or Deptford-le-Stronde before King Henry VIII 1509-1547, Dews acknowledges the non-conformist Ministers there in his book. Having long been a rendezvous for ships, Deptford was fixed upon by Henry VIII in 1513 as a site for a Royal Dockyard. In 1776, Captain Cook was commissioned to command His Majesty's sloop *Resolution*[28] for his third and what proved to be fatal voyage to the Pacific Ocean.

The East India Company received its first Charter from Queen Elizabeth I on 31 December 1600, proceeding to purchase and fit out their ships at Deptford where Samuel Pepys the famous diarist spent much of his time in the middle of the 17th Century as Secretary of the Admiralty during the reigns of Charles II and James II and visiting his intimate friend Mr Evelyn[29] at Sayes Court.

Samuel Pepys[30] worshipped at St Olave's, entering the gate at the end of the Street now named after him from the Navy Office and his own home in Seething Lane, a hop step and jump away from the Tower of London. Pepys

24   *The History and Antiquities of Dissenting Churches and Meeting Houses in London, Westminster and Southwark* by Walter Wilson four volumes published 1810.

25   *The History of Deptford* Second Edition Nathan Dews London 1884.

26   Meaning the languages and culture of Ireland, Scotland, Wales, Cornwall, the Isle of Man and Brittany.

27   People from north-western Europe of German origin including the Dutch and Scandinavians.

28   This ship was built and named after the earlier *Resolution* commanded by Sir Edward Hawke which was lost pursuing the enemy off the French coast. A 16-gun ship was named after him in 1793.

29   John Evelyn wrote a Memoir about his life and the events of the times between 1640 and 1706. His home and garden were called Sayes Court.

30   A FRS, man of many mistresses, Member of Parliament and an Administrator of the Navy, he is famous for his decade long diary which documents *inter alia* the effects of War, the Plague and the Great Fire of London.

was buried in a vault under 'Ye Communion Table' on 4 June 1703. St Olave's Noticeboard records 365 deaths from the Great Plague in 1665.

The Church of England St Alphege (*aka* Alfege) in Greenwich is named after the Archbishop of Canterbury who was martyred where St Alphege sits on 19 April 1012 by the Danes. Henry VIII was baptised in 1491 at this church, which was rebuilt around 1290 and features as a place of worship, baptisms *etc* for Ralph and Nicholas Blundell and their children.

St Nicholas, Deptford Parish's mother church, has existed since at least the 12th Century. In 1696, the church was too small for the rapidly increasing population, and was re-built—Isaac Loader[31] *Esq*, a native of Deptford and High Sheriff of the County, being the greatest benefactor, gave £901 which was recognised in an inscription on a tablet erected in the church. In his Will of 1714, Isaac gave £200 to be invested and the proceeds distributed annually to the poor of the Parish.

John of Bletchingley was a Baptist who held the strong Protestant conviction that the established Church of England was but an arm of the State in disguise. Members of their congregations regarded one another as equals in the Gospel—not persons graded and divided by the conventions of secular society; they could not therefore accept the authority of the State over their religious life.*

The economic, political, religious and social situation in early 16th Century Europe fostered a radical reform movement that led to development of the Baptist version of Christianity. In England, during the Puritan Protestant agitations of Elizabethan and Jacobean times (1558-1625), Baptist adherents regarded Reformation of the Church of England as incomplete and sought to abolish what they regarded as unscriptural and corrupt ceremonies.[32]

---

31   Isaac Loader emerges as a key figure in Chapter Four. He was probably born in Loader's Court, his Father's residence in the Stowage—*ie* a three-acre site at Deptford with frontage to the Thames River.

32   A group of English Protestants of the late 16th and 17th Centuries who sought to 'purify' the Church of England from its Catholic practices, maintaining that Reformation of the Church of England under Elizabeth I was incomplete and sought to simplify and regulate forms of worship. *The English Dictionary of Religion* edited by Mircea Eliade MacMillan Publishing Company NY and London 1987.

Elizabeth I reigned from 1558-1603, succeeded by James I from 1603-1625.

Known in the 17th Century as the Church of Christ, the early Baptists shared Puritan concerns about a Church of England which was still too Papist (*ie* Catholic and beholden to the Pope) and too engrossed with civil enforcement and ecclesiastical preferment; distinguishing themselves by insisting that participation in the church be a voluntary undertaking and by moving away from infant baptism to re-baptism or first baptism later in life as a personal un-coerced expression of faith.

This feature and their belief that the civil government had no responsibility—really, no right to enforce a religious conformity—because it was a private agreement and the conscience must be left free to decide for itself, alarmed more mainstream Christians at the time.

John's independent mind was accompanied by an ironic sense of humour, recorded in Uvedale Lambert's 'Bletchingley Parish History':

'Final sentence in the High Commission[33] in the case against John Blundell of Bletchingly on 6th December 1638. The defendant not appearing was ordered to be attached; for it appeared that on Whit-Monday, he being a special Bailiff with a warrant to arrest Robert Betts, about a quarter of an hour after evening prayers, did arrest Betts in Bletchingly churchyard, and upon some struggling rent a skirt of Betts' doublet; and furthermore, on Easter Day last within the church Blundell did in a saucy and scornful manner desire the Rector, Mr Hampton, to make him a Churchwarden, for that, he said, was a gainful place.

'On these facts, Blundell was held to have violated the liberties of Holy Church and consecrated ground and to have scoffed at the office of Churchwarden, for which he was enjoined to make a public submission in his Parish church, condemned in costs and heavily fined. Three Commissioners fixed the fine at £30 and the other three at £50, so the point was deferred till *the day of mittigation at the end of Hilary Term*. Whether Blundell ever paid the fine or not, no doubt he became a stronger dissenter than ever, and when he died in 1642, left Edmund who was only 15 years of age at the time with even more violent opinions than himself.' *

---

33   One of Charles IIs Prerogative Courts like the Star Chamber.

John's son Edmund's interactions with Rector Hampton are dealt with later.

The High Commission was England's Supreme Ecclesiastical Court. In 1553, Thomas Cranmer the Archbishop of Canterbury sponsored an Act of Parliament which made Puritanism an offence. Parliament abolished the Court in 1641.

A description of the area where John Blundell and his descendants lived at the time is of interest. It is particularly relevant that this quote comes from the 1925 'Surrey and Sussex Border Churches; a Baptist History':

> 'Along the North border of East Sussex stretch a range of low, picturesque hills which at one time bounded the great Andreds Weald Forest. Secluded villages and tiny hamlets stood here and there, such as Worth with its Saxon church, Turners Hill prominent on the ridge, and beyond, southward, Horsted Keynes; looking northward the view is beautiful, where lie the villages of Horne, Burstow and Horley.

> 'Now all so rural, it is difficult to imagine that 200 years ago and before, Weald was a busy iron district where rich haematite ore was dug and smelted in ancient 'bloomery' furnaces, with wood from the great forest, wrought with tilt hammers and rolled by mills worked with water wheels. Now all is changed, the iron masters, their miners and furnace men sleep in the village church yards and their activities have left little trace.'[34*]

One of the largest counties in England, Kent's name comes from the old English word 'cantus', meaning rim or edge. Julius Caesar renamed this to 'Cantium' in 51BC and the name stuck.[35]

John married Katherine Benet (daughter of George Bennett and Anne Culver/Culmer) at St George the Martyr Southwark on 27 November 1618 when he was 38 years old[36] and his wife 18. It was quite normal for better-off country folk to go up to town (London) to marry and St George's was a most popular church for this purpose. That may explain why the marriage was consecrated in Southwark and John wasn't baptised until 1619 in Burstow.

---

34 *A Surrey and Sussex Border Church: Reminiscences of old-time Baptist Assemblies on Turner's Hill, Horley and District 1650-1840 with a short history of the General Baptists* by T R Hooper London Morgan and Scott.

35 *An Economic and Social History of Britain since 1700* by M W Flinn London Macmillan 1975.

36 If the earlier analysis is correct he would have been 23 rather than 38 years old, which seems more likely.

John of Bletchingley was probably living alternately at Bletchingley and Deptford at the time. It may seem surprising that John married so late in life and that the wedding occurred some ten months after their first child (John) was born on 30 January 1618, but men of means wanting children were concerned to ensure their future wife was fertile and Katherine had passed that test. John junior[37] being christened one year after he was born was indicative of the Baptist faith in Mrs Teague's view.

As will soon be seen, John took his Biblical procreation duties seriously and had a child with both of his wives prior to marrying them. Katherine Benet was baptised on 18 May 1600 at St Laurence Thanet Kent and buried on 30 April 1633 at East Grinstead.

Katherine was the Mother of the children up to and including Ralph/Ralf.

Marriage certificates didn't exist at this time, so it's not possible to get the groom's or bride's Father's and Mother's names from that source. John is recorded as Blundle in the church register above, one of the many instances where the name is misspelt. Although we take it for granted nowadays that everyone can read and write, that was not always the case in these ancient times.

Moreover, spelling was quite idiosyncratic, different clerks having their own practices and preferences until Samuel Johnson's *Dictionary of the English Language* was published on 15 April 1755.

The current brick Georgian style St George the Martyr with St Alfege and St Jude was built in 1734-35; the Crypt was cleared in 1899, with the 1484 coffins reinterred at Brookwood Cemetery. The original medieval church was built at the beginning of the 12th Century and rebuilt at the end of the 14th Century. No accounts or minutes have survived prior to 1619, by which time the building was in such a poor state of repair, significant renovations were needed in 1629.

---

37   Sometimes referred to as John of Burstow.

Extract from the Church Baptism's, Marriages and Burial's register

The Southwark and Lambeth of Inner London today are vastly different from the times of our ancestors. It was commonplace for family members to walk significant distances to visit their relatives. For example, the ten-mile trip from Southwark to Bexley started out on what was then the Old Kent Road, traversing footpaths and fields. Market gardens still separated Peckham from Deptford and the associated Deptford Common. Brixton Hill, Honor Oak, Telegraph Hills and Tulse Hill were open country. Catford, Dulwich, Lewisham, Rushey Green *etc* were individual rural hamlets and Bromley was a lively market town, all quite separate from the London metropolis.*

It's also noteworthy that during the 19th Century, the population of England doubled every 50 years. In 1801 it was around eight million, 18 million in 1851 and 36 million by 1901 (including Wales). This sharp increase, combined with people leaving their towns and flocking to the cities—particularly London—meant the obliteration of nearby villages and hamlets which all became part of one vast urban conurbation.*

Aged 56 and widowed for almost three years John married again, to Catherine Ede on 19 March 1636 at St Nicholas' Deptford, when his eldest son was 17 and youngest just five, leading to the children Jane and Nicholas.

Jane (like her oldest half-brother John) was born some 12 months before her parents married. John the Father was probably on the look-out for a new wife to care for the younger children from his first marriage.

Little is known about this Catherine, but Ede was a common name in the Horley District—see Thomas of Cinderfield's section.

John of Bletchingley's children were:

- John born 30.1.1618 and baptised 3.1.1619 St Bartholomew Burstow–c1691 Wandsworth;[38]
- Maria c1621 St Bartholomew Horley–after 1680;
- Edmund born in The Great House Deptford, baptised 5.10.1623 St Mary Bletchingley Surrey–29.11.1699 St Alfege Greenwich;
- Elizabeth 16.10.1625 St Mary Bletchingley–21.12.1626 St Mary Bletchingley*[39];
- **Thomas of Wasps baptised 1626 Horne–3 July 1675 St Mary Bletchingley;**
- Ralph baptised[40] 8.12.1631 St Mary Bletchingley–11.4.1716 St Alfege Greenwich;
- Jane 12.3.1635 St Mary Bletchingley–c1660?; and
- Nicholas 26.6.1639 St Mary Bletchingley–31.8.1683 St Alfege Greenwich.[41]

In 1637, the Episcopalian[42] King Charles I triggered unrest by trying to impose the Book of Common Prayer on Ireland and Scotland, which they rejected, leading to Civil Wars in England, Ireland, Scotland and Wales.

The Scots invaded England after Charles I had another go in 1639, forcing him to call a Parliament to raise the funds to repel them and the situation deteriorated from there. The King and Parliament fell out; Charles I declared war on his own people, was defeated, tried for treason by

---

38   Probate granted 5 January 1692 Wandsworth–Pam Glover. Burial records for the period when he died are not available.

39   Note: The Register doesn't record 'daughter of', so this is uncertain.

40   Mrs Teague has Ralph baptised at St Alphege's Greenwich which was in Kent at the time.

41   Probate granted 11 September 1683 Greenwich–Pam Glover.

42   The Anglican and Catholic theory of church polity according to which the supreme ecclesiastical authority is vested in the episcopal order and not in any individual. *The Macquarie Dictionary*. In other words, church governance is vested in the Bishops.

Oliver Cromwell's Parliament, found guilty and executed at Whitehall on 30 January 1649.

Cromwell ordered Charles Is art collection be sold to pay off debt and as a symbol of the Monarchy's humbling. Leonardo da Vinci's *St John the Baptist* ended up in the French Royal Court. John Embrey, a Royal plumber, received £403 in cash, the balance of the bill to be paid in paintings; he chose 24 including Titian's *Escaping from the Mouth of Satan* valued at £100.

Scotland proclaimed Charles I's son—Charles II—as King on 5 February 1649, but Cromwell defeated him at the Battle of Worcester on 3 September 1651 and he fled to Europe. Known as the English Interregnum, the *de facto* Republic was ruled by Cromwell as a virtual Dictator of England, Ireland and Scotland.[43]

We have already seen evidence of this in the foregoing, but the extent of infant and maternal mortality becomes starker in what follows, as does the practice then to give subsequent children the same names as those who had died. Another Blundell family feature is the strong streak of sterility in both male and female lines and perhaps asexuality in the bachelors and spinsters.

John of Bletchingley was buried on 17 June 1642 at St Mary Bletchingley—his 1642 Will is mainly dealt with in Chapter Four, apart from the earlier extract.

Thomas Blundell of Wasps 1626–1675 The Third Son

Most of John of Bletchingley's children were baptised in Bletchingley's Parish Church of St Mary, except John junior (baptised at Burstow in 1619), Maria c1621 Horley? and Thomas—said to have been baptised in 1626 in Horne where various Blundells held land and were baptised.*

The page containing the years 1625-27 in the Horne Church Register has been cut across and the lower half torn out. Whoever did this probably did so on the basis that it would benefit them if the record of Thomas Blundell's baptism was never found. George Blundell of Burstow, son of

---

43   See also Chapter Two.

John of Hutchens, John of Horley's first son seems the most likely culprit.* This relates to the Blundell Lost Inheritance which is dealt with in the next Chapter.

Thomas of Wasps married Joane Barber (1636—?) on 2 October 1655 at St George the Martyr Southwark, following in his Father's footsteps, including that Thomas' first child—John of Horley—was probably born two years before his parents' wedding, Minister Sam Hyland officiating.

Thomas' children were:

- **John of Horley born 1653?–30 January 1712 St Bartholomew Horley;**[44]
- Thomas I born 11.4.1656, baptised 4.5.1656 St Botolph Aldgate–17.7.1657 St Botolph Aldgate; #
- Sarah 19.10.1657 St Botolph #–1.7.1675 Bletchingley;#
- Thomas II of Burstow 16.6.1659 St Botolph–?;
- Mary 2.4.1661 St Botolph–6.12.1662 St Botolph;
- Hannah 12.10.1662 St Botolph–?; and
- Nicholas 24.6.1665 St Botolph–30.9.1665 St Botolph.#[45]

It will be noted that only John and Thomas II survived until adulthood.

St Botolph sits on a site where there has been a church for over 1000 years, outside the 'Ald' gate on the eastern edge of the City of London.[46]

---

44   Courtesy of Pam Glover as are the entries marked #. The Church of England St Botolph is sometimes just called Aldgate Church. Aldgate in Central London in the historic County of Middlesex is at the eastern most gateway through the London Wall.

45   Pam Glover notes that Nicholas was actually buried at Bedlam which was being used at the time for overflow burials due to the plague, there being some 40 burials per day at the time. St Botolph's Register for Burials includes 'Here followeth those burials which belong to the month of September 1665; in the sad tyme of the visitation.' The 500-year old Bedlam graveyard near Liverpool Street, which was unearthed during Crossrail works, revealed some 20000 skeletons including patients of the infamous Bedlam mental asylum, the poor and **religious non-conformists**.

46   London originally had four such churches, the others being Aldersgate, Bishopsgate and Billingsgate the latter being destroyed in the Great Fire of 1666. All four were named after St Botolph, who died around 680AD, and became known as the Patron Saint of Wayfarers. The Great Fire, started in Pudding Lane about a mile east of the Strand, destroyed nearly three quarters of the City, but stopped short of Somerset House. It cleansed much of the area of any lingering disease associated with the Great Plague.

Travellers prayed here on their arrival and departure. Chaucer lived in rooms above the gatehouse in the 1370s while Daniel Defoe who married there, gave an horrific account of the 1665 Great Plague when over 5000 bodies were buried in a pit dug in the churchyard. Sir Isaac Newton lived opposite the church when he was Master of the Royal Mint.

Following Lord Protector Oliver Cromwell's death on 3 September 1658, the political crisis which caused the Interregnum was resolved and the Monarchy restored. His effigy lay in state for many weeks at Somerset House. Although some mourned his death, many saw it as a relief; John Evelyn the diarist and Royalist called it the joyfullest funeral he ever saw.

Some two years later, as Charles II was about to return to the throne, Cromwell's body was exhumed, hanged at Tyburn, beheaded and the head displayed on a pike at Westminster Hall[47] until the late 1680s.

Charles II resumed the throne on his 30th birthday 29 May 1660. Legal documents were then dated as if he had succeeded his Father as King in 1649.[48]

Charles II returned encumbered by substantial debt incurred during his exile and when Parliament reassembled, they set about remedying this situation by calling on the nation for a 'Free and Voluntary Present' to the King—accompanied by the passage of an Act of Parliament authorising this.

Subscriptions were collected in 1661–62 in various market towns. Although 'voluntary', it was clearly politic to subscribe and most of the

---

47   While William the Conqueror erected the Tower of London, it was his son William Rufus who built Westminster Hall in 1097. The oldest of the Parliamentary buildings the refurbished version stands near where Big Ben is now.

48   The English Civil War and Interregnum meant that many records were lost during the late 1640s through to 1661. In 1653, the Government assumed control of all Church Registers and appointed Civil Officers in each Parish to keep custody of the books. These Officers charged a one shilling fee to make an entry in the Registers, so many baptisms, burials and marriages went unrecorded. In 1654, marriages became the sole responsibility of Justices of the Peace rather than the Clergy. When Charles II was restored to the throne in 1660, these provisions were repealed. In many cases the appointed Civil Officer had previously been the Church of England Clergyman for that Parish and their Registers were generally well maintained. Courtesy of Pam Glover.

better-off members of the community seem to have done so. Our Thomas, Yeoman of Burstow, gave two shillings and six pence. His kinsmen Edmund and George of Bletchingley gave 30 shillings and two shillings and six pence respectively, while James of Burstow[49] contributed five shillings.*

Charles II was King during the 1665 Great Plague and Great Fire of London which started on 2 September 1666 and extinguished the Plague.

Charles II died on 6 February 1685—succeeded by his brother James II who ruled for three years, during which (as a Catholic) he became directly involved in the political battles between Catholicism and Protestantism.

Thomas senior died at the age of 49 in 1675, bequeathing:

> Wasps at Outwood in Burstow Parish and the inventory of '...
> all and singular the Goods and Cattell and Chattles ...' attached
> to his Will and valued at £171.8s.4d to his eldest son John.*

Younger son—Thomas of Burstow—was left £100.*

John Blundell of Horley 1653–1712

John Blundell, Husbandman[50] and bachelor aged 22 years of Burstow married Elizabeth Holmes (baptised 30.11.1655 Horley[51]—buried 4.5.1709 Horley) spinster aged 20 years of Horley on 21 June 1675 at St Peter and St Paul Chaldon. Elizabeth's Father gave consent as she was under the age of 21. Both are buried in the Parish Church grounds at Horley, their tombstone being the earliest discernible of the many Blundells buried there.*

In the 1688-1691 War, James II was deposed by William of Orange who became William III of England and ruled jointly with his wife Queen Mary II—they were cousins and grandchildren of Charles I. In keeping with the 1689 Bill of Rights, they swore an oath to uphold Parliament's laws, the laws of God, the true profession of the Gospel and the Protestant Reformed faith.

---

49   The second of John of Hutchens three sons.

50   A 'Husbandman' was a free tenant farmer/small land owner whose social status was below that of a Yeoman.

51   All of these events in Horley refer to St Bartholomew's Church.

Following a plot on William IIIs life by some Roman Catholics in 1695, men of standing in England were required to take an Oath of Allegiance. Petty Bag Office lists at the Public Record Office show that John of Horley—together with George and James Blundell of Horne—took the Oath.[*]

Yeoman, especially those of Essex, Kent and Surrey increased in wealth due to the rapid growth of London and inflation at this time. As they owned their own land and sold produce, inflation did not unduly affect them, and they became better off. They started to send their children to newly founded schools and these young people were destined to become the middle classes.[*]

From the middle of the 17th Century until the present day, our Blundells have owned many plots of land and four 15th Century open hall Yeoman's houses of Wealden character in Surrey—Benhams, Cinderfield, Hutchens and Wasps—which form an intrinsic part of our family history.[*]

As well as inheriting Wasps, John of Horley also came to own the farmstead of Hutchings/Hutchens, a late 15th Century Open Hall House, by an indenture of 1682 from his father-in-law John Holmes:

> 'In consideration of the mortall love and natural affection which the said John Blundell beareth to Elizabeth his now wife, John Holmes hath settled and made over unto the said Elizabeth Blundell his only daughter and child, and the heirs of her body lawfully begotten by the said John Blundell, one House and lands, tenements and hereditments called by the name 'Hutchings' lying and being in Horley, containing 40 acres etc.'[*]

Hutchings was originally built for a reasonably substantial Yeoman. Now known as 'Hutchens' and 'victorianised' on the outside as can be seen on the next page, Mrs Teague observed that it was relatively unspoiled within and still occupied by a Blundell descendant in 1985.

It was due to the inheritance of this house that the family settled in that John became known as—John of Horley. From the baptism of their eldest child in 1676 until the present day an unbroken line of Blundells have been baptised and buried at St Bartholomew Horley.[*]

John's younger brother Thomas also occupied 'Wasps' for a time, although precise details are not available, and he is known as Thomas of Burstow.*

John of Horley's children were:

- Elizabeth 30.7.1676 Horley–18.1.1706 Horley;
- John of Hutchens 3.3.1678 Horley Yeoman–1.1.1733 Horley;
- **THOMAS of Cinderfield baptised 1 April 1680 Horley–buried 20 November 1740 Horley;**
- Nicholas 27.9.1682 Horley–5.9/10/11/12.1682;[52]
- Sarah 13.8.1684 Horley–?; and
- Mary 4.5.1687 Horley–?.

Signs that John of Horley was in financial trouble emerged in 1699 as he signed a Bill of Indebtedness agreeing to pay his cousin Shadrach the Elder a loan of £50 within the next 12 months plus £1.5s in interest. Small repayments are noted on the back of the document, although it is likely that this loan was never repaid in full. The Bill of Indebtedness and the inability to meet the attendant conditions signaled the start of the eventual financial collapse of this branch of the family.*

John of Horley made his Will on 22 November 1711 and was buried on 30 January 1712. His eldest son John was already living in Hutchens *

*Hutchens in 1860s, drawn by A. Osmond Brown from a photograph *

---

52   Pam Glover notes that the Register has the date but not the month and the entry is between one for 8 September and the next one of 22 December.

at the time, which must have been bequeathed to him prior to his Father making his Will, because there is no mention of John (or Nicholas who died in 1682) in the Will.

Thomas was the principal beneficiary and sole Executor of his Father's Will.

Daughters Elizabeth (wife of Jasper Cox) received £30 of lawfull money of Great Brittain 18 months after her Father's death, Sarah (Worseley) £30 12 months after her Father's death and Mary Blundell benefitting to the tune of £50 one year after her Father's passing. All of these bequests were paid by Thomas.

The Will included:

> 'I give and devise unto my Loving Son Thomas Blundell All that my messuage and herediments containing Barnes, Buildings, Gardens, Orchards and Lands with their appurtenances commonly called or known by the Name of Wasps situate, lying and being in the Parish of Burstow, in the said countie of Surrey.'

Thomas was also given other property in Burstow—all of which was to go to 'his heirs and assigns forever.' The Will has the signatures of three witnesses with John of Horley's mark on it and is sealed with the imprint of a finely carved cameo head of a Roman Emperor.

Probate was not taken out until May 1714, the same year that Thomas II of Burstow (together with his deceased brother John's sons and the husbands of his daughters), raised a mortgage of £127.10s from their Father's cousin Shadrach the Elder on the entire farmstead of Wasps.*

That is, the mortgage was raised by John of Horley's younger brother Thomas II of Burstow, together with John of Horley's sons—John of Hutchens and Thomas of Cinderfield and his daughters Elizabeth with her husband Jasper Cox and Sarah with her husband William Worseley. Mary is not mentioned here, so had probably died before him.

Elizabeth married Jasper Cox on 4 February 1700 at Horne who died in 1725 and left his properties and money to her (two children having been born and died). She remarried Jasper Briant on 9 July 1730 at Bletchingley and was buried on 23 April 1745 at St Bartholomew Horley. Briant died in

1747 and nothing is known about further children or what happened to the Estate when he died.

Sarah married William Worseley on 23 June 1706 at St Stephan Coleman Street London. Nothing further is yet known about Sarah or her sister Mary.

Thomas Blundell of Cinderfield 1680–1740

Thomas, a bachelor, married Mary Ede (26 May 1692 Horley—13 May 1753 Horley St Mary[53] daughter of Richard and Mary Rouse) spinster by licence on 25 November 1713 in Horley.

Marriages were usually by licence or by banns.

Banns (an old English word meaning Proclamation) which date from 1215 required the marriage to be announced publicly on three Sundays before the wedding date in the Parish where the couple intended to marry. This gave anyone the opportunity to raise objections to the marriage proceeding—for example, lack of consent, inappropriate kinship, or a pre-existing marriage that hadn't been dissolved or annulled.

The wording of Church of England banns was:

'I publish the banns of marriage between x and y:

This is the first/second/third time of asking. If any of you know cause or just impediment why these two persons should not be joined in Holy Matrimony, ye are to declare it'.

(*Book of Common Prayer* 1662).

Banns meant that the whole Parish knew your business. For privacy reasons or the need to marry in a hurry, the alternative was a licence, which cost more than banns and was often chosen by those with (or pretensions to) gentility and money.

To obtain a licence, the bridegroom applied at the Registry for the jurisdiction, submitting a statement under oath that there were no impediments to the marriage. The document included the names, ages, occupations and marital status of the parties and any minors had to name

---

53   Most likely, being Mary Blundell widow and at Horne; alternatively, Mary wife of John Blundell gent from Croydon on 9 November 1737 at St Mary Bletchingley.

the parent or guardian giving their consent. A money bond was sometimes required as a surety. For example:

'*Charles,* by Divine Providence, Archbishop of Canterbury, Primate of all England and Metropolitan, by the Authority of Parliament lawfully authorized for the Purposes within written: To our well-beloved in CHRIST, *X of the Parish of A in the County of B, Bachelor and Y of the Parish C in the County of D (status).*

'GRACE and HEALTH. WHEREAS it is alleged that ye have resolved to proceed to the Solemnization of true and lawful Matrimony and that you greatly desire to cause and obtain that the same be solemnized in the Face of the Church; We being willing that these your Desires may be the more speedily obtain a due Effect, and to the End thereof, that this Marriage may be publicly and lawfully solemnized in the Parish Church of ... (town) by the Rector, Vicar or Curate thereof, without the Publication or Proclamation of the Banns of Matrimony, and at any Time in the Year, provided there shall appear no lawful Impediment in this Case by Reason of any Pre-contract, Consanguinity, Affinity, or any other Cause whatsoever, nor any Suit, Controversy, or Complaint be moved, or now depending before any Judge Ecclesiastical or Civil, for or by Reason thereof; and likewise, That the Celebration of this Marriage be had and done publicly in the aforesaid Church between the Hours of Eight and Twelve in the Forenoon. We for lawful Causes, graciously grant this our Licence and Faculty, as well as to you the Parties contracting as to the Rector, Vicar or Curate of the aforesaid Parish who is deigned to solemnize the Marriage between you, in the Manner and Form above specified, according to the Rites of the Book of Common Prayer, set forth for that Purpose by the Authority of Parliament.

'Provided always, that if in this Case there shall hereafter appear any Fraud Suggested to us, or Truth suppressed at the Time of obtaining this Licence, then this Licence to be void and of no Effect in Law, as if the same had never been granted; and in that Case we inhibit all Ministers, if any Thing of the Premises shall come to their Knowledge, that they do not proceed to the Celebration of the said Marriage without first consulting us, or our Commissary of the Faculties. Given under the Seal of our Office of Faculties this R Day of (month) in the Year of our Lord, One Thousand X Hundred and Y and in the First Year of our Translation.

'[Signed] ... Registrar'[54]

---

54   Jane Austen's London.

The site of a former bloomery iron furnace, Cinderfield/Sinderfield—much smaller than Wasps—was built in 1550-1590; smoke from the fireplaces dispersing in the house until the chimney and hearth were added.[*]

Following the mortgage of Wasps to Shadrach the Elder, Thomas occupied this lesser Yeoman's 16th Century farmhouse called Cinderfield—up Meath Lane which leads from Horley among the green fields on the River Mole's banks about a mile and a half north of Horley Parish.[*]

Thomas and Mary Ede were married in November 1713. She probably had one or more miscarriages before Thomas I was born in 1717 and he and the succeeding two children died in infancy as did two later children. It was not until 1725 when Thomas Senior was 45 that he succeeded in producing a third son—who lived to become his heir and was also named Thomas.

Thomas of Cinderfield's children were:

- Thomas I 15.3.1717 Horley–4.8.1719 Horley;
- Mary I 5.8.1720 Horley–20.10.1720 Horley;
- Richard I 18.7.1722 Horley–16.4.1730 Horley;
- **Thomas II of Chelsfield baptised 18 March 1726 Horley–died Chelsfield buried 10 February 1783 Horley;**
- John 1.3.1728 Horley–6.3.1728 Horley;
- Mary II 7.3.1729 Horley–4.5.1730 Horley;[55]
- John II the Cordwainer[56] 18.9.1732 Horley–28.3.1812 Horley; and
- Richard II 27.8.1736 Horley–21.9.1811 Horley, Yeoman and bachelor of Benhams.

Thomas of Cinderfield's older brother—John of Hutchens' male line—came to an end with the death of his youngest son Thomas of Horsted Keynes in 1787.[*]

John of Hutchens' three sons were:

- George of Burstow Hall;
- James–late of Hutchens; and
- Thomas of Horsted Keynes.

---

55   Not proven.

56   A Cordwainer was a shoemaker who made shoes and boots from the finest new leathers whereas a Cobbler repaired them and could make shoes and boots only from old leather.

All three sons died without progeny, so his Estate passed—as bequested—to Richard II* youngest son of his brother Thomas of Cinderfield.

Henry Shove of Betchworth, Husbandman (eldest son and heir of Thomas Shove late of Burstow Husbandman deceased—Jane Blundell's husband?) released the lease of a cottage called Bellweathers at Outwood with a garden and orchard at Burstow Common in his Will for 21 shillings to George Blundell Yeoman of Burstow—the George of Burstow Hall referred to above.

Lesser Yeoman's 16th Century farmhouse called Cinderfield—the home of Thomas Blundell of Cinderfield*

Richard II must have been a very eminent member of the Horley community and church because he was afforded the rare privilege at the time of having a sermon delivered by the Minister at his funeral and burial.

Richard IIs March 1796 Will[57] decreed that all his real and personal estate be sold, and the monies paid first to discharge all his just debts and then:

- the debts owing to him by his brother John (the Cordwainer) were to be repaid to his youngest son Thomas (of Horsted Keynes) no earlier than one year after Richard IIs decease. In other words, Richard IIs older brother John was not relieved of his debts;

---

57   This and the following paragraphs courtesy of Pam Glover who translated the Will.

- the remainder was to be divided among all the children of his brothers John the Cordwainer and Thomas of Chelsfield (deceased 1783) and the children of his nephew (Thomas of Chelsfield's son Thomas) share and share alike when they reached 21 years of age;
- good friends Thomas Best and Thomas Headman both Yeoman of Horley received £5 apiece for their trouble in (inkblot makes it impossible to decipher the last word) and were charged with seeing that the Will was duly carried into execution;
- friend William Comber a Yeoman (presumably a brother of Ann Comber below and her sister Elizabeth who married John the Cordwainer's older brother—Thomas of Chelsfield) was a joint Executor of the Will with Richard IIs nephew George (John the Cordwainer's oldest son); and
- witnessed by the signatures of Ambrose Glover, William Lewis and Thomas Davies.

Among other things it is noteworthy that Richard IIs Will specified that the share and share alike applied to both male and female children. This is unusual as Wills of this time usually benefitted only the male lines.

Moreover, the Will specifies that if any of the intended recipients were to die before achieving their majority, then their share would be divided equally among their brothers and sisters. The nephew Thomas who died in 1804 had married Elizabeth Bassett in 1774 and they had many children—see page 66.

John the Cordwainer married Anne Comber of Charlwood (c1731–13.5.1779 St Bartholomew Horley) on 10 April 1758 at Horley. When John died in 1812, the Parish Registers noted that he was of 'Outwood'—probably 'Benhams'—which was Richard II's house and farm near Hutchens in Horley Row.*

John the Cordwainer's three sons, George, John and Thomas all married and had substantial families. Mrs Teague goes into considerable detail about how George's son Richard went about trying to reclaim the Blundell Estates by fighting the Hughes family in Chancery.[58]*

In 1759, Shadrach II's Widow Ann Blundell defended her possession of Wasps, but following a convoluted court case she suffered a rare loss, Wasps being returned to the Blundells of Horley.*

Thomas of Cinderfield was buried on 27 November 1740 at Horley and his wife Mary Ede also died in Horley and was buried there on 13 May 1753.

Note: Before1752, to accord with Caesar's Julian Calendar, the year was reckoned to change on 25 March in Britain.

The Gregorian Calendar[59]—a refinement of the Julian Calendar— came into effect in 1582, shortening the average year by 0.0075 days to stop the drift of the calendar with respect to the equinoxes and to alter the lunar cycle used by the Church to calculate the date for Easter, restoring it to the time of year originally celebrated by the early Church. To deal with the ten days of accumulated drift, 4 October 1582 was followed by 15 October so that there was no discontinuity in the cycle of weekdays of the *Anno Domini* era.

Britain didn't adopt the Gregorian Calendar until 1752—which came into effect in two parts:

- first, that the year 1752 which began on 25 March should be deemed to end on 31 December that year; and
- second, the day after 1 September 1752 became 14 September 1752.

The implications of this for some dates in our family history were drawn to my attention by Pam Glover and have been changed accordingly.

In Britain therefore, dates before 25 March 1752 derive from the Julian Calendar and references to New Year's Day before 1752 mean 25 March.

---

58   An English Court of Equity that followed a loose set of rules in an endeavour to avoid the slow pace of change and possible harshness (or inequity) of the common law.

59   Named after Pope Gregory XIII, who decreed it in 1582—it was applied by most Catholic nations at the time.

Thomas Blundell of Chelsfield 1726–1783

Thomas Blundell Husbandman and bachelor aged 27 married Elizabeth Comber spinster aged 22 (baptised 29.5.1730 Horley–c1779 Chelsfield daughter of Thomas and Mary) by licence, both being of Horley, at St Mary Magdelene in Reigate on 10 October 1752. James Roffey Cordwainer of Reigate was the witness and both signed their names on the Marriage Licence Application.

Thomas' first three children were born in Horley, the next child's baptism (George) being registered in what was then remote Chelsfield where the rest of their children were born and baptised.

Thomas' younger brother John the Cordwainer married Anne Comber, Elizabeth's sister (John's surname being recorded with one 'l' in the Parish Register). John Cocker was the witness and the marriage was by banns.

About 1758, Thomas' inability to pay his debts led to bankruptcy and he was forced to move out of Cinderfield, the property he had inherited from his Father, after the Hughes family surprisingly gained control of Shadrach II's Estates.*

Aged 34 and no doubt 'encouraged' by the Hughes family, he and his wife Elizabeth left Cinderfield and Horley for Chelsfield twenty-eight and a half miles away.* Why they chose then remote Chelsfield is not known but Settlement Records prove that it is the same Thomas.[60]

Their sons and grandchildren were bereft of property, although Thomas paid window tax of three shillings on seven lights in Lower Chelsfield.*[61]

The window tax, which was introduced in 1696, became a progressive property tax based on the number of windows in the house. Apocryphally the origin of the term 'daylight robbery', the tax was repealed in 1851.

---

60   Personal correspondence with Dorothea Teague.

61   The window tax was introduced by King William III in 1696 to impose a tax relative to the prosperity of the taxpayer, but without the controversy that surrounded the idea of income tax at that time.

It's hard to imagine, but during the second part of the 18th Century more than half of England's population resorted to the Parish for assistance. A pauper was defined as someone given a small amount of dole money by the Parish.*

Although no Blundells appear on Charity Lists, a number are marked 'P' for pauper in accordance with the unpopular Baptismal and Burial Tax of 1783-94 by which three pence was collected by the Clergy and paid to the Government for each baptism and burial. Some compassionate Clergy who disagreed with this tax falling on poor people would ensure it was not collected by inserting a 'P' against the names in the Register as they did in the case of actual paupers who were the only people officially exempt from the tax.*

Thomas of Chelsfield's children were:

- John of Eltham 1.2.1753 Horley–15.3.1826 Eltham[62] married Ann Bunn (1751–14.7.1824 Greenwich) on 18 November 1776 at Chelsfield;
- Thomas 16.3.1755 Horley–2.9.1804 Chelsfield married Elizabeth Basset at ? on 14 November 1774 at Chelsfield;
- Mary 20.2.1757 Horley–26.4.1757 Horley;
- George 28.12.1760 Chelsfield–15.3.1835 Shoreham married Anne Johnson (1760–?) on 3 November 1788 at Shoreham;
- William 27 February 1763 Chelsfield–died 1807 Shoreham when thrown from a horse married Ann Johnson (a cousin of his brother George's wife) on 2 May 1785 at Chelsfield;
- Elizabeth 18.1.1765 Chelsfield–? married John Anderson on 9 November 1787 at Shoreham;[63]
- Mary 19.7.1767 Chelsfield–?;
- Sarah 1771–1771 Chelsfield; and
- **JOSEPH baptised 7 August 1774 Chelsfield–died 2 May 1840 and buried 8 May 1840; both at Maidstone.**

---

62   John's headstone in the Eltham Anglican churchyard records his Father as Thomas of Sinderfield in the Parish of Horley County Surrey.*

63   Pam Glover cites plenty of records for John (property, criminal etc); nothing further is known about Elizabeth.

George, who we will return to in the next Chapter, had seven sons all of whom settled near the Kent-Surrey border at Halsted, Keston, Knockholt *etc.* One of his sons was named Shadrach, whose Memorial in East Bergholt church bears the same squirrel crest as that worn by the Ince Blundells. This is probably a grandiose fabrication as no link has ever been found between our Blundell line and the famed Lancashire Blundells of Ince and Crosby near Liverpool who have held lands there since 1154.[64]

John of Eltham, his younger brother William and cousin George the Miller of Horley were among those who signed an agreement with John the Cordwainer's three sons—John, Thomas and George (replaced by his son Richard as reported earlier)—seeking to regain the Blundell Estates, all being descended from Thomas of Cinderfield, the true beneficiary of Shadrach II's Will, despite the fact that the Hughes family had been in possession of all the property for nearly 50 years when they set off on yet another doomed frolic.*

Thomas of Horley in the preceding table—sometimes called of Cinderfield (as with his Father)—was for obvious reasons later described as of Chelsfield; the ancestor from whom sprang the Kentish Blundells.* Pam Glover who has given so generously of her time and efforts descends from this line.

As succeeding generations of this Thomas' five sons, two surviving daughters, 18 grandsons and 14 granddaughters multiplied, they settled in the towns and villages surrounding Chelsfield, such as Bromley, Chislehurst, Cudham, Eltham, Halstead, Knockholt, St Mary Cray, Shoreham and West Wickham. Most of these now lie within the London Borough of Bromley with one or two over the boundary in Sevenoaks.*

They were all within a day's walking distance of one another, except where Thomas of Chelsfield the Elder's youngest son—our direct ancestor Joseph senior ended up—and founded the Blundell clan in the Maidstone area of Kent.

---

64   From the Horley Local History Society.

The ten Blundells in the Bromley Trades Directories from the earliest in 1866 to 1900 are all Thomas of Chelsfield's grand or great grandsons.*

Thomas of Chelsfield died in 1783 aged 57 years rightly believing he was the designated heir to large estates (Clarke Mansion House at Foxhall Suffolk [now known as East Bergholt Lodge], Kirdford in Sussex, other real estate in Sussex and Surrey [Burstow and Horley], Stratford, Little Yeldon and Toperfield in Essex and Kent) which unequivocally should have come to him and his heirs in accordance with his Father's second cousin Shadrach Blundell's directions 27 years earlier. Thomas was carried back to Horley for burial.*

Shadrach II's Will—with its series of caveats, should have led, through the death of various parties and their failure to produce legitimate male heirs—to his Estate passing:

> '... to the male heirs of Thomas Blundell late of Cinderfield, share and share alike and to the male heirs of their body lawfully begotten.'*

Shadrach's grievous oversight of not leaving an authorised Will led to protracted litigation over two Centuries as well as a considerable change in lifestyle and much bitterness for those who considered that they had been tricked out of their rightful inheritance, as is dealt with in the next Chapter.* Many people wasted a lot of effort and money attempting to gain for themselves and their families a share of Shadrach II's wealth—all without success.*

Motivated partly by greed and spurred on by romantic impulse, the portion that they could have achieved, with the effluxion of time, would have been very small indeed, for by 1850 Thomas Blundell of Chelsfield had 67 grand-children and that is only the Kentish total to which must be added the Horley numbers.*

Pam Glover has provided the following details re George Blundell in the table on page 65 who married Anne Johnson at Shoreham on 3 November 1788, producing:

- William 1789–1863 Lime Merchant;
- Thomas 1791–1866 Wood Cutter and Agricultural Labourer;
- George 1793–1887 Brickmaker;
- Rosamund 1795–1864 married Daniel Whitehead, Agricultural Labourer;
- Joseph 1797–1879 Agricultural Labourer married Ann Sargent;
- Richard 1800–1892 Agricultural Labourer;
- John 1803–?;
- James 1805–1892 Fruitier and Agricultural Labourer; and
- Charles 1807–1899 Fruitier.

Their occupations and lifespans are noteworthy.

When Thomas of Chelsfield's penultimate son William came to marry Ann Johnson in 1785, neither could sign their names—a retrograde step in this family—indicating the level to which their station in life had fallen.

Joseph Blundell Senior 1774–1840

Joseph, born in 1774 at Chelsfield, the youngest child of Thomas and Elizabeth Comber, trekked much further afield than his siblings searching for work before settling in Thurnham (*aka* Thornham)—the picturesque village in the North Downs near Maidstone*—over 26 miles from Chelsfield.

Here he met and married by Banns Elizabeth Presnall/Presnell (c1781—died 28.4.1845 buried 4.5.1845 both at Maidstone) both of this Parish on 17 November 1797 at the Thurnham Parish Church 'Saint Mary the Virgin', by the Vicar John Hodson. Joseph made his mark, Elizabeth signed her name and the witnesses were Daniel Hadlow and Richard Catt (a frequent marriage witness).

Their first son Joseph was baptised there almost a year later on 7 October 1798, while their second child Sarah was born on 24 April 1800 at Boxley and also baptised nearly 12 months later, suggesting Joseph junior had been born some time before his baptism and that the family were still part of the Baptist faith.

By the time of Sarah's baptism, the family were in Sandling North Maidstone, the County town of Kent, Joseph senior and Elizabeth ended their days there in the 1840s. Joseph of Pleasant Row was buried on 8 May 1840; Elizabeth of Week Street on 4 May 1845—both in Maidstone.

Joseph and Elizabeth's children were:

- **JOSEPH 7 October 1798 Thurnham–responsible for the Australian Blundell dynasty see Chapter Six;**
- Sarah 21.6.1801 All Saints Maidstone–23.11.1828 All Saints Maidstone;
- Jane born Maidstone 27.1.1804 baptised 25.3.1804 All Saints Maidstone–19.4.1870 Ricketts Folly Halstead Sevenoaks;
- Maria Eleanor ('Ellen') born 17.3.1806 baptised 18.5.1806 All Saints Maidstone–14.5.1868 Maidstone;
- George born 16.9.1807 ^ baptised All Saints Maidstone–8.4.1855 Maidstone;
- John born 22.3.1812 Sandling North Maidstone baptised 15.4.1812 All Saints Maidstone–3.7.1882 East Malling; and
- William 25.3.1814 ^ baptised All Saints Maidstone–?.3.1897 Maidstone.

It is notable that none of Joseph senior's sons was named Thomas after Joseph's Father which may indicate there were difficulties between them and why he moved so far away from the family home.

The Thurnham Registers five years prior to Joseph junior's baptism and 20 years after, revealed no other Blundells, but many Presnalls. The 1851 Census shows John as born in Sandling but the 1861 Census records him as having been born in Boxley. No settlement records exist for Thurnham Parish so it's not possible to prove when Joseph senior moved to Thurnham from Chelsfield. Examination of the nearby Boxley Registers revealed nothing of interest.

A search of the original Baptism Registers at All Saints Maidstone from 1799 to 1818, revealed the information in the previous table. Although all entries recorded the parents as Joseph and Elizabeth Blundell, only Sarah's (the second born child) entry recorded their place of abode as Boxley. A search of marriages from 1819 to 1826 and burials from 1816 to 1840 at All Saints proved fruitless.

The 1801 Census revealed Maidstone had 8000 people, Adford 2600, Hythe 1400 and Sevenoaks 2600—small numbers—living in the District at the time.

The Bishop's Transcripts at the Cathedral Library (East Kent Archives Office) Canterbury revealed the following baptism dates:

- Sarah 21 June 1801;
- Jane 25 March 1804;
- Maria Eleanor 18 May 1806; and
- John 15 April 1812.

^The dates in the table on the previous page (except for our Joseph) include birth dates where known as well as baptisms. It was quite unusual at the time to record birth dates as religion and church occupied such a central position in people's lives. The Bishop's Transcripts show how George fits in and reveal another son William, whose baptism shows his Father Joseph as a blacksmith. Summary details relating to Joseph and Elizabeth's children their marriages and issue follow (except for Joseph junior who is dealt with in Chapter Six).

Sarah married James Stanhope Stevens (1794–1862) on 21 November 1824 at Thurnham, producing:

- George 1828 Maidstone–?.

Jane married (Sergeant) William Watts (1788–1875) on 11 September 1826 at All Saints Maidstone and had:

- William 13.2.1825 Maidstone–;
- George 1827–1828 Maidstone;
- John 1828[65]–;

---

65   Pam Glover can find no census record for him after 1841, but she has a possible marriage record in Dover in 1849. He certainly went to Australia, married Judith Stapleton on 16 September 1861 at Bathurst and died at Orange in 1862. No issue from the marriage.

- Sarah 23.8.1830 Maidstone–;
- Mary Ann 1832 Maidstone–;
- Frederick 1835–1835 Maidstone; and
- Emily 1836 Maidstone–.

Maria Eleanor married George Rose on 19 January 1827 at Thurnham.[66]

George married Margaret Hills on 27 June 1830 at Birling, producing:
- George 1832[67] Shoreham–1910;
- William 1835–;
- Mary Ann–;
- John 1838 Shoreham–;
- Shadrach! 1840 Shoreham–1919;
- James 1843 Shoreham–; and
- Ellen–.

John married Sophia ('Sarah') Bishop (1820–?.4.1892 Malling) on 26 October 1846 at East Malling, producing:
- Joseph 19.9.1841 Maidstone–12.3.1843 Maidstone;
- George–;
- Elizabeth 1849–18.10.1855 Maidstone;
- John 13.12.1854 Maidstone–1919; and
- William 17.8.1856 Maidstone–1930 ?.

William married Sarah Nelson (1811–1891) on ? October 1845 at Maidstone, producing:
- Elizabeth ?.9.1847 Maidstone–1907;
- Mary Ann ?.9.1849 Maidstone–1861; and
- Emily ?.4.1856 Maidstone–1889.

Joseph Blundell senior's second son—George[68] of Shoreham—was also a Blacksmith. None of the other Blundells that Mrs Teague came across in the Kent branch of the family are Blacksmiths. Again, none of these children

---

66   Nothing further known.

67   Another Blacksmith.

68   Renowned as an immensely strong and energetic man.

are named after George's parents, although one was called Shadrach—perhaps in the flickering hope that the family fortune would be restored?

From Census Returns for 1851 and 1861, after his marriage, John (Joseph senior's third son) continued to live in Sandling, a hamlet on the outskirts of Maidstone and at least until 1840 all baptisms, marriages and burials were registered at All Saints. John and his wife 'Sarah' Bishop were Farm Workers.

Their son, William—who died in 1930—recalled the poverty that the family suffered and that they were often hungry. This may have been after his Father John fell off a haystack and broke his neck when William was a boy. John's other children included Joseph, George, John and Elizabeth—unlike his siblings naming two after his parents.[69] George must have died in infancy because the family bible doesn't have any dates for him unlike the other children, just an entry to say that he was born. John junior lived in East Malling and died from cancer during World War I.[70]

Kent Economic and Social Conditions when our Joseph grew up[71]

Prior to the Agricultural and Industrial Revolutions, work was governed by the sun and the seasons, not the clock. This pattern of work was also true for many early Australians and continued to be the case for most of the Blundell descendants, particularly those involved in farming and transport until towards the end of the 1800s and in some cases into the early 1900s.

From about 1760 to somewhere between 1820-1840, the Industrial Revolution in the United Kingdom saw the replacement of small-scale labour intensive subsistence farming with large-scale high-volume commercial agriculture through new technology. Agricultural employment

---

69   The subsequent Inquest recorded 'Accidental Death' arising from a fall from a farm cart while loading tares (meaning a weed found in grain)—courtesy of Pam Glover.

70   Personal correspondence with Sybil Pugliese, a descendant of John Blundell and Sarah Bishop.

71   *Economic and Social History of Britain* by M W Flinn.

fell from 75% of the work force in 1688 to 50% by 1780 and 25% by 1840. The application of steam power to manufacturing, mining, textiles *etc* which began in the 1780s led to industry surpassing agriculture as the major employer around 1815.

Employment based at or near home declined and was replaced by work at central locations such as factories and shops. The new concept of 'going to work' arose. Urban numbers grew very rapidly—and in conditions of great squalor in the first decades—reaching 50% of the total in 1851.

This was accompanied by a population explosion, from 9.7 million in 1780 to over 21 million in 1830, largely because of the fall in infant mortality and control over disease in children flowing from improvements in public sanitation and medical practice. At the same time, the percentage of people living in towns and cities more than doubled from a base of 15% between 1780 and 1830.

The Industrial Revolution produced massive and long lasting structural unemployment and instability accompanied by horrendous societal fall out. Vast increases in pauperism after 1780 led to the breakdown of traditional systems of Parish and County-based poor relief and rapid urbanisation forced adoption of national policies.

The 1834 Poor Law Act was designed to force people to seek work—however degraded and wretchedly paid—rather than resorting to 'charity' in 'work houses', a situation exposed by Charles Dickens in his novel *Hard Times*.

From 1780 to 1840, child labour was institutionalised before diminishing slowly. Male wage rates fell dramatically after 1810 but employers still preferred part-time rather than full-time workers, and children and women rather than men.

> When trade fluctuated between boom and depression, and years of good harvest were followed by periods of poor crops, poverty was always present, for few workers earned sufficient to set aside for bad times.'[72]

---

72   *Visionary and Dreamer* by David Cecil. Princeton University Press 1969.

February 1811 saw the start of a wave of machine breaking and other acts of violence across the country. The authorities reacted in 1812 by making frame-breaking a capital offence. Many 'Luddites' were hanged while others were transported or gaoled. By 1817 Luddism had largely disappeared, although many became Chartists.[73]

The Luddite movement was based on skilled workers, descended from medieval craft traditions, who put heavy emphasis on the importance of maintaining high quality products. They were opposed to the deskilling involved in destroying craft industries rather than the machines themselves, rightly forecasting that the new technology would destroy their livelihood and opportunities for work.

Rural life was not particularly idyllic:

> '... the peasantry were overworked and underfed ... it was not surprising that they should break machines and burn ricks ... in the 1820s and 1830s.'[74]

Indeed, George Blundell (a cousin or nephew of our Joseph the younger) was charged with having conspired to set fire to certain stacks of corn belonging to Samuel Love the younger and others at Filston Farm Shoreham. He was discharged by proclamation, but two of his confederates were transported.[75]

This then was the social climate that our Joseph forefather grew up in. His work as a Farmer's Man was under threat and newly married given that he and his wife[76] were recorded as having no children. Aged 28, his prospects and future must have seemed decidedly bleak. C J Sansom's 'Tombland' and Phillipa Gregory's 'Wideacre' trilogy describe the plight of the ordinary people at the time and the extraordinary gap between their standard of living and those above them in the social order.

---

73   A working-class movement for reform of the political system to make it more democratic.

74   See footnote 72 *op cit.*

75   *Maidstone Journal* 19 March 1883 page 3 column 4 'Kent Assizes at Maidstone.

76   No details known.

Joseph, with no education, no trade and no prospects (unlike his Father and brother George) symbolised the depths to which many Blundells had descended from a proud and wealthy background and birthright.

Maidstone was the County Centre (the largest unit of local government) and Kent Assize town (one of seven circuits where civil and criminal trials took place) and chief agricultural centre. Kent derives from the Anglo-Saxon word 'Maegthanstone' meaning mighty or strong stone and the earliest documented reference is in 975AD when Edgar Dunstan the Archbishop of Canterbury owned the Maidstone Manor (which was the administrative centre).[77]

Little more than a hamlet (a small human settlement) at this time, Maidstone was grouped around St Mary's Church (later to become All Saints), a site well above flood level and protected on two sides by the rivers Len and Medway.

It was dominated by the church until Tudor times (the Royal Family that usurped the Plantagenets and ruled England from 1485 to 1603). Its development during the middle ages was mainly due to its central position in the County and because nearby Penenden Heath (now a suburb of Maidstone) was the ancient meeting place of the Shire where executions took place.

Of particular interest to the Blundells is the Unitarian Church, the oldest non-conformist church in Maidstone erected in 1736.

Boxley was a pleasant hamlet, near The Pilgrims' Way, in the Parish of the same name, beautifully situated near the foot of steep wooded downs on a barren ridge of chalk hills. It takes its name (like Box Hill in Surrey) from the box trees that flourish on the downs. It is situated about three miles NNE of Maidstone and was once a market town. The area comprises 5754 acres and had a population of 1470 and 289 houses at the time of writing. It also has a 13-15th Century English Church (*ie* Anglican).

Vestiges of the Abbey built in 1146 are still evident.

This whole area is strongly associated with the poet Tennyson whose

---

77   *Webster's International Dictionary.*

sister married a friend of his—the scholar Edmund Lushington. She is buried in the attractive partly medieval (500 to 1500AD) Parish Church of All Saints in Boxley with its Galilee porch (waiting room). Tennyson's works based on the village include 'In Memoriam', 'The Brook' and 'Prologue to the Princess.'

Thurnam (*aka* Thornam) Parish and village is about one-mile ENE of Maidstone comprising 3319 acres, population of 531 with 110 houses and an English (Anglican) church which has been restored.

Above the village and by The Pilgrims' Way on one of the highest points of the North Downs, on the brow of the hill stand the ruins of Thornham (or Godard's) Tower, supposed to occupy the site of an ancient Roman watch-tower.

This was a 12th Century 'motte and bailey castle' near a series of mounds thought to be of Roman origin. Motte and Bailey come from Norman French words meaning mound and enclosed land. Such a castle was a fortification with a wooden or strong and secure stone keep (a fortified tower) situated on raised earthwork (motte) accompanied by an enclosed courtyard (bailey), surrounded by a protective ditch and palisade (fence made from wooden stakes).

A tradition exists that the castle was built on top of a Saxon named Godard. St Mary's Church about a mile down the hill south of The Pilgrims' Way contains a late medieval carved font. The lane at the front is part of a Roman Road that led from Sittingbourne to Maidstone. Alfred Mynn the famous England and Kent cricketer is buried in the churchyard.

William the Conqueror's Norman invasion of England in 1066 led to the building of stone castles and rectangular stone keeps such as the White Tower at the Tower of London which was started in 1070. These keeps were protected by boundary walls of stone inside the familiar moat and drawbridge depicted in movies and documentaries.

As mentioned in Chapter Two, The Pilgrims' Way was the route that people took to visit St Thomas a Becket's tomb—the Archbishop of Canterbury from 1162 until his murder in 1170 and who came to be regarded as a Saint and Martyr by both Anglicans and Catholics.

Now part of the growing conurbation, Bearsted is two miles east of Maidstone town Centre, The Pilgrims' Way lying to its north along North Downs Way.

Up until the 1850s, more than half of England's population had never travelled more than 50 miles from where they were born and that's why there were and still are such different dialects—even in neighbouring hamlets.

Before returning to the link between our English and Australian ancestry (*ie* Joseph Blundell) the next Chapter delves into the Lost Inheritance—a fascinating episode in our family history.

Four
The Lost Inheritance

Dorothea Teague's *Shadrach Blundell—His Family and Property 1580 to Modern Times*[1] goes into considerable depth about how our direct ancestor Thomas of Chelsfield (the Australian Joseph's grandfather) came to be dispossessed of the Blundell family fortune that he was entitled to.

Mrs Teague's book which is drawn on in this Chapter plus Pam Glover's research and additions by the author shed new light on what happened.[2]

The involvement of John of Bletchingley's children is central to the saga, *viz*:

- John;
- Maria;
- Edmund;
- Elizabeth;
- **Thomas of Chelsfield**;
- Ralph;
- Jane; and
- Nicholas.

---

1   Referenced in the Acknowledgements page which also indicates how the reader can obtain a copy of this book. The* in the text means that the sentence/paragraph *etc* were sourced from Mrs Teague.

2   To simplify the myriad dates, some are baptisms rather than birth dates and some are burial dates rather than death dates.

Elizabeth probably died before 1642 and was not mentioned in her Father's Will. The surviving daughters—Maria and Jane and son Ralph—who were not critical to the Lost Inheritance are dealt with below, before explaining the other children's part.

Maria Blundell c1621—after 1680

Maria in her Father's Will, Mary/Marie by some interlocutors and Marye on her Marriage Register entry, received 20 shillings in her Father's Will.*

Maria married Thomas Woodman (23.5.1619 Horley[3]—24.8.1680 Horley) at St Mary Bletchingley on 20 February1640, producing:

- Thomas 12.8.1641 Horley—1708 Horley;
- Katherine 14.5.1643 Horley—before 1680?;
- John 20.11.1650 Horley—20.3.1677 Horley;
- Charles 19.2.1654 Horley—26.4.1662 Horley;
- James 21.6.1656 Horley—before 14.5.1730 Horley;[4]
- Robard 8.5.1659 Horley—1662;
- Jane 1660—8.5.1660 Horley; and
- Mary born/died 4.7.1663 Horley.

Thomas Woodman descended from an established wealden family of the stock of Protestant martyrs.* A Yeoman Farmer and Tanner when he married Maria, he later became tenant of Horley Manor for 20 acres of land called 'Notts' for which he paid 20 pence *per annum* rental. He was assessed for four hearths for which he had to pay tax in 1664 and a quitrent of 11 shillings for Holylands, Horley Manor in 1668.[5]

Thomas the first son of William Woodman (1593—?.10.1657) and Ruth ? (1593-1638) had three siblings—Joane (14.11.1613—9.12.1633), Katherin (12.11.1615—?) and William (18.4.1625 St Bartholomew Horley—29.5.1686 St Bartholomew Horley).

---

3   All references to Horley in this table refer to St Bartholomew Church.

4   Probate granted 14 May 1730 Horley—Pam Glover.

5   Granted to Charles II in 1662 as a permanent tax, requiring every occupier to pay two shillings annually for each hearth or stove on their property. Quitrent was an annual land-based rental tax.

Thomas' Will of 19 May 1680 left Maria £10 per year for the rest of her natural life plus specified household goods in their home. By this time, Thomas owned 'Huets' *aka* 'Lakelands' together with a barn on 24 acres near the Horley Common as well as other unspecified lands and tenements. Nothing further is known about Maria after Thomas died in 1680.

The Will provides for the two surviving children. James—19—who received household goods, while most of Thomas senior's Estate went to the first son Thomas who was also a Tanner and sole Executor.

The wealden protestant martyr referred to above is almost certainly Richard Woodman, an ironmaster and Churchwarden, who employed 100 people and was burnt at the stake with nine others on 22 June 1557 at Lewes—the largest number to be burnt at the one time—designed to serve as a warning to others.

Woodman had the temerity to challenge a local preacher who had switched from proselytising the Church of England to Catholicism, occasioning a charge of heresy under legislation designed to protect such people. Having been found not guilty, Woodman returned home to itinerant preaching, causing a warrant to be issued for his arrest. He escaped to Flanders and France and returned home three weeks later to be betrayed by a brother who owed him money. This is a captivating event, but somewhat peripheral to us, as Thomas doesn't seem to descend directly from Richard the Martyr.

Richard Woodman was tried at the Churches of St George the Martyr[6] and St Mary Overie at Southwark in London under the direction of the Catholic Cardinal Reginald Pole[7] as Archbishop of Canterbury.

Pole, who had fled to Europe to escape the clutches of Henry VIII, returned to England and favour under the auspices of the Catholic Queen Mary I in 1553.

---

6   The very same Church that features in some Blundell family weddings.

7   Pole had denounced Henry VIIIs annulment of his marriage to Catherine of Aragon and usurpation of the Pope, causing Henry to execute his elderly Mother Margaret, the Countess of Salisbury, without her knowing what crime she had been accused of or how the sentence was passed. Gwynne *op cit.*

His Mother Margaret was the niece of King Edward IV and King Richard III—when the latter was killed, the House of Tudor usurped the Throne from the Plantagenet line as explained in Chapter Two.

Ralph Blundell 1631–1716 the fourth son

By 1650, when Ralph was only 19 years of age, he was a Mealman[8] with connections to Croydon (south-west of Bromley) and for the next 100 years the Blundells owned property there.*

Ralph married Frances Allard (1635—?) on 10 November 1651 at St John the Baptist Croydon Surrey. This means he was about 20 and Frances only 16 years of age, suggesting a pre-nuptial pregnancy and as there are no known issue of the marriage she probably died in childbirth.

Ralph married a second time to Ann Baker (1635–15.2.1661 St Alfege Greenwich) on 27 August 1655 at St Alfege and they had:

- John 7.7.1656 St Alfege—30.8.1660 St Alfege;
- Ralph 13.3.1658 St Alfege—3.4.1658 St Alfege;
- Mary I 17.6.1659 St Alfege—before January 1661; and
- Mary II 24.1.1661 St Alfege—24.1.1661 St Alfege.

Ann presumably died from complications some three weeks after the stillborn birth of her daughter Mary II.

Ralph widower of Greenwich married for a third time to Mary Allen of Sholden near Deal who was over 21 years of age on ? 1661 at ?, producing:

- William 7.6.1663 St Alfege—died at sea;[9]
- Ralph II 29.1.1665 St Alfege—died 1704 Woolwich;[10]
- Mary I 22.7.1666 St Alfege—16.4.1668 St Alfege;
- Thomas I 20.2.1668 St Alfege—before October 1674;
- Katherine/Catherina 11.4.1669 St Alfege—after 1698?;
- Mary II 12.6.1670 St Alfege—6.7.1734? St Alfege;

---

8   A Mealman was a dealer in meal—*ie* corn, grain or flour—a lucrative 17th Century trade, supplying the Navy and the East India Company from Deptford.

9   Probate 24 April 1700 Deptford—Pam Glover.

10   Probate 11 May 1704 Woolwich—Pam Glover.

- Humdra? (daughter) 16.12.1672 St Alfege—?;
- Thomas II 20.10.1674 St Alfege—25.1.1699? St Alfege;[11]
- Susan 22.10.1676 St Alfege—2.1.1680 St Alfege;
- Susanna 16.11.1679 St Alfege—? ;
- ?Edmund 15.4.1682 London—29.11.1699 St Alfege; and
- Euah (Sarah?) 15.4.1683—?

This sequence is incomplete, omitting Eve and Gue? twins who were buried on 27.11.1678, Ene 17.12.1682 and others buried on 26.3.1678 and 27.11.1679—all at St Alfege.

Mrs Teague had the Wills of three of Ralph's sons—William, Edmund and John. The eldest—William a bachelor of Deptford—was a Captain in the East India Company, but where John fits in is not yet known. Notably, at least 17 of Ralph's children died quite young.

William's Will of 1698 was to be equally divided between his siblings Ralph (*aka* Ralf), Edmund, John, Mary, Katherine and Susannah.

Thomas—a Mariner—left everything to his wife Frances but doesn't feature in William's Will.

The Greenwich Palace was a favourite of Henry VIII and he used it extensively in the 1520s.

Jane Blundell 1635—c1660?

John of Bletchingley's eighth and youngest child Jane received £100 of lawful English currency on her 21st birthday. Not much is known about her.

Pam Glover suggests Jane married James Witaker (?—1660[12]) on 17 November 1653 at Bletchingley and had a son John around 1660 at Dartford/Deptford.

She then married Henry Shove (20.1.1627 Horley—son of Henry and ?) at St Bartholomew on ? because of the comment on page 87 which

---

11   Probate 2 April 1700 Woolwich—Pam Glover.

12   James died seven years after the marriage, the same year the son was born leaving no Will—Pam Glover.

refers to Maria and Jane and their respective husbands Thomas Woodman and Henry Shove.[13]

John of Bletchingley's Will

Returning to John of Bletchingley's 1642 Will, the opening religious paragraph, which was common before about 1750, is particularly interesting, reflecting the belief that people at the time held about their relationship with God:*

> 'In the name of God Amen the seventeenth day of June of the reane of Our Lord God one thousand six hundred and forty and two. I John Blundell of Bletchinglie in the County of Surrey, Yeoman, being sicke and weake in bodie, but of perfect sense and memory (thanks be given to God) doe ordaine and make this my last will and testament in manner and forme following, that is to say first and before all things I commend my soule unto the hands of Almightie God my Creator through whose mercie in Jesus Christ my alone Saviour I hope and look for Salvation.

> 'Next, I give unto the most needie poor of Bletchingly tenn shillings which I Will, shall be distributed by my executor on the day of my burial.

> 'Item. I give unto my sonne John Blundell one shilling of lawful money of England to be paid by my executor within one year next of my decease.

> 'Item. I give unto my daughter Maria Woodman twenty shillings.

> 'Item. I give unto my sonne Edmund Blundell 400 pounds of lawful English money to be paid by my executors when the said Edmund shall accomplish the age of one and twenty years.

> 'Item. I give and bequeath unto Ralph Blundell my sonne all my land called the Whitelands and one cottage belonging to it which were the land of one Richard Smith which said lands and cottage lying and being in the Parish of Burstow aforesaid and in the countie aforesaid and to the heirs of the said Ralph Blundell forever. Provided always, and it is my will notwithstanding of my gift that he my said sonne Ralph Blundell shall have the rent of the said lands and cottage until he shall accomplish the age of twentie six years.

---

13   No record of this marriage for Jane or the Conventicle Dorothea Teague refers to can be found by Pam Glover.

'Item. I give and bequeath unto Nicholas Blundell my sonne two hundred pounds of lawful English money to (be paid at 21 years of age).

'Item. I give and bequeath unto Jane Blundell my daughter one hundred pounds.

'Item. Those of my goods and chattels unbequeathed my debts being paid, and legacies faithfully performed, and funeral discharged I give and bequeath unto Catherine my loving wife (this bit unclear) ... and she Executrix of this my last Will and testament. ...'*

Some observations about the above and what is not included there (the Will running to three and a quarter closely written pages of instructions) follow.

First, the Will deals with each child in the sequence of their birth.

John Blundell's first-born son—John—is cut off with the proverbial shilling!

Maria Blundell/Woodman's husband Thomas and 'my good friend Jasyn (who?) to be paid unto them tenn shillings a piece'.

The Will is precise and in exactly the same form in stipulating what would happen to Thomas, Ralph, Nicholas and Jane's portions in the event that they

'... doe dye without issue of his bodie lawfully to be begotten ...'

their portion was to be equally distributed between all the others and their heirs forever. As might be expected John is not favoured. As we saw earlier Jane received £100 on her 21st birthday while Maria married before her Father's death and received 20 shillings.

Edmund is not mentioned in the preceding paragraph, probably because he had already been generously catered for as we will see on the next page, although this sits oddly with the provision for him in the next paragraph.

If Jane died before reaching 21 years of age her share was to be equally divided between Maria, Edmund, Thomas, Ralph and Nicholas. If she married before reaching 21 and had 'issue lawfully begotten of her bodie' then her £100 was to be divided equally among those siblings.

Last, John's third son, **Thomas**—our direct ancestor—was principal beneficiary, inheriting messuage (a dwelling house with outbuildings and land) tenements and lands in Burstow in County Surrey with the property known as Wasps depicted below and to his heirs forever. It seems that John of Bletchingley purchased this house from John Seyliard together with the Priestland property.*

Wasps on the fringes of Outwood Common at Burstow (now near Gatwick Airport), built around 1479, is a four bay, open hall house, typical of its time and the District—an example of a good quality Yeoman Farmer's dwelling.*

Wasps on the fringes of Outwood Common at Burstow *

When erected, the house had no chimney, the fire being set at the centre of the hall on the earth floor, with openings left at either end of the roof through which the smoke would eventually escape.*

Unlike the other brothers, the property bequeathed to **Thomas** and his younger brother Ralph was to be held in trust for them until they were 26 years of age.*

The default position for Wills at this time favoured the first-born son as major beneficiary with the other children bequeathed a minor share of the spoils.

John II was not to be so fortunate.

Usually this would mean Edmund—the 2nd son—would be principal beneficiary but he too is passed over for the next younger brother **Thomas** meaning their Father—John of Bletchingley—left deliberate instructions to that end.

Although we cannot be absolutely certain about the rationale behind these decisions, we know John II was cut-off with the proverbial shilling—probably because he had eschewed the Baptist faith.

As to Edmund's circumstances, he was 21, unmarried and a devout Baptist when his Father died and was probably already largely provided for. He had received property at Deptford (including The Great House where he was born) as well as a further £400 in his Father's Will.

Edmund also seems to have been a very significant beneficiary from his Great Uncle Edward's 1633 Will and his son Josephe's [14] 1634 Will, both of which named John of Bletchingley as Sole Executor. So, John was acutely aware of what Edmund was to receive from these sources and this may have led to the next son in line—Thomas—being so favoured in his Father's 1642 Will.

Edmund was Overseer for his half-brother Nicholas' Will (where he was forgiven a debt to Nicholas) and may well have been particularly close to that side of his family adding to the conjecture of how and why Shadrach II's assets came to Mary—Edmund's daughter—as we will see later.

Maria got only 20 shillings because she was already married to Thomas Woodman whereas Nicholas and Jane were to receive £200 and £100 respectively when they turned 21. Ralph was also well provided for.

Whereas Edmund, **Thomas**, Ralph and Nicholas all refer to one another in their Wills, inventories and other writings, their brother John is never referred to.*

Their sisters Maria and Jane and their respective husbands—Thomas Woodman and Henry Shove—and all of the brothers except John (and Ralph?) appear in the Surrey Quarter Sessions Lists concerning

---

14   These Wills have been dealt with more fully in Chapter Three.

Conventicles, meaning that they were all practicing Baptists whereas John II obviously was not, supporting the prior comment about why he was not a beneficiary of his Father's Will.

It might also explain the circumstances that led to cousin George—Churchwarden of Horne Parish—gifting five shillings to John junior in 1705.*

As with his sisters, Ralph played no part in the Lost Inheritance. He had already inherited property in Burstow from his Father and his occupation as a Mealman suggests he would have been relatively well off. When Ralph died he was Clerk of the Customs House in London—another well remunerated position.*

Because the story is so complicated, I have attempted to assist understanding by treating the remaining sons and their progeny differently from their birth order, dealing first with Nicholas, followed by Edmund, John and last—our **Thomas**.

Nicholas Blundell 1639–1682 the fifth son and last-born child

Nicholas and his descendants are the centrepiece of the Lost Inheritance.

A Mealman of Deptford East Greenwich, like his older brother Ralph, Nicholas married Elizabeth Sturt (*aka* Elisibeth Stert/Stirt/Ebert in some sources); born 28.5.1648 St Mary Guildford Surrey—1756?) at St Mary Somerset in London on 23 February 1665, three months before she turned 18, producing:

- Shadrach 31.3.1666 St Alfege Greenwich—21.11.1735 East Greenwich, buried 24.11.1735 Bletchingley St Mary; and
- John of Goldstone, a bachelor, 2.4.1668 St Alfege who died in 1750 at East Bergholt Lodge.

Nicholas' wife Elizabeth's parents were Shadrach Sturt (1615–1662) a Miller of Deptford and Elizabeth Gosden (1618–1672).*

When Nicholas died in September 1682, he left his son Shadrach (who was named after his father-in-law Shadrach Sturt):

> 'All my lands, House and barnes in the Parish of Horley, also all that my Estate lying in Burstow Surrey ... (and) Four hundred pounds of lawful money of England.' *

This was subject to Nicholas' wife Elizabeth enjoying them for the term of her widowhood—their sons Shadrach and John being 16 and 14 years of age respectively at the time.*

Nicholas also left lands in Bletchingley and Greenwich, £400 to his second son John of Goldstone, forgave the debt that his brother Edmund owed him and appointed his brothers Ralph and Edmund to oversee his Will.*

Shadrach Blundell the Elder 1666–1735

Shadrach, who was Senior Boy at Colfe's Grammar School in Lewisham in 1682—went on to Jesus College Cambridge on 7 July the same year— being admitted to the Inner Temple on 15 January 1683 and called to the Bar on 2 June 1690 (as Shadrack!).

Originally established in 1574, the Lewisham Hill School was re- founded by the Reverend Abraham Colfe (Vicar of Lewisham) in 1652 to educate the sons of the Blackheath Hundred—a local Government division based on the Parishes of Deptford, Greenwich *etc* in Kent.

The Inner Temple is one of the four Inns of the Court; professional associations for barristers and judges that provide legal training, selection and regulation for their members. The Inner Temple and its three Associate Inns are the only bodies that can call a Barrister to the Bar and allow them to practice.

The Thames washed up against the old wall of the Temple Inn Gardens—four miles upstream from Deptford and six miles downstream from Wandsworth.

Following the English Restoration in 1660 when the English, Irish and Scottish Monarchies were restored under King Charles II, a strict Anglican orthodoxy ensued, and the Court of the Star Chamber enforced religious edicts against Catholicism within the Inner Temple:

> '... no pyson eyther convented or suspected for papistrye shulde be called eyther to the bench or to the barre.'

Shadrach was thought to have taken 'silk' as a King's Counsellor—being selected to appear for the Crown and entitled to wear the customary black silk gown with a long full periwig in either grey or white. It was during the 1720s to 1750s that this judicial wig became part of their official dress.

Some claim that he rose to be a King's Serjeant or King's Prime or Ancient Serjeant—those posts ranking in precedence before a King's Counsellor.

However, Sir John Sainty's list doesn't mention Shadrach in either of the foregoing or as a King's Counsellor.[15] Moreover, he doesn't appear in any of the Inner Temple's records with respect to these claims.[16]

Shadrach Blundell, Steward[17] of the Manor of Shoreham at Chelsfield, practiced law into the 1730s, often consulted as an Adjudicator in legal disputes, including at the Manor.

Someone so descended had already prospered, but Shadrach was fated to possess an extraordinary amount of property.*

Edward Clarke junior was a member of the Inner Temple with Shadrach—explaining how the latter came to meet Edward's half-sister Frances.

Frances' Father Edward died in 1693, bequeathing her his house and lands at Coggshall Essex and a capital sum of money—with another house, farm and lands at Stratford in Suffolk to be shared between Frances and her half-sister Mary/Margaret.

---

15   Sir John Sainty's *List of English law officers, King's Counsellors and holders of patents of precedence* London Selden Society 1987.

16   Personal correspondence with the Inner Temple.

17   An official appointed to represent the Manor's owner—probably Snelling Thomas who succeeded Shadrach as Senior Boy at St Colfe's. Thomas became a large landowner in Chelsfield and High Sheriff of Kent.*

Edward the Father left the bulk of his Estate to his son Edward who died in 1747—he and his wife Catherine having had no children, that Estate passed to his nephew Shadrach junior.*

The Clarke name was well known in the East Bergholt district of Sussex as a family of Clothiers (cloth makers)—two Edward Clarkes becoming High Sheriffs of Suffolk—one in 1650 and the other in 1720.*

Marriage Allegation

Shadrach declared the following **Marriage Allegation**[18] on 10 February 1693.

The Marriage Allegation translates as follows

> Appeared personally Shadrach Blundell of the Inner Temple[19] London Esquire bachelor aged above 26 years and alleged that he intends to marry with Miss Frances Clarke of the Parish of St Sepulchre London spinster aged above 23 years at her dispose,[20] not knowing of any lawful tort or impediment to hinder the said intended marriage of the truth of which he made oath and prayed licence for them to be married in the Parish Church of St Mary le Savoy London in the County of Middlesex.'

Below the sworn statement is Shadrach Blundell's signature. At the side of the document are the names Blundell and Clarke, the line below

---

18   London and Surrey Marriage Bonds and Allegations Reference No:10091/30 sourced from Ancestry.

19   Note that most records wrongly translate 'Inner' as 'Junor'. The Church associated with the Inner and Middle Temple Inns of the Court is called the Temple Church, built by the Knights Templar in 675, the oldest church in London.

20   The three words 'at her dispose' (as her parents had both died by then) in the translation are suggested by Pam Glover as they have defied other attempts to discern them.

that meaning 'sworn before me' and then the Clerk's[21] signature—Thomas Pinfold senior. Another entry on the page shows that Thomas Pinfold also took an allegation from another parishioner of St Sepulchre as the Clerk of that Parish.

The Marriage Allegation—signed by Shadrach Blundell on his behalf and that of his wife to be—swore that there were no impediments to the marriage. It would have been accompanied by a Marriage Bond that set a deliberately high financial penalty on the groom and his bondsman in case the allegation should prove to be false and to deter irregular marriages.

Bonds and allegations were only required for couples who applied to marry by licence rather than banns. Frances Clarke was a parishioner at the Anglican Church of St Sepulchre Parish, located just outside the now demolished old City Wall in Holborn Viaduct almost opposite the Old Bailey, close to the Inner Temple. Shadrach would have lived in that vicinity, the Strand—which linked the City of London and the Royal and Monastic settlement at Westminster—being lined with sumptuous town houses of bishops, nobility and the like.

Marriage by licence was often preferred by the better off to protect themselves from the common knowledge of their affairs through the public announcements associated with the banns process.

The Marriage Bond

While I have been unable to locate a copy of Shadrach's Bond,[22] the following template would have been used, noting that until 1733, this part would have been in Latin. The bondsman was usually a friend of the groom or a relative—in this case being his close friend and soon to be brother-in-law—Edward Clarke.

---

21   A man appointed by the Archbishop to issue Marriage Licences.

22   The Bond would normally have been digitised at the same time as the Allegation, so it seems likely that a record of the bond no longer exists.

The sum declared would only be paid if the bond conditions broken:

'Know all men by their presence, that we Shadrach Blundell of the Inner Temple in the County of Middlesex, Barrister-at-Law and Edward Clarke of this same place Barrister-at-Law, are bound and firmly obliged to the Right Worshipful (name of the Minister) Doctor of Law, Vicar General, and Official Principal of the most Reverend Father in GOD (name of the title that follows) by divine providence, Lord Archbishop of York, Primate of England at a Metropolitan. Lawfully authorised in the sum of Two Hundred Pounds[23] of good and lawful money of Great Britain to be paid to him the said (name of the Minister above)—his Executors, Administrators, Successors and Assigns; for the payment whereof well and truly to be made, we oblige ourselves and each of us by ourselves for the Whole, and the Full, our Heirs, Executors and Administrators firmly by their presence, Sealed with our seals. Given this (x) Day of the Month of (x) in the Year of our LORD GOD, One Thousand and Six Hundred and Ninety-Three.'

The next part is known as the condition, stating the nature of the promise. It gives the names of the prospective bride and groom.

'The Condition of this Obligation is such: That if the above-bounded Shadrach Blundell and Frances Clarke—now Licenced to be Married together be neither of Consanguinity or Affinity the one to the other, within the Degrees prohibited for Marriage: If also there be no precontract of Matrimony betwixt either of the said parties and other Person or Persons whatsoever, but that they may be lawfully Married together, both by the Laws of God, and this Land: Moreover if the Parents of both the said Parties (if they be living) or otherwise their Tutors and Governors (if they have any) be thereunto agreeing: And lastly if the said Marriage be done and Solemnized in such manner as in the Licence to them granted is Limited: Then this Obligation to be void or else to remain in full force and virtue.'

On the left-hand side of the Condition 'Sealed and Delivered in the presence of' two witnesses, one of whom is the Archbishop's surrogate. On the right-hand side the signatures of the groom and his bondsman with their seals affixed.

---

23 The value of £200 in 1693 in today's terms would be between £26440 in historic standard of living terms and £5479000 in economic power ie the value of that wealth now.

Recorded separately as The Marriage Licence:

'Blundell Shadrak, *esq* of Inner Temple bachelor, 26 and Mrs (*sic*) Frances Clarke of St Sepulchre, London, spinster her parent's dead— at St Mary Savoy 10 Feb 1693.'[24]

Shadrach proceeded to marry Frances Clarke (c1670-1724 Greenwich) on 10 February 1694 at the church specified in the Allegation, *ie* St Mary le Savoy in the Savoy Precinct between the Strand (originally *Stronde*) and the Thames, precisely one year after the Marriage Licence was issued.

In the infamous Battle of Culloden near Inverness, Dr Archibald Cameron of Lochiel Culloden (brother of Donald) survived the slaughter and escaped to France in 1746. Persuaded by the English of his safe return, he came back to Scotland, was caught and executed in 1753 and then interred beneath the altar of the Chapel in the room adjoining the Queen's Chapel.

Charles Dickens lived in Savoy Street beside the Church's burial ground and wrote *Oliver Twist* at that time; his parents John and Elizabeth having married at St Mary le Strand on 13 June 1809.

Henry VII seeking redemption from a well-deserved purgatory built the hospital in 1505 and set up a fund to pay all the operating expenses. In typical fashion, Henry VIII ignored his Father's wishes and arrogated the operating expenses fund for himself in 1509, although Queen Mary I reversed this practice when she came to the throne in 1553. Covent Garden, the garden of the Abbey and Convent, was also seized by Henry VIII and granted to the Earl of Bedford in 1552. On 17 September 1860, the Church of St Mary le Savoy burned to the ground and all its records were destroyed.

The Medieval Parish Church of St Mary le Strand was demolished in 1548 to allow the Duke of Somerset to build his new house on the site, so the parishioners decamped down the Strand to St Mary le Savoy (now known as The Queen's Chapel of the Savoy[25]) while their new church was constructed.

---

24   This paragraph courtesy of Pam Glover.

25   In 1937, King George VI also decreed it as the Chapel of the Royal Victorian Order.

Edward Seymour was the first Duke of Somerset, the eldest brother of Queen Jane Seymour (Henry VIIIs third wife) and was Lord Protector of England[26] during the minority rule of his nephew King Edward VI from 1547 to 1549.

Despite Seymour's supposed popularity with the common people his policies often annoyed the gentry—he was subsequently found guilty of treason and decapitated on Tower Hill on 22 January 1552. See also Chapter Two and the background section of Chapter Three.

Princess Elizabeth then took up residence in Somerset House. When she became Queen in 1558, she preferred the St James or Whitehall Palaces, using Somerset House as a lodging place for foreign diplomats sent to negotiate her hand in marriage, all to no avail.

The congregation returned to St Mary le Strand in the centre of the Strand (on a small island of its own opposite King's College and Somerset House on one side and Australia House on the other side) when it was consecrated in 1724. Said to be the loveliest Baroque Church in England, traces of Roman, Saxon and Medieval London were found when the foundations were laid around 1714.

Shadrach and Frances (c1670—c1724) produced:

- Shadrach(k) II 29.7.1697 St Alfege Greenwich—10.9.1753 East Bergholt Lodge;[27] and
- Elizabeth 25.12.1698 St Alfege Greenwich—?.

Shadrach subscribed to Lexicon Technicum (a Universal English Dictionary of the Arts and Sciences) and the Reportorium Ecclesiasticum Parochiale Londoninense (a history of the Diocese of London containing an account of the Bishops, Deacons, Archdeacons, Prebendaries and Parish churches).

Shadrach Blundell Esq (the Elder) died on 21 November 1735 at East Greenwich and was buried on 24 November at St Mary's Bletchingley.

---

26   Vested with virtually the full powers of a King. Substantial bribes were involved in securing the position.

27   Shadrach II was buried six days after his death in the East Bergholt Church nave under a flat gravestone.*

His 1735 Will displayed a strong obligation to provide for his **kinswoman Elizabeth Land** the sum of £20 *per annum* while his son Shadrach II lived and £40 *per annum* if he died before her.*

Shadrach II extended this same sense of responsibility to Elizabeth Land.*

Shadrach Blundell the Younger 1697–1753

Shadrach the Elder's son—Shadrach II—even more than his Father became extraordinarily wealthy.*

Shadrach II, also a Lawyer, was admitted to the Inner Temple in 1713 and entered Pembroke College at Cambridge a year later aged 15. He remained a Member of the Inner Temple without being called to the Bar. At first glance, that might seem a tad unusual, but it was common for people to use the Inns of the Court as a form of finishing school at the time to gain rudimentary legal training and to socialise with others in their class of society. Shadrach II's wealth probably meant that he didn't actually work for a living or practice law.

Upon his Father's death in November 1735, Shadrach II inherited estates in Burstow and Horley in Surrey, Kirdford in Sussex and others in Essex. Just when he came to own the Clarke Mansion at Foxhall East Bergholt which was built in 1503 (now known as East Bergholt Lodge Suffolk and depicted on the next page) is not clear, but he lived and died there.*

Shadrach II's Uncle John died 15 years after his brother Shadrach in 1750 while living with his nephew in East Bergholt Lodge.* Now Cullum Street East Bergholt Suffolk it's not far from Holton St Mary on the A12, just north of the Essex border, ten miles north of Colchester and eight miles south of Ipswich.

Known as John Blundell, Gentleman of Goldstone,[28] he never married and had no children. His Estate comprising the Manor of Broadham near Oxted Surrey with a farm known as 'Chirps' at Goldstone, parts of Greenwich, the properties inherited from his Father

---

28   A small hamlet in East Shropshire.

*East Bergholt Lodge**

in 1683, together with Estates at Fletching and Worth in Sussex thus also passed to Shadrach II.*

On 10 September 1753, Shadrach II (aged 56) lying ill in his bed in the presence of his 'cousin' **Elizabeth Land** dictated his last Will and Testament to Dr John Edwards of Colchester[29] Essex who was attending him.* Pam Glover presciently observed that there was no mention of his wife Ann being present!

James Laysell, who was employed[30] as a Husbandman[31] by Shadrach was sent to summon Jeremiah Heard (a Farmer and near neighbour) as the other qualified witness. Heard had locked himself in his house and took some time to get out. When he arrived and at the very instant that Shadrach II was poised to sign his Will, he moved his hand towards Heard and said—'You should have come before'—sank back upon the pillows and died.*

Dr Edwards testified that while he was writing the Will, Shadrach II said: 'I have been very neglectful' and 'Lord God that I should defer this to the last.'*

---

29   About ten miles south of East Bergholt.

30   Probably at his wife Ann's urging. John II's son Edward had a daughter Jane who married John Dumsday—his Mother was Elizabeth Laysell/Lazell, related to Ann Slater/Blundell.

31   A Farmer.

Why an educated lawyer of such standing was so irresponsible and indecisive (uncharacteristic of this family) to have not made a Will until he was on his deathbed is as equally puzzling as his decision to marry when he was 56 years old to Ann Slater (who was 36) of Culham Street London. How did they meet? The reference to Cullum Street East Bergholt a few paragraphs earlier is eerily coincidental.

John Slater (?—?.5.1727 London, son of John and Ellin) married Mary Akerman/Acreman (25.1.1689—? daughter of James and Mary) on 4 October 1716 at St Dionis Backchurch London, producing:

- Ann born 1.7.1717 London baptised 18.8.1717 St Dionis Backchurch London—1777 Colchester Essex;
- Edward 24.7.1721 London—1788; and
- Mary 3.12.1727 London—1794.

Ann Slater and Shadrach II had no children and they were married for just over three years at the time of Shadrach II's death. His predecessors' profound religious beliefs are strangely absent in Shadrach II.*

Shadrach II surrendered all Copyholder lands in Essex and Suffolk in a pre-marriage settlement of 9 June 1750 to Ann Slater for life. An alternative explanation is that these lands were a dowry from Ann's Father and Shadrach surrendered them back to her as a condition for the marriage to proceed.

This form of land tenure was called 'Copyholder'[32] because the Title Deed was a copy of the relevant entry in the Manorial Court Roll kept by the appointed Steward. If it wasn't a dowry marriage settlement, then the conditions of the next paragraph would apply.

Copyholder titles were usually not mentioned in the Wills of the Owner (Shadrach II in this case) because the Executor of his Will was supposed to retain the Copyholder title for one year after the death of the Copyholder (ie Ann) at which time it should have gone to Shadrach II's intended beneficiary (Thomas Blundell of Cheslfield). The inimitable Ann became the Executor of her husband Shadrach II's Will and that was to change everything.

---

32   As opposed to Freehold title.

In these early times, a marriage for most property-owning people did not require a church ceremony. Instead, a private contract provided protection for the woman in case her husband died or abandoned her. That might explain why Shadrach II and Ann Slater's marriage record hasn't been found. It also helps to explain how Ann came to possess considerable assets of her own as will be seen towards the end of this Chapter when we get to her Will.

It wasn't until 1754 that a church ceremony became central to the legal concept of marriage.

Most married women couldn't own property in their own right before the 1882 Property Act came into effect. Until then, married women forfeited all that they had to their husband on marriage. This legal doctrine of 'coverture' meant that women's identities were simply subsumed by their husbands.

Following depositions from Elizabeth Land, Dr Edwards and Jeremiah Heard on 11 December 1753, Probate was granted to Shadrach's widow Ann Blundell (*née* Slater) four days later.*

There's no doubt '**Elizabeth Land, Spinster, Cousin German once removed—who claimed to be Shadrach Blundell's sole next-of-kin**'—was at the bedside when he died or that Shadrach II intended that his Estate pass to the descendants of **Thomas of Wasps** who was the principal beneficiary of his Great Grandfather John of Bletchingley's Will and elder brother of Shadrach II's Grandfather Nicholas.*

Shadrach II had willed the Kirdford Estate in Sussex to Elizabeth Land with the wish that on her death it pass to his wife Ann and following her demise, revert to **Thomas of Wasps'** descendants.*

Elizabeth Land honoured this obligation four days after Shadrach II died. On 14 September 1753, she made her Will giving 'unto my cousin Ann Blundell of East Bergholt aforesaid Widow and her heirs and assigns ... all my real estate whatsoever and wherever ...' and appointed Ann Blundell Executrix.[33]

There's an interesting round robin involving the Kirdford Estate going on here as Elizabeth inherited half of this Estate (the other half went to

---

33   Courtesy of Pam Glover.

Shadrach I) from her brother Abednigo's widow in 1731 which she then assigned to Shadrach I.

Elizabeth Land died in 1756 and on her instructions—Ann became the beneficiary. Promptly ignoring her late husband's wishes that the Kirdford Estate should be bequeathed to Thomas Blundell of Chelsfield, she sold it to Earl Winterton for £900 in 1767 * and presumably pocketed the proceeds? Kirdford is a village and Parish in the Chichester District of West Sussex. £900 in 1767 would be worth about £150000 today.

Edward Turnour Garth, a Member of the House of Commons, the first Baron of Winterton in 1761, was created Earl Winterton, the third rank of the Peerage, in 1766, the same year he was conferred with the Viscount title. Does this sale go with Ann's seeming enchantment with those above her in the social order?

Elizabeth Land is variously referred to as Shadrach I's kinsman, Shadrach II's cousin, Shadrach II's Cousin German once removed and sole next-of-kin.

The term 'Cousin German once removed' is usually taken to mean a relative descended from a common ancestor by two or more steps in a diverging line but it was also used to describe other forms of kinship at the time.

Elizabeth Land's importance to both Shadrach I and II appears in the considerate and careful mention of her in each of their Wills.*

The Sturts

The question arises as to why Elizabeth Land was such an important person in the lives of both Shadrachs? The following analysis answers this.

Shadrach (*aka* Sidrak!) Sturt (Stirt/Stert) Miller of Deptford (1615–1662) m Elizabeth Gosden (1618–1672) on 27 April 1647 at St Mary Guildford Surrey, and had:

- Elizabeth 28.5.1648 St Mary Guildford—?.1756 ? who married Nicholas Blundell;
- Sidrak/Shadrach 17.11.1650 St Mary Guildford—before 1672;

- Abednigo c1651 St Mary Guildford—1689;[34]
- Meschach 13.6.1652 St Mary Guildford—16.4.1676 St Botolph Aldgate London; and
- Ann 1653—?.

The precise birth/baptism and death/burial dates of Ann Sturt are not known but she and Elizabeth were left £100 apiece at 21 years of age or marriage—whichever was the earlier—in their Father's Will.*

As well as the first-born Elizabeth and last-born Ann, Shadrach Sturt had three boys—Sidrak/Shadrach, Abednigo and Meschach—all three sons' biblical names indicative of a Puritan household.*

The latter two children would have experienced the 'inundation of unparalleled magnitude'[35] when a terrible storm from the north-east swept over the Deptford District on 1 January 1651.

They also survived the Deptford Plague in 1665-1666 where one third of the Parish perished, but they and their families subsequently passed away and eventually, all they had went to Shadrach Blundell I and II.*

Chapter Three of the Book of Daniel records that Shadrach, Meshach and Abednego were three Jewish men thrown into a fiery furnace by Nebuchadnezzar (King of Babylon) when they refused to bow down to the King's image. The three are preserved from harm when the King sees four men walking in the flames, the fourth embodying the image of the Son of God.

Abednigo, a Cooper, married Mary Hensley[36] on 7 December 1682 and produced:

- Elizabeth[37] 11.10.1683 St Dunstan London—? ;
- Mary 23.10.1687 Rotherhithe—?; and
- Shadrach (no records found)—?.

---

34   Probate granted 24 May 1689 at Rotherhithe Surrey—Pam Glover.

35   *The History of Deptford in the Counties of Kent and Surrey* Second Edition by Nathan Dews 1884 London J D Smith printer.

36   Pam Glover hasn't found death records, but the last two of the three children are mentioned in his undated Will which included 'intended on a voyage across the seas'.

37   Not proven.

Meschach, a Cooper,[38] of St Bottolph's Aldgate London, married Elizabeth Dale of St Olave's London on 24 April 1675. No known issue.

When Meschach, of the Minories in London died in 1676 (the year after his marriage) his property passed to his wife and then to his younger sister Ann who went to live with her sister Elizabeth around 1682.*

It will be recalled that Elizabeth Sturt's husband Nicholas Blundell died on 5 September 1682—leaving her a widow with two sons—Shadrach aged 16 and John who was 14. Comparatively well off, Elizabeth might well have welcomed her younger sister Ann—who had just married—into her household.

Ann Sturt had married Thomas Land (1644—?) on 25 January 1682 at St George the Martyr Southwark Surrey and they had a son Shadrach baptised on 17 July 1687 at St Dunstan and All Saints Stepney and daughter Elizabeth Land who was born in 1692 in Putney and died as a spinster in 1756. Stepney is in the East End of London; Putney is contiguous with Wandsworth and the Thames.*

Therefore, Elizabeth Land was Shadrach I's first cousin (his Mother Elizabeth Sturt's sister Ann's daughter) and Shadrach II's first cousin once removed. 'Once removed' means that Shadrach I and Elizabeth Land share the same set of Sturt grandparents, but Shadrach II is from the next generation.

In 1731, Abednigo's widow—by then Mrs Mary Thorner—granted the property she inherited from her husband to Shadrach the Elder and **her sister-in-law's daughter Elizabeth Land**—supporting the analysis above. The Sturt Estate in Kirdford then came to Shadrach the Elder *via* his first cousin Elizabeth Land.* It then passed as intended to Ann Slater-Blundell on Elizabeth Land's death.

By a series of chance events, Shadrach II became a very wealthy man possessing a considerable amount of property. He precisely—if belatedly—bequeathed those Estates but the intended beneficiaries didn't receive them.* The peculiar dilatoriness of Shadrach II not making and signing his Will until before he was on his death bed is inexplicable.

---

38   Mainly supplying to the Navy.

Who got the family fortune, the participants in the saga and how they came to be the favoured ones with the acquiescence/connivance of Shadrach II's Widow underlies Dorothea Teague's research and books.

Within the next few months the entire Blundell Estates as they came to be known were won by a family named Hewes (Hughes) who claimed to be Shadrach's Heirs-at-Law—the repercussions of which have reverberated through the lives of succeeding Blundell generations.*

Although Probate was granted to Shadrach II's widow on 15 December 1753, by the Spring of 1754 he was declared Intestate[39] and his Will overturned.*

Ann Blundell may have been smitten by the Hewes family's connection with Royalty—Queen Anne having bestowed Knighthoods, positions of influence and other favours on them—as well as their standing in society and as high-ranking officers in the Royal Navy. Or she may have been 'leaned on' by the Loader/Hughes families who were no strangers to the various Courts.[40]

Early in 1754, George Blundell of Burstow Hall brought a Bill of Complaint against Widow Blundell claiming that Shadrach II had died Intestate and that he was Heir-at-Law to the Estates.

George's Father was John of Hutchens, eldest son of John of Horley, the eldest son of Thomas of Wasps, whose Father was John of Bletchingley. The latter was also the Father of Nicholas Blundell, whose son was Shadrach the Elder and whose son in turn was Shadrach junior. No lawful issue of Nicholas and his line had survived so **Thomas of Wasps** being Nicholas' older brother, he George was the rightful heir.*

Ann responded that her late husband was:

> '... seized in Fee of divers(e) lands and hereditments in the counties
> of Suffolk, Essex, Kent, Surrey and Sussex, though what particular
> lands I do not know ...'

---

39   Granting Probate meant that the intended Will was officially approved. Intestate
      meant that Shadrach II was declared as having not made a Will.

40   Pam Glover.

Which seems unlikely, but going on to point out that John of Bletchingley had three (*sic*)[41] sons, John his first born, Thomas and Nicholas (Father of Shadrach senior); the son John being Father of another John and Adam, Adam having a son John who was still living

'... he I believe to be the True Heir-at-Law of Shadrach (II) Blundell.'*

She then added what seemed to be a curious off-hand postscript that Edmund—the second son of John of Bletchingley—had a daughter Mary who became the Mother of Mary Hughes and Catherine Newland.* How the widow Ann Blundell knew about this is intriguing.

If Shadrach II's intentions in his unsigned Will were judged invalid, then custom and practice would have it that John of Bletchingley's first born son John II's descendants would be the beneficiaries—which would have been an ironic and paradoxical twist of fate given John II had been cut off by his Father with the proverbial one shilling.

We will come back to John V, son of Adam, but this is the first mention that Edmund ever married and had a child *ie* Mary.*

Edmund Blundell 1623–1699 the third son

Five Blundell families had 21 children christened at Bletchingley between 1597 and 1633. Edmund and his brother Thomas (and the others?) attended the old Bletchingley Grammar School (refounded in 1632) where he was one of four children whose parents paid 16 shillings *per annum*; the others paid less.

A Master was procured to teach them to:

'... reade and wryte and for to caste accompt as also to catchyse them;
and such of them as are capable to instruct and teache the grounds
whereby they may come to understand the latin townge.'*

William Hampton came from Reigate Priory where Lord Nottingham lived to be Rector of Bletchingley in 1625 where he stayed for 51 years through all the 'troublous' years of Civil War. He married Elizabeth

---

41   Ignoring the sons Edmund whom she knew about as well as Ralph.

Rhodes of Reigate and his son Charles born in 1631 followed him as the Rector of Bletchingley.[42]

Enter Henry Smith, a quaint character who made his fortune in London and set up 'Smith's Charity' for the poor in Surrey Parishes. Smith took to testing each Parish Priest by calling on them dressed as a beggar and if he was well-treated, the Parish became a beneficiary of his Charity's largesse. The sum of money in Bletchingley's case was an extraordinary £1800 *per annum* at the time.

Rector Hampton was recorded as a simple-minded Royalist who took little part in politics and looked after his Parish which was mainly inclined to Parliament's side in the Civil War.

In February-March 1642, Edmund signed the Bletchingley Protestation Return. This attempt to avert Civil War required all men over 18 years of age to take an Oath of Allegiance:

> '... to live and die for the true Protestant religion, the liberties and rights of subjects and the privilege of Parliaments.'

Those who refused to sign were also recorded to establish the number of Roman Catholics (and Puritans?) so as to tax them more heavily.

In 1648, when Edmund was 25, Lord Holland led an abortive Royalist uprising from Kingston to seize Reigate Castle—but he and his followers were easily dispersed—and he was duly executed by order of the Parliament in 1649.

Eight years later, Rector Hampton was still subject to an Inquiry of alleged complicity in the uprising and of hiring witnesses to swear falsely against his accusers, Edmund Blundell and Nicholas Norton. In 1656, however, two members of the Barebones Parliament,[43] elected for Surrey by the congregations, signed a declaration which stated:

> 'We cannot finde any proofe to be made against the said Mr Hampton either of his hiring witnesses or of his being an abetter [someone who abets or incites] att the late rising of the Lord Holland.'

---

42   From the Bletchingley Church booklet which records the Rectors and something about their lives.

43   A cynical nickname for Cromwell's Parliament, which he succeeded in establishing and controlling.

and so, Rector Hampton escaped censure, remaining in charge of the care of the souls of the Bletchingley inhabitants.[*44]

Charles II's Restoration to the Throne in 1660 was celebrated by buying and installing in the church a new Royal Arms. Rector Hampton was again able to display the *Book of Common Prayer*, having removed it from the Pulpit, but still reciting the prayers therein from memory during the Interregnum.

It's also of passing interest that in 1668-1669 there were only five celebrations of Holy Communion: Whitsun, December 29th, Palm Sunday, Easter and low Sunday. Normal Sunday services were Matins, Litany and Evening Prayer.[45]

From the Surrey Quarter Sessions 1661-1663, we learn that:

> 'Edmund Blundell of Bletchingly, Yeoman, Nicholas Blundell, Richard Best and William Batchelor servants to Edmund; Thomas Woodman of Horley and his wife (Edmund's sister Maria) James Blundell and Nicholas Blundell of Burstow and eleven others were charged under the Conventicle[46] Act of 1664, with unlawful assembly in the house of Edmund Blundell on a Sunday.'[*]

Surrey Quarter Sessions Records for 1663-1666 list people summoned to appear at the next quarter sessions in July 1664 at Guildford:

> '... the following being 16 years or more and have not repaired to their several Parish Churches for the space of three months.'

Thomas Woodman, a Tanner who was Maria Blundell's husband; Edward Blundell Yeoman; and Thomas Shove, a Weaver who was Jane Blundell's husband are among the names listed. They were fined three shillings each.[*]

The position of Baptists during this time of political and religious upheaval was fraught, as we saw earlier with John of Bletchingley.

---

44   Following a 24 August 1653 Act of Parliament, Thomas Chapman of Bletchingley, Mason and Clerk of the Parish, was approved and sworn by Robert Holman of Pendhill as a Justice of the Peace and the Parish Registrar of Bletchingley.

45   Whitsun or Whit-Sunday is the name for the Anglican/Methodist festival of Pentecost, the 7th Sunday after Easter to commemorate the Holy Ghost's descent on the Disciples of Jesus Christ. 29 December celebrates the Holy Innocents such as the martyrdom of Thomas a Becket.

46   A Conventicle was a prohibited meeting of a religious sect, particularly Puritan, also used contemptuously to describe the building they used.[*]

The motive behind the investigation into Rector Hampton's actions relating to Edmund Blundell was revealed in the 1669 Diocese of Winchester list of conventickles (non-conformist places of worship) which reads:

> '... there hath been noe meetings in Bletchingley since Edward Blundell, the Anabaptist[47] went away ...'

although there were still dissenters in the Parish. Edmund would have been aged about 43 and over the next 30 years his name crops up in a number of family documents, as will be seen.*

In 1676, from a Town Deposition of the Court of Chancery,[48] we learn that he was living in Rotherhithe; his signature is firm and clear. His burial is recorded in the Lee (adjacent to Greenwich) Kent, registers:

> '1699, November 30th Edmund Blundell from Greenwich buried.'*

It seems Edmund left behind him something far more tangible than mere signatures and a reputation as a forceful advocate of the Baptist faith.*

Shadrach II's widow Ann asserted that Edmund had married and produced at least one child—Mary—born in 1649.*

Mrs Teague was unable to find any evidence of Edmund's marriage. It followed that if he didn't marry then his putative daughter should have no claim on the Blundell fortune, while custom and practice at the time meant that daughters were deemed ineligible if there were male heirs.

Pam Glover is yet again to the fore here, discovering that Edmund married Anne Negus (25.7.1627 St Giles Cripplegate London) on 24 May 1646 at St Botolph Bishopsgate London, producing:

- Anne 4.5.1645 Horne[49]—14.4.1649 Horne; and
- Mary born 22.6.1648 London and baptised on 2.7.1648 at All Hallows Barking by the Tower, City of London—24.5.1705 St Nicholas Deptford Greenwich.

---

47 Literally re-baptisers, but also used as a pejorative term

48 A Court authorised to apply principles of equity as opposed to the law in cases brought before it.

49 Born 12 months before her parent's marriage.

Mary Blundell married Abram Constable 12.7.1648 Lee—3.10.1669 St Nicholas Deptford[50] on 21 December 1668 at St Margaret Lee, producing:

- Mary Constable (1669?—before 1728?) married Thomas Chapman at ? on ? :
  - ~ Isaac Chapman (?—1763)[51] married Martha Johnson ?—? on 8 March 1715 at St Mary Lewisham Kent.

Both buried Wandsworth. No issue.

Isaac Chapman became the oldest Master in His Majesty's Navy and on his death in 1763—there being no issue—left his share of Shadrach II's Estates half to Sir Richard Hughes II and half to John Hartford—if the latter had no heirs, then his half was to revert to Richard Hughes II. And that's what happened.*

Mary Blundell/Constable's daughter Mary's marriage to Thomas Chapman raises an interesting question. Is this Thomas, a descendant of Thomas Chapman the Parish Clerk of Bletchingley Church—a Cromwellian who scribbled doggerel in the Parish Registers until called to order by the Restoration? Thomas Senior's son, also Thomas in 1678 was keeping careful accounts for washing church linen and 'oyllin the klocke and belles and cleaning the dial.' The Chapmans all lived in the 'Clerk's House' which belonged to the Parish at the time and then to the Church itself.[52]

Abram Constable died only ten months after his marriage to Mary Blundell.

As a relatively young widow with a child (Mary Constable), Mary Blundell/Constable married again just over a decade later on 7 August 1679 at Holy Trinity Minories London to Isaac Loader of Deptford, producing:

- Richard 8.2.1681 Deptford—1708;[53]
- Mary 2.12.1683 Deptford—?.2.1728;

---

50   No Probate found.

51   Probate granted 16 January 1764 Wandsworth.

52   From the Bletchingley Church booklet which records the Rectors and something about their lives.

53   Probate 19 June 1708—Pam Glover.

- Catherine 8.7.1686 Deptford—25.12.1756 St Nicholas Deptford; and
- a stillborn boy in 1687.

Isaac Loader (20.2.1653 Kent—1715 son of Henry) rose from modest beginnings to great wealth. By 1690, he was principal supplier of iron ware (50% of the total) to the Navy. Isaac contributed generously to the Parish poor in 1682, to building Greenwich Hospital in 1695 and he gave £900 to refurbish St Nicholas' Church at Deptford where he was buried in a vault following his death in 1715. He became High Sheriff of Kent in 1701.*

Isaac and Mary's oldest child—Richard—does not feature in the rest of this story as he did not concern himself with this grandmother's legacy (perhaps the inheritance from his Father had already made him a wealthy man?).*

On the other hand, Richard's sisters Mary born 1683 and Catherine born 1686 and his elder half-sister Mary Constable born 1669 were greatly concerned with the fate of this inheritance.*

Together with Shadrach II's widow Ann, the three sisters and their husbands emerge as the central figures in gaining the Blundell family fortune and dispossession of who Shadrach II had intended to leave his Estate to.*

Indeed, Mary Blundell/Constable/Loader—Edmund Blundell's daughter—turns out to be the critical figure on which the Hughes family staked and won its claim to the Blundell Estates.*

It's also of more than passing interest that the Loader family of Deptford were Baptists. A committed upholder of that faith, Edmund Blundell was born in 'The Great House' at Deptford in 1623 and lived there for some time.

Alfred Dunkin[54] gives the following account:

'... The Great House in Hughes' Fields, formerly occupied by Admiral Richard Hughes, hosted a Sunday school on the ground floor since 1833. Built before 1623, the Admiral was born there in 1729—a water colour of the house is reproduced at Page 19.'[55]

Note the link to Admiral Richard Hughes.

---

54   *History of Kent* Volume II Alfred J Dunkin published 1854.
55   From *Reminiscences of Old Deptford* by Thankfull Sturdee—also quoted in Dorothea Teague's book.

Peter the Great resided in the house in 1698 when working in Deptford Dockyard and 'a portion of the building was used as a Chapel fitted up with a curiously carved pulpit.' In 1836, a large portion of Hughes' Fields was compulsorily acquired by an Act of Parliament to construct a pier and surrounds and The Great House was demolished around 1858.

At the British Archeological Association meeting on 26 February 1862, Mr Baskercomb exhibited *inter alia* an apple scoop found concealed in this house when it was demolished. The scoop, about seven and a half inches long, was made of cherry wood, the whole surface elaborately carved with zig-zags. The flat end being fashioned into a whistle with the letters 'E B' and the date 1682.

The initials are those of Edmund Blundell born in the house in 1623[56] and known to have lived there so The Great House probably belonged to his Father—John of Bletchingley—and was part of Edmund's inheritance, passing to his daughter Mary and on her marriage to Isaac Loader, it became his property.*

Dews' corroborative evidence reveals the Sunday School was non-conformist and provides a direct link between the Blundells and the Hughes.[57]

Isaac Loader's Will of 1715 left large bequests to his son Richard and in trust for his daughters Mary and Catherine. Isaac doesn't mention his wife's first daughter Mary Constable, but there's no doubt her son Isaac Chapman got his share of Shadrach II's Estate.*

Mary Loader/Hughes and Catherine Loader/Story/Newland filed a suit in the Court of Chancery[58] seeking a more immediate return from their Father's Will. Mary died in 1728 and the suit was settled in 1734 when Catherine's husband Francis Newland purchased the Deptford Estate for £600.*

---

56   It was not unusual for Blundell family members to be baptised or buried in Bletchingley, the birth or death having occurred elsewhere.

57   See footnote 35.

58   One of the three divisions of the High Court to provide remedies not available in the Courts of common law and which had jurisdiction over all matters of equity.

Around 1741, Francis Newland mortgaged his purchase and assigned the property to his son William in an endeavour to keep it in the family. The Creditors foreclosed in 1748, compelling William to relinquish the whole Deptford Estate to them. Francis was declared bankrupt, probably because of gambling debts.*

In a further twist, Shadrach Blundell II acquired the Deptford Estate, which for some considerable time was the subject of a Court of Chancery dispute.

The Loaders and Hughes

The second marriage of Mary Blundell/Constable 22.6.1648 London—24.5.1705 St Nicholas Deptford to Isaac Loader produced:

- Richard Loader 8.2.1681 Deptford—1708;
- Mary Loader 2.12.1683 Deptford—?.2.1728 married Captain Richard Hewes I Esq[59] 1674–1756 at St Nicholas Deptford on 30 April 1702:
  - ~ Mary Hewes/Hughes 1.8.1703 St Andrew Holborn Camden London—? married Henry Osborn[60] 1697 Chicksands Bedfordshire—4.2.1771 Hill Street Berkeley Square London at ... on ... No known issue;
  - ~ Catherine—no records found; and
  - ~ Admiral Sir Richard II 5.4.1708 St Nicholas Deptford[61] ?—23.9.1779, buried in a St Nicholas' Church vault on 30.9.1779 married Joanne Collier/Collyer (1710–?) of Deptford at St Michael Cornhill London on 1 June 1728:

---

59   Richard Hughes' Will of 1756 left all his property to his two daughters Mary and Catherine, suggesting his son Admiral Sir Richard III had a separate settlement—courtesy of Pam Glover.

60   Later Admiral, third son of Sir John Osborne Baronet of Chicksands, Bedfordshire. Henry served in the Admiral White Squadron of His Majesty's Fleet in 1771 when his residence was St George Hanover Square in Middlesex.

61   First Baronet of East Bergholt (NB); a Baronet sitting between a Baron and a Knight in the Royal Order of Precedence. Richard III became 2nd Baronet and Robert 3rd Baronet.

> › Admiral Sir Richard III Barnabus[62] ?.3.1729 St Alphege
>   Greenwich—5.1.1812 East Bergholt; and
> › Admiral Sir Robert 17.9.1739 Portsmouth—8.6.1814 Holyrood
>   Southampton married Mary Collingwood at ... on ... ;
>   » John 1775 London—13.2.1835
>   married Ann Ware
>   on 25 September 1796 at St Botolph Aldersgate.

- Catherine Loader (8.7.1686 Deptford—25.12.1756 St Nicholas
  Deptford) first married Thomas Story/Storey 1st Lieutenant
  HMS *Dunster* (17.10.1691 Kent—15.1.1716 Deptford) at ... on ...
  No issue.

  second marriage to Francis Newland ?—11.4.1756 Deptford on 24
  July 1718 at St Margaret Pattens London:

  ~ Francis ?—before 1741? married Dorothy ?—? at ... on ... ; and
  ~ William ?—?.6.1778 Greenwich.

Mary Blundell/Constable/Loader's husband Isaac—who was also a
prominent Baptist of Deptford—bequeathed in his Will of 5 September
1715:

> 'To my kinsman Shadrach Blundell (senior), I give six compleat
> Authors out of my Books such as he shall choose.' *

Mary Loader aged 19 married Captain Richard Hewes I Gent at St
Nicholas' Deptford on 30 April 1702. Their children were all baptised in
Deptford and the family was living in Church Street there in 1722.*

Mary Loader was destined to become one Royal Navy Commissioner's
wife, Mother of another—Sir Richard Hewes II—and grandmother of
two more Admirals—Sir Richard Hewes III and Sir Robert Hewes—and
Mother-in -Law of Admiral Henry Osborn.

Mary Blundell/Constable/Loader died in 1705; her daughter Mary
Constable/Chapman prior to 1728, and Shadrach I's death in 1735.

---

62   Pam Glover has a reference to Nelson writing: 'Sir Richard Hughes is a fiddler;
      therefore, as his time is taken up with tuning that instrument the squadron is cursedly
      out of tune.'

The Hewes family—of ancient Welsh stock—arrived in Deptford about 1645.*

Mary Loader's husband, Captain Richard Hewes/Hughes, became Commissioner of the Portsmouth Dockyard on 5 May 1729 and was succeeded by his son Richard II from 12 February 1754 until 25 August 1773.

Sir Richard Hughes II was born at Deptford and the locality where he first saw the light of the day still bears his family's name in the riverside portion of St Nicholas' Parish, although the Mansion was demolished in 1858 because of its dilapidated and unsafe condition.

When King George III visited the Royal Naval Arsenal, he was entertained with a magnificence suitable to so high a rank at The Great House and so well pleased with the conduct and behaviour of the then Captain Hughes II (Mary Blundell/Constable/Loader's grandson), he knighted him on 17 July 1773 just prior to his cessation as Commissioner the next month. He died aged 71 on 23 September 1779.

Sir Richard Hughes II, his Aunt Catherine Loader/Story/Newland and Richard's first cousin once removed—Isaac Chapman—became Shadrach II's Heirs-at-Law, each inheriting a one third share of each single Estate. Put another way, Catherine Loader was the daughter, Richard Hughes the grandson and Isaac Chapman the grandson of Edmund Blundell's daughter Mary Constable/Loader.

By about 1800, Sir Richard Hughes II's two sons possessed the lot.*

The puzzling aspects relating to Shadrach II's Will being set aside and declared Intestate are matched by the descendants of Mary Blundell/Constable/Loader (Edmund Blundell's daughter) being awarded Shadrach II's Estate when other claims failed. We're also left with questions about why other Blundell lines didn't pursue their claims and the extraordinary decision to confer the Estate on a female at that time when there were other male heirs of higher precedence such as John Blundell II's line available and against Shadrach II's express wishes that the Estate should go to **Thomas Blundell of Wasps'** heirs.

Mary Blundell/Constable/Loader's descendants argued that Edmund took precedence over his other brothers and as he died in 1699, then his daughter Mary (who had also died in 1705) and the heirs of her body lawfully begotten were the rightful inheritors. It defies belief that that's what the Court found.

Shadrach II also intended to leave the four surviving daughters of Christopher Baynes (supposedly Canon of Gloucester Cathedral and minor Canon of St Paul's) Estates in Essex and Suffolk to be divided between them after the death of his wife Ann. His 'Will' remembers them immediately after his widow Ann and Elizabeth Land but nothing more is known about their connection or whether they received their bequests. No claim from any of them was ever found and it wouldn't be surprising if Ann didn't tell them about it or chose again to follow her own path.*

These bequests were to be enjoyed by the Baynes sisters for the term of their natural lives and then pass to the three sons of John of Hutchens (George, James and Thomas—all of whom had passed on by 1787.). In that event, the Estates were to devolve to Thomas of Cinderfield (who died in 1740) and his sons.

As we saw earlier, this sequence would have meant that the sons of Thomas II of Chelsfield (our Australian Joseph's grandfather), John the Cordwainer and Richard II would have been the beneficiaries instead of the Hughes usurpers. What a difference that outcome might have made to our distant ancestors.*

But, Widow Blundell seemed determined to go against the explicit wishes and written (but not signed) Will of her late husband.* Why she did this is anyone's guess, but it smacks of malevolence.

John Blundell II 1618–1692[63] the first son

The first child of John of Bletchingley—John II—was clearly in Wandsworth by 1649 when he married there, and the Parish Registers show Blundell baptisms as early as 1625, the Father being Ralph, a Waterman.[*64]

How this Ralph is related to John of Bletchingley is not yet known.

As mentioned earlier, John II learned in 1642 that he had been cut out of his Father's Will with the proverbial shilling—his siblings also disowned him.

John II went to Wandsworth three months after Ralph died on 17 September 1649. Pam Glover has raised whether this was to take over Ralph's properties and business? Ralph's widow never re-married and John and his wife left substantial property holdings in their Wills.

Another variation on this theme is that John II went to Wandsworth around 1642 when he was 24 years old to learn to be a Waterman under the tutelage of his kinsman Ralph. If not, there is an unexplained seven-year gap in what John II did between 1642 and 1649.

Further confusing research here is the many Blundalls in the church registers and that the burial records from 1678 to 1727 are missing.

Wandsworth was a small town at the River Wandle-Thames confluence, six miles upstream from the City. A Waterman/Wherryman was someone licenced to navigate a small boat called a wherry or skiff carrying passengers/goods along and across The Thames. At that time, there were no other bridges between the Kingston upon Thames and London Bridges which were 12 miles apart. Combined with poor rural roads and congested city streets, The Thames was the major convenient thoroughfare.

---

63   Probate most likely granted January 1692 but could have been 1693 according to Pam Glover. As pointed out elsewhere burial records for this period when he died are not available.

64   Pam Glover has plotted this latter family group in a separate Ancestry tree and her research has been pivotal to many of the details in the names, places and dates that follow over the next five pages.

John II was never referred to as a Yeoman or mentioned in his sibling's Wills.*

John II married Anne Tharpe 27.2.1625 Wandsworth—1699 Wandsworth on 27.12.1649 at All Saints Wandsworth, producing:

- John III 17.10.1650 Wandsworth—1715 Wandsworth;[65]
- Richard[66] 21.11.1652 Wandsworth—?;
- Nicholas 24.11.1654 Wandsworth—25.12.1729 Wandsworth;
- Charles 21.12.1656 Wandsworth—30.4.1665 Wandsworth (plague);
- William 3.4.1659 Wandsworth—15.8.1663 Wandsworth;
- Anne 8.9.1661 Wandsworth—8.5.1666 Wandsworth (plague);
- Edward 11.10.1663 Wandsworth—11.5.1716 Worth;
- Elizabeth I 6.1.1665 Wandsworth—?;
- Elizabeth II 14.4.1667—?;
- Thomas 22.8.1669 Wandsworth—9.7.1677 Wandsworth; and
- Margaret 1671[67] ?—?

John II was said to be 54 years of age[68] when pressed[69] into His Majesty's Service on the Ship *Cambridge* which was launched in Deptford in 1666. Watermen were often conscripted to the Navy because of their skills, but it was unusual for someone of Blundell's age to be pressed.*[70]

John III married Mary ? c1650–5.12.1744 Wandsworth -on ? at ? producing:

---

65   Probate granted 13 October 1715.

66   Nothing further known about Richard, Thomas and Margaret, although Pam Glover notes she was mentioned in her Father's Will.

67   So, Anne was 46 and John II 53 when their last child was born.

68   This would mean he would have been born in 1612 instead of 1618, so John II may have tried to avoid being pressed by claiming he was older than he actually was?

69   Meaning the act of taking men, particularly sea-farers or others with required experience, into naval service by compulsion, with or without warning.

70   John II's 1690 Will was granted probate in January 1716, appointing his wife as his Lawful Attorney.

- John IV(a) 3.8.1677 Wandsworth—before March 1680;[71]
- Mary 26.9.1679 Wandsworth—before December1744;[72]
- John IV(b) 17.3.1681 Wandsworth—29.4.1720 Croydon;
- Martha 26.2.1682 Wandsworth—?;
- Adam 28.7.1688 Wandsworth—26.1.1729 Wandsworth; and
- Ann ?—?

John IVb married Mary Slater 23.1.1680 Middlesex—? on 21 January 1717 at Godstone (near Bletchingley). No issue and it will be noted from the above that he died in April 1720, less than three years after the marriage. We knew from Mrs Teague that John IVb's wife Mary was related to Ann Slater, Shadrach II's wife, but not how until now.

Pam Glover discovered Mary's surname was also Slater and it turns out that her older brother John married Mary Akerman and they had a child—the very same Ann Slater—in other words John IVb's wife Mary[73] was Ann Slater's Aunt.

This explains how Ann Slater/Blundell knew about John II and his progeny and argued that Adam's son John (who was still living) was the true heir to her husband Shadrach's Estate. The puzzle then is why this side of the family never pursued a claim against Shadrach II's Estate.

Martha in the previous table married John Savory on 23 June 1710 at St Mary Magdalen, Old Fish Street, London. They had at least four children in Wandsworth (Joyce, John, Mary and Joseph)—nothing further known.

Martha's sister Ann married Joseph Merit on 20 April 1707 at Holy Trinity Clapham. Nothing further known.

---

71   No burial record as per above reference but must have died before John IVb born.

72   Must have died before her Mother as she is not mentioned in her Mother's Will, which states that she had already settled gifts on her children (meaning her sons John IVb and Adam) and then to her grandson John Blundell, granddaughter Rebecca; daughters Martha (m to John Savory) and Ann (m to Joseph Merrit).

73   Mary Slater's parents were John and Ellin. As well as her older brother John, she had a younger sister Elizabeth (6.6.1682 London—?) who married John Bothem (1682- ?).

Adam in the John III table above married Catherine Stables (?—?) on 3 April 1721 at Clapham, producing:

- Adam 24.6.1722—;
- John V 22.9.1723 Wandsworth—13.7.1778 Wandsworth;
- Rebekah 31.10.1725—before 1729;
- Samuel 25.9.1726–20.8.1727; and
- Rebeccah 27.1.1729 Wandsworth (one day after her Father's burial)—?.

Catherine Stables-Blundell remarried George Blackbourne on 5 February 1730.

John V married Susannah Upfield 26.9.1725 Wandsworth—? on 24 December 1758 at Wandsworth, producing:

- Mary 31.1.1761 Wandsworth—?;
- Anne 1.8.1762 Wandsworth—?; and
- John VI ?—2.6.1766 Wandsworth.

John II's son Nicholas married Rebecca Torrington ?—? on 7 October 1686 at St James, Duke's Place, London, producing:

- Rebeccah 4.9.1687 Wandsworth—?;
- Sarah 30.12.1688 Wandsworth—?;
- Mary 6.4.1690 Wandsworth—?;
- John 20.8.1693 Wandsworth—?;
- William 13.1.1695—?;
- Mary 21.6.1696 Wandsworth—?; and
- Deborah 25.1.1698 Wandsworth—?.

John II's son Edward 11.10.1663 Wandsworth—11.5.1716 Worth first married ? on 4 July 1701 at Worth who died ?.8.1706 at Worth—No issue. married second Mary Cornish ?—13.10.1762 East Grinstead Sussex on ? 1707 at Worth, producing:

- Mary 27.11.1708 Worth—;
- Elizabeth 29.12.1710 Worth—; and
- **Jane** 19.1.1713 Worth—2.5.1779 East Grinstead.

Jane Blundell's Father Edward died when she was three years old and it seems that she (and her two sisters Mary and Elizabeth? although they both may have died?) were brought up by Shadrach the Elder and his wife Frances who died in 1724. Why, we don't know. But, after Shadrach 1 died in 1735, Jane received an annuity from Shadrach II until her death in 1779, but which the Blundell family continued to pay to her husband until he died in 1802.*

Jane, spinster, aged 29 married John Dumsday Staymaker[74] of East Grinstead (1724 Bures Suffolk—1802 East Grinstead) at The Fleet on 13 December 1742—later registered at St Nicholas' Deptford. John Dumsday was the son of John (1699-1728) and Elizabeth Laysell (*aka* Lazell 1704-1742 Deptford). Ann Slater/Blundell was related to the Laysells.

Irregular or clandestine marriages called 'Fleet Marriages' were performed at The Fleet Prison in London by priests who were serving time there and amenable to being bribed to conduct the ceremony outside the normal marriage hours of 8am to noon and which were often unregistered. Such marriages were secret because the couple wanted to keep it from family and friends and were not conducted in accordance with the rites and banns of a public ceremony. For some, it was because of a pre-nuptial pregnancy; for the gentry it usually meant one of the parties was marrying someone from the lower classes—a subject of shame and grief to their families.

The Prison was on the Farringdon Street side of the Fleet River which entered the Thames between the Pier and Blackfriars Bridge on Victoria Embankment near the Inner Temple. Of notorious nature, it was used for people sentenced by the Star Chamber and Court of Chancery and as a Debtor's Prison.

Jane's marriage to John Dumsday produced:

- Hannah 1743 East Grinstead—9.10.1780 East Grinstead;
- Sarah 1745 East Grinstead—1801?;
- John 4.5.1748 East Grinstead—?;
- Ann 8.5.1750 East Grinstead—?;
- Mary 1752 East Grinstead—?; and
- William 1755 East Grinstead—?.

---

74   A corset maker.

The Widow Ann Blundell argued that her husband Shadrach's true Heirs-at-Law were John of Bletchingley's first-born son John II and the heirs of John III, but there is no evidence they ever made a claim and by 1778 that whole line had died out. Perhaps they were unaware of Widow Blundell's testimony? As already observed, it would have been the ultimate irony if John II's line got the fortune, given his Father had cut him off with the proverbial shilling.*

John II's son Nicholas married Rebecca Torrington ?—? on 7 October 1686 at St James, Duke's Place, London, producing;

- Rebecca 4.9.1687 Wandsworth—?;
- Sarah 30.12.1688 Wandsworth—?;
- Mary 6.4.1690 Wandsworth—before June 1696;
- John 20.8.1693 Wandsworth—?;
- William 13.1.1695 Wandsworth—?;
- Mary 21.6.1696 Wandsworth—?; and
- Deborah 25.6.1698 Wandsworth—?.

John II's daughter Elizabeth II 14.4.1667 ?—? married George Young ?—? on 2 January 1682-83 at St James, Duke's Place, London, producing:

- George Young ?—?

As Shadrach II lay dying in 1753, it was his servant James Laysell (Elizabeth Laysell/Dumsday's brother?) who was sent to fetch the neighbour Jeremiah Heard to witness Shadrach II signing the Will. On his return, Laysell helped to support his Master's head on the pillow until he expired. A trusted and loyal servant, Shadrach II left him £20.*

James Laysell's 1755 Will leaves everything to his wife with the rider

> '... if after my decease there should appear any one to trouble her in the enjoyment of my said estate I declare that I give them one shilling for all pretensions for such is my pleasure ...'

Does this precaution have regard to what happened to Shadrach II's Will?[75]

---

75   Courtesy of Pam Glover.

Soon after John Dumsday died in 1802 and the annuity to the family ceased, his and Jane's son—John—brought a claim against the entire Blundell Estates; doing so in the full knowledge that they were all by then snugly in the possession of Admiral Sir Richard Hughes II.*

This suit failed 'through a technical fault' presumably because the pedigree presented did not convince the judges and was thus judged faulty.* The Court records[76] also note that the Appeal fell outside the 60-year time limit to bring such claims but curiously it still heard the case.

Although the details pertaining to John II's son Edward and his daughter Jane *etc* are correct, they were deemed too slender for her son John Dumdsday's claim to stand up in a Court of Law against John II's verifiable line of descent through John III which ended when John Blundell V of Wandsworth died in 1778.*

That such a technical fault could disqualify John Dumsday's claim again raises the oddity of the law (and Ann Slater/Blundell) settling Shadrach II's fortune on the Hughes family through Edmund's daughter Mary.

The mystery surrounding a legal decision in favour of a woman (Mary) against the explicit wishes of Shadrach II that the money go to his male blood relation Thomas of Chelsfield seems destined never to be solved.

Thomas Blundell 1626–1675 the third son

John of Bletchingley's third son and principal beneficiary of his Father's Will, **Thomas of Wasps**, and his successors are dealt with in the previous Chapter.

To simplify all that for the purpose of this Chapter, it's clear that **Thomas of Wasps'** principal beneficiary—his eldest son John of Horley—in turn left the bulk of his Estate to his eldest son John of Hutchens and then provided for his second son Thomas of Cinderfield.

---

76   Courtesy of Pam Glover.

John of Hutchens' line came to an end in 1787 with the death of his youngest son Thomas of Horsted Keynes, the Estate passing to Richard II, the youngest son of Thomas of Cinderfield.*

When Richard II died in 1811, his Estates were to be sold and divided equally between his two brothers Thomas of Chelsfield and John the Cordwainer and the children of his late nephew Thomas, a son of Thomas of Chelsfield.[77] *

Mrs Teague explains how these circumstances should have led unequivocally to Thomas of Chelsfield becoming Shadrach II's principal beneficiary, but such was not to be!

Ann Slater/Blundell[78] 1717–1777

Ann's Father John Slater divided his Estate into three parts:

- his wife Mary (*née* Akerman);
- share and share alike to all his living children; and
- the remaining portion to be invested with the interest to be paid to his wife Mary until her death or remarriage at which point it was to be divided among their children.

Ann died at her Residence in Colchester Essex, around 1777. Her Will was also declared in Colchester on 3 September 1777. *Inter alia,* she distributed:[79]

- property in Colchester where she was living to her brother Edward and forgave him all the debts he owed to her;
- £1800 to Edward Slater and Isaac Akerman[80] to manage as an investment with the interest being paid to her sister Mary (wife of Ralph Heale the younger—a Wiltshire Clothier) the total

---

77   Thomas of Chelsfield's other children didn't rate a mention, including the last-born Joseph, Father of Joseph the Australian Patriarch.

78   I am indebted to Pam Glover for the summary of the following two Wills. Ann's Will covers five closely written pages.

79   The connection between Ann and some of the beneficiaries above is not known.

80   Ann's Mother was Mary Akerman.

investment to be paid to Mary if Ralph dies before her or to her children if she dies before Ralph;

- £1400 to her sister Elizabeth Hamworth,[81] spinster of Clapham Common;
- (indecipherable) to her brother John Hamworth and £50 to each of his children;
- £50 to Isaac Akerman;
- £20 to Mrs Mary Halls—who was living with Ann;
- £10 to John Crisp of Chichester;
- £30 to her maidservant Amy Hyam;
- £5 to Ann wife of Philip Buckingham; plus
- various small bequests.

---

81   This would seem to mean that Ann's Mother Mary married again to ? Hamworth.

Five
Background to Convict Transportation

Transportation overseas as the punishment for many criminal offences next in severity to death was first introduced into English law by Queen Elizabeth I for the punishment of Rogues, Vagabonds and Sturdy Beggars in 1597—pursued further by Charles II, George II and George III from 1660 to 1820.[1]

Successive Governments regarded building penitentiaries as prohibitively expensive whereas transportation offered many advantages; it was cheap and a deterrent to potential criminals; it removed those criminals it failed to deter and at the same time assisted their redemption by providing them with opportunities in a new environment away from criminal connections. It also provided a labour force to assist economic development of new settlements.

Transported prisoners were sent to the 13 North American Colonies from 1718 until the 'American War of Independence' from 1776 to 1783 ended the traffic there. Although carefully shrouded in mystique, this was really a Civil War between those who supported British rule and those that didn't.[2]

---

1   This draws on *Early Australian History* by Charles White Free Press Office George Street Sydney 1889.

2   See N M Gwynne – reference 1, Chapter Two

Great numbers of convicts were sent, and their service deemed so valuable that in the latter stages of the system Plantation Owners readily paid £20 per head, not only relieving England of the £5 cost that they allowed for each transported person but earning the homeland some £40000 *per annum* for these outcast beasts of burden.

Disused warships (known as 'hulks') moored in the Thames and at Chatham, Plymouth and Portsmouth then became more than temporary convict housing:

> '... for the more severe and effectual punishment of atrocious and daring offenders.'

The authorities were always keen to keep costs down and avoid giving prisoners a better life than the poor people had outside the hulks.

Although introduced as a temporary measure for two years by the Parliament in 1776, they existed for over 80 years and between 1776 and 1795, one third of the total number of 5772 prisoners died in the hulks, which were notorious for despair, overcrowding, sickness and violence as an 1835 Inquiry showed.

With North America no longer available as a destination, the Government was forced to look for other ways of handling the thousands of felons awaiting disposal in Britain's gaols and prison hulks.

In doing so, it would have been acutely aware that Captain Cook had arrived in Botany Bay on 22 August 1770 and claimed the East Coast for Great Britain as New South Wales. In 1644, Abel Tasman—the Dutch seafarer—had discovered the Southern Continent which he named New Holland ('*Novia Hollandia*').

After considering many proposals, orders in Council were issued in 1786 to establish a Penal Colony in NSW at the urging of Thomas Lord Sydney—Secretary of State for the Colonies 1784-1789.

The First Fleet[3]

The First Fleet of 11 ships, carrying 582 male and 193 female convicts, sailed from Portsmouth on 13 May 1787 arriving in Botany Bay on 18-20 January 1788–543 male convicts and 189 female convicts survived the voyage.

The low mortality rate of 5.4% was due to the contract being a cost-plus agreement which allowed all the costs to be claimed. The Contractor hoped—in vain—that by doing a good job he would win future contracts.

Most of those convicts were young people from England's agricultural districts—only 55 had been sentenced to longer than seven years servitude, usually for poaching and smuggling. A meagre 39 of the 778 sent out had been sentenced to penal servitude for life. Far from being the worst offenders, the First Fleet convicts were hand-picked from the gaols. Five years after arriving a remarkable 650 of the 773 (84%) who had landed had served their sentences and been set free.

The Second Fleet[4]

The First Fleet was closely controlled by the Government, overseen by Captain Phillip (see page 130) and his Naval colleagues.

While Australians generally know something about the First Fleet there's very little awareness of the notoriety surrounding the Second Fleet, which should have turned out to be a salutary lesson of privatisation gone wrong.

The British Treasury was outraged at the cost of the First Fleet, deciding that the Second Fleet and future transportations would be on a fixed price basis and awarded to the lowest bidder. This created a series of perverse incentives—*eg* payment was not dependent on how many reached Port Jackson—the fewer that survived the greater the profit for the Company.

---

3   *Contracts and convicts: how perverse incentives created the death fleet* by David Donaldson The Mandarin 22 November 2018.

4   Footnote 3 plus *Australia's tragic beginnings: The grotesque story of the Second Fleet* by L J Charleston news.com.au 3 December 2018.

The First Fleet stopped three times on the Voyage which took 250 days; the Second stopped only once and took 160 days—again increasing the profit at the expense of the health and welfare of the convicts, the six ships arriving at the Colony in stages from 26 June 1790.

Camden, Calvert and King, the slave trading company was the Contractor. An inglorious 40% of the prisoners died *en route* or soon after landing.

Governor Philip was deeply shocked at the sight of such 'gross inhumanity' and immediately despatched a message to the British Government condemning those responsible. Officials reported that conditions for the slave trade were better than those for the convicts, some Ship Masters were especially cruel and some deliberately withheld food so that they could sell it at inflated prices in Sydney and pocket the proceeds. Records were amorally falsified to disguise the dates of deaths to enhance their profit.

Although the outrage prompted calls for criminal charges, the Company was never indicted and had already been awarded the Third Fleet contract before news leaked out about what had happened. The Attorney General recommended an Inquiry but Government concerns about exposing further details of the problems associated with transportation meant that that never went ahead.

Instead, a private prosecution was brought against the Captain and Chief Mate of the *Neptune*. They were 'somehow acquitted', and the Government defended them when the matter was raised in the Parliament.

John Blundell (Blendell 1760–1831) was sentenced to seven years transportation for the theft of 360 half pence. He arrived on the *Neptune* and on 30 July 1790 married Elizabeth Anderson (1762–1831) and two days later they sailed with other convicts to Norfolk Island. Anderson had been sentenced to seven years for the theft of half a guinea and eight shillings, arriving in Sydney on the *Lady Juliana* as part of the Second Fleet.

The marriage broke up and Elizabeth went to live with John Carroll a soldier—a common experience on Norfolk Island. Blundell remained as a Farmer on the Island until transferred to Van Diemen's Land in February 1908. By 1909 he was living at Clarence Plains on an 18-acre land grant with a wife and no children. This may mean that his wife Elizabeth had resumed living with him as she was certainly recorded as living in Tasmania in 1811.

These 'People Australia' extracts from the National Centre for Biography at the Australian National University raise many questions. They are somewhat peripheral to this book, but of interest to us because of the Blundell name.

Selection for Transportation[5]

In 1812, a House of Commons Select Committee reported that when the hulks fill up to their establishment the authorities issue a vessel tender and then accept the lowest cost tender as a matter of course.

Unlike the First Fleet, the prisoners were selected as follows—in the first instance all male convicts under 50 who are sentenced to life/14 years and then filled up with such of those sentenced to transportation for seven years who are the most unruly in the hulks or convicted of the most atrocious crimes.

With respect to female convicts, it was customary to send without any exception all whose state of health will admit it and whose age does not exceed 45 years.

Transportation was inflicted upon thousands whose offences would nowadays be regarded as trivial. The Courts punished small offences with great severity.

About 200 were embarked on each ship with a guard of 30 men and an Officer. The Surgeon received a gratuity of ten shillings and six pence for each convict landed at NSW and the Master of the Ship £50 from the Governor. The Contractor was paid six pence per day for the food allowance

---

5   Footnotes 1 and 3 *op cit.*

for each prisoner—their greed only being matched by their deceitfulness ensuring they gamed the system so that speedy delivery of the cargo was not considered as important as maximising their daily financial yield.

Before leaving the Hulk, the convicts were roughly clothed in new suits and placed in irons. They were each allowed a pair of shoes, three shirts, two pairs of trousers and other warm clothing plus a 'bed', pillow and blanket.

Much of the well-being of the prisoners depended upon the quality and compassion of the Surgeon Superintendent.

Under the worst Surgeons, the convicts were brutally treated, cheated of their full rations, kept in leg irons for the whole voyage, penned below deck for most of each day with nothing to do and allowed up on deck only at set times to drag around in a circle for exercise—each man chained to the next. They were cold in winter, parched in the tropics, neglected in illness and publicly flogged for misbehaviour.

Under a humane Surgeon, things were very different. Irons were struck off soon after leaving England; the men were well fed, cooking their rations in small mess groups; the ship kept scrubbed and rather better ventilated; lime juice was issued regularly to prevent scurvy; those who fell ill had proper treatment in the hospital; there was school every day and there were books to read.

The Ten Governors[6]

The NSW Colony Governors' are virtually unknown to modern day Australians, so the commentary below is intended to provide context for what follows.

Captain (later Admiral) Arthur Phillip RN 26.1.1788–11.12.1792

The First Fleet arrived at Botany Bay on 18-20 January 1788. The French explorer Jean-Francois de La Perouse arrived soon after. He had been on a four-year journey to emulate Cook's voyages and investigate the new

6   The material in this section comes largely from 'The Story of the Ten Governors' by Charles White 1889 supplemented by the *Australian Dictionary of Biography*.

British Colony. After camping on the area now named after him in Sydney for six weeks he sailed off and vanished. Having learnt of this, the British authorities would have been concerned about foiling any attempts by the French to gazump their claims on the new NSW Colony.

Realising that there was no shelter from the easterly winds, the land was swampy and there was a poor supply of fresh water, Captain Arthur Phillip explored the coast to the north where he discovered 'one of the finest harbours in the world'. He named this Cove after Viscount Sydney who had sent him on the mission and on 26 January 1788 The Fleet assembled in Sydney Cove to witness the hoisting of the British Flag.[7] The Assembly drank to the King's health as a group of Aboriginals watched on from a respectable distance.

Known as 'First Landing Day' and then 'Foundation Day' it wasn't until 1935 that the Australian States-Territories declared 26 January as Australia Day, which became a public holiday in 1994. The Australian Flag was legislated in 1953 followed by the Aboriginal Flag in 1955 and amazingly we continued to sing the British National Anthem 'God Save the King/Queen' until 19 April 1984.

As Governor and Captain General of NSW and Commander in Chief of the 200 marines, 200 soldiers and their Officers, Phillip addressed them and the assembled convicts on 7 February 1788 about His Majesty's Commission.

In January 1789, a conspiracy involving soldiers to rob the public store was discovered; seven were caught in the act and summarily hanged by the Governor despite the rabid protests of their Officers.

During the two or three straitened occasions when crops failed and re-supply was tardy, Governor Phillip lived on the same weekly rations as everyone else—two and a half pounds of flour, two pounds of rice and two pounds of pork.

---

7   From Circular Quay, the Flag Pole is in Loftus Street on the right-hand side of the
     Old Customs House.

In August 1791, convicts whose sentences had expired were allowed for the first time to select small parcels of land to clear and cultivate for their own use.

Major Francis Grose arrived in the Colony as Commander of the NSW Corps on 14 February 1792, but it was no Valentine's Day present.

Governor Phillip commented acerbically on Grose's Army (*sic*):

> 'They were observed to be very intimate with the convicts, living in their huts, eating, drinking and gambling with them, and perpetually enticing the women to leave the men.'

The whole Military Detachment (with a few exceptions) took an oath to stand by each other and resist any attempts by anyone to punish a soldier no matter the crime committed against an inhabitant. On one occasion, part of the Detachment left the barracks with their bayonets fixed and attacked unarmed people in open and avowed mutiny for four days.

Phillip left the Colony due to ill health in December 1792 and was praised for his uprightness of character, kindness of heart, firm discipline and administrative ability. On return to England, he settled in Bath[8] on a £500 *per annum* pension for his services in establishing the Colony.

The Interregnum 11.12.1792–10.9.1795

The three years after Phillip's departure can best be characterised as military despotism—first Major Francis Grose and then Captain William Patterson of the 102nd Regiment of the NSW Corps. Their incompetence, militarism and condonement—if not active support—of profiteering by the Corps established an evil order of things which affected the Colony for at least the next 100 years.

Raised in England, the Corps didn't attract Officers of repute—the ranks were filled with unscrupulous hucksters inclined to maximise their pecuniary interests and satisfaction of gross sensuality. Characters who had been disgraced in other Regiments were hand-picked by Grose's men as fit and proper recruits. Grose (by name and nature) received emoluments and honours in return for this 'service' to the Secretary of State.

---

8   Where he died in 1814.

Grose's first move after Phillip's departure was to merge the military and civilian authorities, giving the Corps absolute power and control of the Courts.

The Corps appropriated land to themselves and their friends, took control of the King's stores and made rum the currency.[9] They relied on monopolistic control of all real and personal property, price fixing and other corrupt practices to ensure their disproportionate share of the spoils from the 4000 or so inhabitants at the time. Grose, then Patterson did nothing to control this rapaciousness or the tendency of their men to take the law into their own hands.

Under Governor Phillip, John Macarthur was Captain and Paymaster of the Corps. During and after he left the Corps, supported to the hilt by his cronies, Macarthur became a wealthy and powerful figure through land grants, assigned convict labour, appointment to official positions of influence—including appointing himself as Colonial Secretary—and other favours.

Governor Phillip had alienated about 3000 acres of public land to individuals according to an established set of criteria during his term. By comparison, Grose and Patterson promptly appropriated more than 15000 acres to themselves and their friends (including Macarthur) in no time flat.

The British Government was not enamoured of Major Grose's administration of the Colony and he was ordered to return home in December 1794, only to be sent to Ireland and incredibly promoted later to Lieutenant General.

Captain John Hunter RN 11.9.1795—27.9.1800

Hunter—a well-meaning man of good judgement and benevolent character—arrived on 7 September 1795 and soon realised that civilian authority had to be restored. He tried in vain to combat the serious abuses by the military who were succoured by the growing and powerful 'Colonial Aristocracy' fostered and controlled by Macarthur.

9　The NSW Corps was heavily involved in the trade of rum in the Colony as a surrogate for money which was in short supply—hence their nickname the 'Rum Corps'. They dominated Colonial business through corrupt dealings until Governor Macquarie tempered their insidious influence and arguably surreptitiously after that.

Hunter found himself helpless in the face of overt and covert opposition, finding his opposing forces more troublesome than the convicts.

A stronger man would have arrested and sent the Rum Corps Leaders home, but this might well have triggered the Rebellion that came later. Instead, Macarthur's coterie contrived successfully to remove Hunter.

Hunter established the first school and church (St Phillip's) and stimulated agriculture and coastal discovery—leading to subsequent settlements around the Hunter River, Illawarra, Shoalhaven, Twofold Bay and Wilson's Promontory.

At the end of 1800, 5500 people were in Sydney including 776 children.

Captain Philip Gidley King RN 28.9.1800–12.8.1806

Hunter's antithesis, King was rough, uncouth and lacking perseverance—he faced misconduct, military arrogance, disobedience by the Corps and the rum selling pinnacle. Dissolution of morals, relaxation of penal discipline, runaway convicts and bushrangers not brought to brook by the police marked his term.

An insurrection by 250 convicts at Castle hill in 1804 was put down by Major George Johnston and 24 Soldiers in 15 minutes, leaving 16 convicts dead, 12 wounded and 30 taken prisoner—five ringleaders were later executed.

Macarthur got so far ahead of himself that he winged his superior Colonel Patterson in the shoulder in a duel. In an endeavour to redress the systemic problems that had arisen and break the circle, King sent Macarthur back to England to face a Court Martial because he thought (probably rightly) that Macarthur would be acquitted by his fellow officers in Sydney, but he failed to receive any support from the authorities in Britain either.

During King's time, the explorer Matthew Flinders circumnavigated the entire Continent in 1801-1803 and proposed it be named *Terra Australis,* later suggesting 'Australia'. When Lachlan Macquarie was Governor of the NSW Colony, he recommended Flinders' suggestion in a letter of

21 December 1817 and the name Australia was officially adopted by the British Admiralty in 1824.

King had some successes, including advancement of the material resources of the Colony, trade with New Zealand and the South Sea Islands and what became the Ticket of Leave system—overshadowed by the impact that the Rum Corps had on him and his professional reputation.

His incapacity to break the antagonism of the military was matched by their influence in also having his period of service shortened.

Just prior to his resignation, King granted his successor Bligh 1000 acres of land and Bligh returned the compliment by giving Mrs King 1000 acres.

Captain (later Admiral) William Bligh 13.8.1806—26.1.1808

The clashes that Macarthur and others had with the second and third Governors—Hunter and King—presaged Bligh's appointment. He was, of course, the very same person who commanded the *Bounty* and dealt with the Mutiny through dauntless courage and stern determination.

Offsetting these fine characteristics, Bligh lacked moderation and humanity, being motivated by self-advancement, the accumulation of money and prestige. His thrusting nature, overbearing personality and abrasive temper ensured he never earned the respect of those who served under him.

Governor Bligh arrived on 6 August 1806 determined to pursue vigorous conduct of public affairs and a firmer hand with the military and civil elite—in marked contrast to King's hesitancy. King who had not yet departed briefed Bligh on the devious military personnel and their succouring officials.

If only Bligh's zeal coupled with excessive bluntness and outbursts of passion had been moderated, a different outcome could have been in the making. His career was marked by frequent misjudgements, a great deal of bastardry and occasional brilliance.

He came into conflict with Macarthur almost immediately and eventually took him to trial over an incident involving one of his trading ships. The Jury of Corps Officers refused to recognise the Court, so Bligh threatened to charge them with treason. As Commanding Officer of the NSW Corps, Johnston defended his men, arguing it was Bligh who needed to be removed from office.

Paradoxically, it was 26 January 1808 when Bligh was arrested by Johnston who had taken unto himself the Lieutenant-Governor title, declared Martial Law and set about removing opposing forces in public office and replacing them with people friendly to their cause. Bligh remained under house arrest until 20 February 1809 but didn't leave Australia for England until 12 May 1810.

This infamous Military Coup led by Johnston—orchestrated by the venal Macarthur self-appointed as Colonial Secretary, but virtually the Governor—which came to be called the 'Rum Rebellion' was really a quarrel about power.

Although Bligh's behaviour and demeanour contributed to the outcome, words such as mutiny, sedition and treason were justifiable, and it remains the only example of armed insurrection in Australia.

Britain eventually awoke from its slumber after this incident and the associated anarchy, cashiering Johnston, prohibiting Macarthur's return to the Colony for eight years, recalling the NSW Corps and replacing them with a new cohort of troops. It was also decided not to send another Navy Officer on the basis that the military might respond better to a Commanding Officer of their own genre.

A Short Interregnum 1808–1809

Lieutenant-Colonel Joseph Foveaux returned from England (where he had been on leave attending to his personal affairs) as Lieutenant-Governor in July 1808 to find Bligh had been put under house arrest, a situation he ignored.

Foveaux's time on Norfolk Island was marked by brutal, sadistic and perverted treatment of the convicts as dealt with in Robert Hughes' *The Fatal Shore*—a very good and instructive read about Colonial history.

Even more extraordinary was the the Rum Corps decision to put Colonel William Patterson in charge from January 1809 until Macquarie's arrival.

Patterson had been the Principal Officer of the NSW Rum Corps under Major Francis Grose who rescinded many of Phillip's decisions to favour himself, his favourite fellows and troops. Grose regarded those under sentence as well as those who had been emancipated as convicts and treated them accordingly. It was Grose who made the infamous John Macarthur Paymaster of the Corps.

Colonel (later Major General) Lachlan Macquarie 28.12.1809–1.12.1821

By now there were 11590 people in the Colony.

The first Army Governor, Macquarie was energetic, self-reliant, and determined with good intentions, but a poor financier and self-conceited—affixing his name everywhere and anywhere he could. True to form, the Sydney establishment conspired from the outset to have yet another Governor removed from office.

On one occasion Macquarie remarked that

'... there were but two classes in the Colony to choose from—those who had been transported and those who ought to have been.'

After breaking the dominant Rum Corps clique and appointing himself Colonel of the Regiment, Macquarie elevated the Emancipist class, stimulated the pursuit of agriculture and erected many new buildings. He pursued geographical discovery with such remarkable determination and vigour to be meritorious of itself to warrant a place on the first page of Australian colonisation.

'He found New South Wales a gaol and left it as a Colony; he found Sydney a village and left it a City; he found a population of idle prisoners, paupers and paid officials and left a large free community thriving on the produce of flocks and the labour of convicts.'

The undying enmity of the wealthy freemen led them to harass Macquarie continuously and send home fabricated charges of various kinds against him.

These eventually sufficed for John Thomas Bigge to be sent out from England to conduct a Commission of Inquiry in 1819.

Bigge's task was to assess the effectiveness of transportation as a deterrent to felons and whether Macquarie's humanitarian policies detracted from transportation as an object of real terror through ill-considered compassion for the convicts. That seems a clear set of riding instructions to me.

Macquarie's interactions with Bigge were fractious on both sides and it's probably no real surprise that Macarthur and his wife went to some lengths to entertain, socialise and seduce him to their cause. Bigge's enquiries were conducted informally and often in secret with no record of the testimonies.

Bigge's reports to the House of Commons did have a positive effect on Australia's future, notwithstanding it led directly to Macquarie's recall after 12 years of unstinting effort directed towards the Colony's material advancement.

From today's vantage point it seems extraordinary that the British Government didn't recognise the underlying cause of removal of Governor after Governor.

Macquarie died two years after his return and his tombstone in Scotland is inscribed 'The Father of Australia.'

Major General Thomas Brisbane 1.12.1821–1.12.1825

At the start of Brisbane's term there were 38778 inhabitants.

Eminently unsuitable for the office—weak, vacillating and given to delegating duties and decisions to others that he should have made, Brisbane came on the scene at the very time that the struggle for supremacy between the different classes was at its height.

He dogged this challenge—militarism and the 'pure merinos' reasserting their position and power in the scheme of things in this vacuum. Without the courage or tact to manage the contending forces, he retreated to the sanctuary of scientific studies, turning a blind eye to officials helping themselves and each other to place and power and dividing the land in great slices between them.

Formation of a Legislative Council, liberty of the press, discoveries of new country, trial by jury and a steady flow of immigration from England following Bigge's Reports marked Brisbane's largely unremarkable term.

Brisbane was relieved of his duties after four years.

Major General (later General Sir) Ralph Darling 19.12.1825—22.10.1831

Darling was an *aficionado* of the red-tape school—a man of precedents and forms, neat, exact, punctual, industrious, spiteful, arbitrary and commonplace.

True to his venomous disposition, he ruled the convicts with an iron hand and great severity and tried to crush the newly-born free press which dared to raise its voice against gubernatorial cruelty.

Opposed to immigration, he couldn't stop the arrival of people with moderate means, being disdainful of these lesser beings and modifying the system of land grants to make the rich even richer.

Darling's contempt and high-handed actions were supported by sickening fulsome flattery of the Gazette newspaper as the Government's mouthpiece.

This outraged the Australian and Monitor newspapers who condemned his actions. He responded by trying to gag them, a move which caused them to make even more extreme agitations, prompting Darling's recall.

At the close of his administration the population was 51155.

Lt General (later General Sir) Richard Bourke KCB
3.12.1831—5.12.1837

Bourke was born on 4 May 1778 in Dublin and died on 13 August 1855 at Limerick. Educated at Westminster School (in the precincts of Westminster Abbey in London) and Oxford University, he graduated with a BA in 1798.

A distant relation of Edmund Burke (the great Irish Statesman with whom he spent his vacations) Richard joined the Grenadier Guards (the most senior infantry regiment of the Guards Division) serving in the Netherlands in 1799 where he was badly wounded through the jaws. Bourke married Elizabeth Bourke on 1 March 1800, going on active duty to South America in 1806 before acting as Lieutenant-Governor of the Cape of Good Hope from 1826 to 1828.

The most able and popular of the early Governors, Bourke's, Anglo-Irish cultural identity to the fore during his rule was marked by firmness, humanity, liberality, vigour and zeal.

Very soon after taking office, he encountered opposition to his reformist disposition by political opponents and personal sorrow when his wife died on 7 May 1832 at Parramatta where she was buried.

He reformed the regulations relating to land, initiated trial by jury, substituted civilians for military personnel in criminal cases, and met further opposition when he proposed that Emancipists[10] serve as Jurors. Magistrates in the Hunter District, where Joseph Blundell was situated, were bitterly resistant to these changes on the basis that isolated settlers had a genuine fear of assigned convicts committing atrocities.

Bourke directed public funding to the major religious denominations in proportion to their number of adherents. He also enacted major change to religious freedom, education funding and elective Government.

His six-year rule was full of measures and events of utmost importance in shaping the Colony's destiny, including steps to abolish transportation and

> '... the Bounty Scheme to encourage landowners and businessmen to sponsor immigrant employees from Britain.'

Agitations from the Colony for free men and women succeeded with the despatch of the first shipload of assisted migrants in 1832. 'This coincided with a mighty social upheaval in the Old World. Industrialisation caused poverty and distress'[11] to the working classes.

Many Southern England Parishes (particularly Sussex and adjoining Kent where the populations had risen rapidly) saw assisted migration of rural labourers and their families as a way of reducing their populations and calls for assistance from the Parish purse.

Between 1836 and 1847 Sussex sent 3914 such people while Kent sent 1213.

Rural Villages of about 1000 inhabitants such as Burwarsh, Northiam,

---

10   Convicts who had served their term or been pardoned and were free to own land and no longer subject to penal servitude.

11   *The Enlightened Years,* Department of Immigration Local Government and Ethnic Affairs AGPS Canberra 1988.

Rolvenden and Tenterden which feature in Chapter Seven sent more than 50 each to Australia. Parishes and Poor Law Unions equipped the emigrants and paid to transport them to the departure point where Commissioners for Land and Emigration used money from land sales in Australia to pay for their passage.

Governor Bourke[12] issued regulations about the allotment of convict labour to settlers. They allowed for one man to every 160 acres, plus one more for every additional 40 acres—not exceeding 640 acres—that were under hoe or plough cultivation. Over 1280 acres, the allowance was for an additional two men for every 640 acres. A tradesman rated as two or three men and no Station could have more than 70 men.

His high place in the eyes of the public was reflected in the size of the crowd and sound of their ovation when he departed the Colony in December 1837.

In a measure of the esteem with which he was held, a voluntary fund was rapidly filled, raising £4000 to erect his bronze statue, which stands proudly on the corner of Bent and Macquarie Streets in Sydney.

Lt Colonel Sir George Gipps 24.2.1838–11.7.1846

A military man with a superior education, Gipps had trouble coping with the transition between serfdom and freedom. He possessed repulsive manners, an arbitrary disposition, overbearing demeanour and propensity to make enemies of those he could have befriended to good purpose.

The discovery of favourable land at Port Philip attracted a steady stream of superior class immigrants such that by 1841 the population was 149669 and at the end of his administration it numbered 196704.

When the returns from land revenue were small, the policy was to apply them wholly and exclusively for the benefit of the Colony. Swelling returns attracted the cupidity of the Home Government and Governor Gipps was just the man to enforce the return of the revenues to the parental lap.

---

12   *Australian Dictionary of Biography.*

This disastrous decision smashed the economy, ruined many people and led to strife between the Governor and the elected Legislative Council members who prosecuted the people's cause such that the Imperial authorities and Governor were forced to yield to Colonial grievances. Gipps' animosity led to his recall.

Sir Charles Augustus FitzRoy 2.8.1846—20.1.1855

FitzRoy was simply a cipher for those who still held the reins and whose vassal he was. He had no official aptitude, his intellectual attainments—like his morals—were of a low order and he was as bare of common sense as of refined tastes.

He had no opinions of his own, acting as a mouthpiece for the powerful vested interests as well as being a 'hoary lecher' and womaniser after his wife died in Sydney in a horse carriage accident.

His claim to be a gentleman rested on a large income, fashionable dress and a polished exterior and he was content to pursue other interests while leaving his official advisers to manage the Colonists. No doubt, this was influenced by his descent from Henry Fitzroy the first Duke of Grafton, an illegitimate son of King Charles II and Barbara Palmer whose exploits deserved their notoriety,

In 1851 FitzRoy wrote to Earl Grey, the Secretary of State, pleading for an extension of the normal six-year term, claiming this would be well received throughout the Colony. Grey didn't agree.

As an elected member of the Moreton Bay Legislative Council, John Dunmore Lang[13] successfully moved an amendment to an Address of Farewell motion describing FitzRoy's rule as

> '... a uniform conspiracy against the rights of the people, extravagant, inefficient, dilatory in pursuing exploration and discredited by a moral influence emanating from Government House deleterious and baneful in the highest degree.'

As a Presbyterian Minister, Lang was only too well aware that FitzRoy had forced his attentions on a servant in Berrima and got her pregnant.

---

13   *Australian Dictionary of Biography.*

During FitzRoy's time there was a failed attempt to reintroduce the convict transportation system, discovery of gold, separation of Victoria from NSW and establishment of two deliberative chambers—the Legislative Assembly and the Legislative Council—after 68 years of successive Governors.

From being a Crown Colony of the severest type, NSW became a self-governing community—through Earl Grey not FitzRoy who was the last of the old school—ending the autocratic arbitrary rule of Governors.

The Governors' Legacy

The Australian Dictionary of Biography generally portrays a sanitised picture of most of these ten Governors but only a few were genuinely worth their salt.

Charles White's work shows that the 'darker and bloodier stains which deface this period of Australia's history'—were the very men who came out free and exploited those who were sent out—assisted by complicit or ineffectual Governors and perversion of the whole system of Colonial administration. Indeed, one could be forgiven for observing that traces of these villains' DNA manifests itself in various ways in modern day Australia.

On the other hand, the Colony's history is filled with examples of steady advancement towards prosperity despite disastrous administrations.

Governors Phillip and Hunter pleaded with the British Government for free settlers to no effect, largely due to war and economic factors back home. Macquarie opposed free settlers, so nothing really happened until after his departure on 1 December 1821.

Thenceforth, immigrants who could pay their own passage, had capital to develop the land they were granted and to absorb convict labour were sought out. Numbers increased and demand for labour outstripped the available supply.

In 1831, the British Government ended the practice of land grants and began selling land, using the profits to finance the immigration of free land owners.

Governor Bourke's arrival in December 1831 led to significant reforms but it wasn't until Convict Assignment to NSW was abandoned that a new era dawned. Prior to then, NSW had among the largest slave plantations that the world had ever seen—attributed by some commentators as more degrading than had existed anywhere—during ancient or modern times.

When transportation to NSW stopped in 1840, some 80000 convicts had been sent to the Colony. The last transportation shipment arrived in Western Australia on 10 January 1868—by then 806 ships carrying 160000 men and women convicts had arrived in Australia—about 25% were on life sentences, 25% on 14-year sentences and 50% on seven-year sentences. Apart from NSW, 66000 went to Van Diemen's Land and 9600 to Western Australia, the balance being deployed elsewhere.[14]

The 1850s gold rushes caused a huge increase in self-funded migration defeating the purpose of getting a labour pool to be used throughout the Colony.

In 1856, with new self-governing constitutions, NSW, Victoria, South Australia and Tasmania were released from Colonial Office control as was Queensland when it separated from NSW in 1859. These Governments then allocated funds from general revenue to stimulate assisted immigration.

The NSW population grew from:
- 1821–   30000;
- 1846–   187413;
- 1854–   251315;
- 1859–   336572;
- 1871–   503981;
- 1887– 1044000;

there being 3543032 in all of Australia in 1887.

There were 798 NSW schools in 1861 with 34767 pupils and by 1886 these figures were respectively 2833 and 226860. 1860 saw 70 miles of railway, which by 1886 was 1971 miles.

---

14   Footnote 1 *op cit.*

From the 1820s to the 1860s the assisted migrants were mainly rural labourers, encouraged to come out in family groups as we shall see later.

Convict Assignment on Arrival in Australia[15]

It was during Governor Hunter's five-year term from 11 September 1795 that the Assignment System was developed. The Government took first pick of the convicts as they arrived. The rest were placed with free settlers for employment, usually by an Assignment Board which met regularly to receive applications from settlers and decide which convict would go to which Master.

Convicts who were well behaved, but had no trade, were usually allocated to a private settler as a farm labourer/servant—a fate that prisoners understood was much more preferable than being retained by the Government or allocated to public labour.

Officials in Sydney constructed a scale of work for an Assigned Convict, the minimum workload being known as the 'Government Task'. The early 1800s weekly task for an assigned convict labourer consisted of one of the following:

- felling of forest timber—one acre;
- planting of corn—1.5 acres;
- burning of forest timber—1.8 acres;
- chipping-in of wheat—1.5 acres;
- splitting of 2-yard palings (two men)—800; and
- threshing of wheat—140 gallons.

Convicts had to be under the supervision of a free overseer and the settler was required to supply suitable housing. In most cases, this consisted largely of slab and bark huts that could be erected easily at no great expense. The cost of rations for each convict was estimated at £15 per year.

---

15   *The Bushranger of Bungendore* George Dick published by the Bungendore and District Historical Society. *The Story of the Convicts* Charles White Free Press Office 1889.

Assigned convicts worked a 50 hour week, nine hours a day from Monday to Friday and five hours on Saturday. Masters did, of course, use their assigned convicts on any kind of work that needed to be done.

In return, the regulations required Masters to provide each man with two frocks or jackets, three shirts, two pairs of trousers, three pairs of boots, and a hat or cap each year. These were to be issued in the following order:

- on the first day of May—one woollen jacket, one shirt, one pair of woollen trousers, one pair of shoes and one hat or cap;
- on the first day of August—one shirt and one pair of shoes;
- on the first day of November—one woollen or duck frock,[16] one pair of woollen or duck trousers, one shirt, one pair of shoes; and
- always one good blanket and one mattress.

They were also required to provide the following weekly rations:

- 12 lbs of wheat or 9 lbs of flour;
- 7 lbs of beef or mutton;
- 4 oz of salt; and
- 2 oz of soap.

These rations did not suit the severe winter climate in Canberra and the wider region, so the lot of the assigned men in their draughty huts was a hard one.

Masters were not supposed to beat their servants (though many did) but could bring them before a Magistrate if they misbehaved. Punishments ranged from a reprimand for a minor offence, time on the treadmill[17] or for slightly worse offences assignment to hard labour on the road gang, solitary confinement on bread and water, or flogging with the lash. For serious or frequent offences, the most severe punishment short of execution was to be transported to a penal settlement: Moreton Bay, Newcastle, Norfolk Island and Port Macquarie.

---

16   A water repellent, durable and versatile canvas material.

17   Steps set into two cast iron wheels that drove a shaft used to mill corn, pump water and the like as a form of hard labour punishment.

The corruption of the 'Pure Merinos', Magistrates and Upper Classes was endemic. Many settlers resented and largely ignored any restrictions aimed at stopping them from continuing to use convicts as slave labour. From 1838, Station Managers had to hire free men at the equivalent of about 52 dollars a year, plus rations and quarters.

As with the voyage to Australia, convict welfare was a lottery. Some were treated little better than slaves or animals, overworked and harshly beaten despite the regulations. Others were fortunate enough to be sent to good Masters, who looked after them as valued domestic servants and paved the way for their reintegration into society as good citizens.

For some convicts who experienced only poverty and prison in England, life as an assigned convict to a good Master was better than anything they had ever known before. They had a bed to sleep in, regular food, a comparatively pleasant climate and kind treatment. For these, transportation really was the start of a new and better life; for others it was sheer misery.

Six
Joseph Blundell—the Patriarch

Family Legends and Myths

Stories about ancestry are usually passed down through the generations by word of mouth—often embellished to hide undesirable aspects.

For example, where a family descended from a convict ancestor, there was considerable social pressure to conceal the associated stigma until the 1970s. Since then, a more enlightened view has emerged as *inter alia* such an ancestor provides insights into the early days of Australia's settlement.

Various stories about Joseph Blundell's past which became family folklore 'recollections' are related here as a backdrop to what follows.

My great grandmother Rosanna[1] thought her Father was born in 1786 in Maidstone, a market town in Kent eight miles south of Rochester, the son of Joseph Blundell (a blacksmith and Susan?), marrying Susan Osborne (daughter of Abraham) at Boxley or Thurnham in Kent in 1840 when she was 28 and he 54 years of age. They arrived in the Colony soon after, living at Liverpool on the outskirts of Sydney for some years before coming to Canberra where Joseph was employed by Charles Campbell of Duntroon.

Audrey, 17th and last child of John,[2] told me that Joseph was a Gentleman's Valet born in Maidstone England in 1786, convicted

---

1 The tenth of Joseph's 11 children.

2 Joseph's first born.

to Australia and subsequently aged 54 married Susan Osborne aged 28 at Boxley in the NSW Colony in 1840. They lived at Liverpool Plains, later moving to Canberra.

The Liverpool Plains was a vast agricultural area in the north-western slopes of NSW, bounded to the east by the Great Dividing Range and to the west by the Warrumbungle Range. The major watercourse is the Namoi River and the principal towns are Gunnedah, Narrabri, Quirindi and Tamworth.

Harold 'Nobby' Blundell's[3] version was:

> 'Joseph Blundell, a stockman and gilly farmer of Duntroon Scotland and his wife Susan were assisted to migrate prior to 1818 by Robert Campbell who wished Joseph to take charge of his Australian stock.

> 'While Joseph was in charge at Bathurst in 1821-23, a prolonged drought forced him to seek more pasture. Joseph and his shepherds travelled with the stock as far as Lake George and while there, their Aboriginal stock men befriended the local blacks who spoke of a big river to the southeast.

> 'Joseph and two companions, whose names are not recorded, rode in search of it. They reached the Molonglo River (near Duntroon— in the Winter of 1827) and camped below where Duntroon homestead now stands, thinking they had reached the river spoken of by the blacks. The party was impressed by that area as a bitter cold wind with sleet and light snow was blowing down from the Snowy Mountains to the South. The hardy Scots said it was a 'bonny place just like home'. The stock was shifted to the area and a permanent camp established. It was nearly a year before they learned that the local Aboriginals were referring to the junction of the Molonglo and Murrumbidgee Rivers at Uriarra Crossing where a large black camp existed (Uriarra being an Aboriginal name).

---

3   Grandson of George—Joseph's third child. Nobby subsequently wrote *Moments in History—A Nation's Pioneer Heritage* instigated by the Far North Queensland Australia Remembers Committee for the 1995 Australia Remembers Year to commemorate 50 years after the end of WWII. Coincidentally, I was responsible as Secretary of Veterans Affairs and President of the Repatriation Commission for that idea/program and series of events all around Australia and overseas in 1995 and the smaller Anzac Cove Ceremony in Turkey to mark the 80th Anniversary of the Gallipoli landing by the ANZACs in the early stages of WWI.

'Although it is now known that early explorers had passed through the District on their way to the south coast of NSW, it is believed that Joseph Blundell and party were the first white settlers to reside there.

'By 1830 Joseph had charge of Campbell's stock which ranged over a vast area from Delegate to Mount Cooper (some 156 Km south of Canberra in line with Nimmitabel in the Snowy Mountains).

'At this time, Joseph lived in a cottage near the Yarralumla wool shed (which is still there at 208 Cotter Road) close to where the Prime Minister's residence now stands. Joseph lived there for 30 years, far longer than any Prime Minister and in far less comfort.

'As part of his close association with the Campbell family, Joseph's bullock team was engaged in carting stone for St John's Church commissioned by George Campbell in 1841 and the stone building adjacent to the church (originally a shepherd's hut) which was later used as a school house and residence for the teacher; all of Joseph's eight grand-children by his son George attended school there.'

Nobby Blundell's book records that 'Joseph's assignment to Dr Townson was transferred to Robert Campbell almost immediately on disembarking from the *Marquis of Huntley* in Sydney Cove.' His Aunt Alice claimed to have 'sighted records at Duntroon where Joseph Blundell was in charge of stock belonging to Robert Campbell at Camden in 1826.'

Lyall Gillespie, a former City Manager and Canberra Historian, recorded Joseph as having been born in Kent; soldier, shepherd, later farmer; who resided in Canberra from 1837 with his wife Susan (*née* Osborne) where he reared a large family of seven sons and five daughters.

Some other references also mention 12 children, but I have only been able to find four of the purported five daughters.

Bulletin 1 of the 1986 Queanbeyan District History Society brought forth a response from a descendant that Joseph was a soldier, who while chasing a rabbit had trespassed on another man's property, was apprehended and transported to the Colony of NSW. The Bulletin quoted Archives as showing a Joseph Blundell aged 28, labourer, protestant, life sentence for assault, arriving per ship *Marquis of Huntley* in 1826 and assigned to Richard

Jones of Cabramatta—Joseph arrived with wife only. The records were also said to show an 'R A' Blundell, a 'Farmers Man' from Kent, being tried on 2 January 1826 at Maidstone and arriving on the same ship as Joseph.[4]

Two obvious questions, which arise from this narrative, are addressed in this Chapter—*ie* are Joseph and 'R A' Blundell one and the same person and what of the putative accompanying wife?

Gloria O'Neill [great grand-daughter of George (Joseph's third child)] recalls her Father Horace Collogan saying that Joseph was brought to Australia by the Campbells to look after the sheep.

These stories turn out to be a mixture of fact and fiction, embroidered with poetic licence to disguise the reality.

The Facts

We know that Joseph Blundell was baptised on 7 October 1798 at Thurnham (*aka* Thornham). The trying economic and social conditions at the time he grew up in the Maidstone District are also covered at the end of Chapter Three.

The next part of Joseph's story was recorded 27 years later:

'On 22 November 1825 (Saturday), a little after seven o'clock in the evening, George Pearson, gamekeeper for Mr Charlton of Pim's Court (near Maidstone) on going into one of his Master's Coverts found there two men, named Joseph Blunden (*sic*) and Samuel Knight, the former armed with a gun. The keeper collared Blunden, and asked what business they had there? He replied they had got nothing, and desired Pearson to let him go. Pearson refused. Blunden then thrust the muzzle of the gun, with great force into the corner of the right eye of Pearson, and a scuffle ensued, and Blunden was thrown to the ground. Knight then began to beat the keeper with the gun, but the latter left Blunden and tripped Knight up. Blunden seized the opportunity to rise, and with the gun levelled Pearson to the earth, and beat him in the most savage manner, till the stock was broken to pieces. They also stabbed him in the right leg, with some sharp instrument. When the attack commenced, the keeper sent another man, who was with him, for assistance, but he did not return until the outrage had been perpetrated, and poor Pearson was found insensible, and in a most dreadful state. He was conveyed home, and medical aid immediately procured. For several days his life was in imminent danger, and it was believed that the first blow had destroyed his eye, but we are happy to learn, that he is so far recovered as to be able to rise from his bed, though it is expected that the wound in the leg will make him lame for the remainder of his life.

'Mr Charlton sent to Maidstone for Constable E Poolly who from the information obtained on Wednesday morning last, about nine o'clock, apprehended Knight in the Fish Market, Maidstone, and shortly after, took Blunden near the Rose and Crown, with three pheasants in a sack on his shoulder. On taking the prisoners to Pearson's house, he spoke positively as to 'Blunden being one of the men that attacked him, and expressed his belief, that Knight was the other.'

'The prisoners were then brought back to Maidstone and having been examined before J Jacobson Esq were remanded until Pearson should be sufficiently recovered to give evidence against them. They were accordingly placed in the watch-house.

'On Sunday morning (4 December 1825) O S Davis Constable of Maidstone went to visit the prisoners to give them some broth when he found they had made their escape. The place was very strong, but by taking off the iron brackets from a seat, they had prized out some stout iron bars lining the roof and by that means forced a passage through.

'Their operations must have occupied a considerable portion of time and made much noise, but they were favoured by the night being very tempestuous and it is supposed that they were assisted by confederates outside.[5]

'The following Saturday night (10 December 1825) around midnight, Bryant and Dawson, two of the town's watchmen were called to the Plough Public House to clear the tap room, there being several persons whom the widowed landlady could not get rid of. While so engaged, the watchmen gained some information that led them, with two others, to visit the house of Samuel Knight, in Stone Street; one of the men who had broken out of the watch-house.

5   *Maidstone Gazette and Kentish Courier* Tuesday 6 December 1825.

'The watchmen searched the house, and at last found Knight concealed in a coal-hole under the stairs. On attempting to secure him, three of his brothers swore he should not be taken, and a contest took place, which was at last terminated by Knight being secured. The prisoner was then taken to the Plough, and was followed by his brothers, and a battle again took place, but after nearly an hour's contest, the watchmen were victorious, and conveyed Knight to the watch-house.

'About five o'clock, the following morning (Sunday), the same party went to Bearsted, where Blunden (the other man who escaped from the watch-house) lodged. On searching, they found Blunden's half-boots in bed with a young woman, and shortly after, they discovered him up the chimney, and he was dragged down covered with soot, and having on only his shirt and a round frock. He made no resistance and was conveyed to Maidstone.

'Both prisoners were examined before J Jacobson Esq on Monday 12 December 1825. George Pearson, Mr Charlton's gamekeeper, was sufficiently recovered to attend and he swore to the men as being those who so cruelly beat him. They were accordingly fully committed for trial at the approaching Assizes.'[6]

As to the reference '... they found Blunden's half-boots in bed with a young woman'—was this the wife I have been unable to find?

The Prison, which is near where the Kent County Council County Hall in Maidstone is located, where Joseph was detained is depicted on the next page. This gaol replaced the original County Prison which had been in the High Street in the 17th Century but had moved to a new building in King Street in 1746.

Some of the following might at first glance seem a tad repetitious but has been included to provide a full account of what happened and as an interesting description of the language and proceedings at the time.

The Special Goal Delivery of 2 January 1826 for Maidstone includes a Gaol Calendar, *ie* a printed list prepared before the Court sat, listing the prisoners for trial and giving the accused's age and trade or profession. This includes:

---

6   *Maidstone Gazette and Kentish Courier* Tuesday 13 December 1825.

Maidstone Gaol, circa 1828

- No:135—Joseph Blundell, aged 27; and
- No:136—Samuel Knight, aged 21; both labourers.

'Committed 12th December by P Le Geyt, Clerk, charged on the oaths of George Pearson and others with having unlawfully entered into a certain wood at East Farleigh, with intent illegally to kill game, armed with a gun and bludgeon.'

On the back of this Gaol Calendar, the names of the prisoners with their fates, sentences or acquittals *etc* have been written, including:

'Repealed. Transported for Life. Joseph Blundell attainted of Maliciously and Unlawfully Stabbing George Pearson with intent to prevent the Prisoner's lawful apprehension.

'Acquitted and discharged. Samuel Knight, misdemeanour.'

The Kent Special Goal Delivery, Winter 1825, began at Maidstone on 3 January 1826. The number of prisoners was described as lamentably heavy, there being already 120 of these unhappy persons as at 6 December 1825. The cases tried in the *Nisi Prius* Court[7] on Wednesday 4 January included:

'No:18—Joseph Blundell (27) puts himself (*ie* pleads not guilty)— Jury say Guilty on the last count only—no goods—to be hanged— judgement recorded.' At the side is a further entry "Repealed", Transported for Life.'

---

7   A Trial Court for hearing civil cases before a Judge and Jury.

At the end of the record for this Gaol Delivery is a list of 'Bills for Costs' for the various cases, including Joseph Blundell and another—£23.4s.6d.[8]

The indictments against Joseph were:

- 'Joseph Blundell, late of the Parish of East Farleigh, Kent, labourer puts himself—Jury say Guilty on last Count—Not Guilty on remaining Counts—No Goods—To be hanged by the neck until he be dead;

- Second Count repeats the above details, but the charge is that the stabbing was 'with intent to disable the said George Pearson;'

- Third Count again repeats the same details as in the first Count, the charge being that the stabbing was 'with intent to do some grievous bodily harm to the said George Pearson;' and

- Fourth Count repeats the same details again, but the charge is malicious stabbing "with intent to obstruct, resist and prevent the lawful apprehension and detainer of them the said Joseph Blundell and Samuel Knight at the Parish aforesaid ... for the committing of which said last mentioned offence they were liable by Law to be apprehended, imprisoned and detained".

On the back of the document:

'George Pearson, Joseph Sargent, George Birchall, John Fearne, John Craddock, Edward Wright, George Golding, Edwin Poolly, Henry Kipping, Richard Wedd. Sworn 10 (the witnesses). True Bill.[9]

A document in the bundle next to the above, provides further detail:

'Joseph Blundell, late of (place lost—damaged), Kent, labourer, (Judgement on another Indictment), and Samuel Knight, late of the same, labourer (puts himself—Jury says—Not Guilty—Acquitted) on 22 Nov. (6 George IV 1825) ... with force and arms, at the Parish aforesaid ... unlawfully did enter into a certain wood

8   ASSI 31/24 Agenda Book Kent and elsewhere 1821-1825.

9   ASSI 35/256/3.

there called Hall Wood, of and belonging to Richard Vachell Esq,[10] and then in the occupation of John Charlton, with intent ... illegally to destroy, take and kill game, and were then and there found at night ... being ... Armed with a gun and bludgeon ... The said Joseph Blundell and Samuel Knight afterwards, to wit on the said 22 Nov (6 George IV 1825), with force and arms, at the Parish aforesaid ... unlawfully did enter into a certain other wood there called Hall Wood, of and belonging to the said Richard Vachell, and then in the occupation of the said John Charlton, with intent ... to aid, abet and assist each other illegally to destroy, take and kill game, and ... were ... found at night ... armed with a gun and a bludgeon ... (A total of eight counts listed, including the above first two. All relate to the same time and place, and similar offences.) (At the side of the document, at the bottom, is 'Poaching'.)'

On the back of the document:

'John Charlton, George Pearson, Joseph Sargent, George Birchall, John Fearne, John Craddock, Edward Wright, George Golding, Edwin Poolley, Henry Kipping (Richard Wedd—deleted).[11] Sworn 10. True Bill.'

The George Pearson referred to above was probably the same one recorded in the 1851 Census as still living in East Farleigh aged 55 with his wife Jemima (50) and children from Jemima (25) down.

KENT WINTER ASSIZES Maidstone Thursday 5 January 1826 before Mr Baron Hullock:

'Joseph Blundell and Samuel Knight were indicted under Lord Ellenborough's Act, for maliciously cutting George Pearson, with intent to murder him, at East Farleigh on 22 November last. The prisoners had been committed under the Poaching Act 57 Geo III.

'It appeared in evidence that the prosecutor, who was a servant in the employment of a gentleman of fortune, named Charlton, at East Farleigh, was out in one of his Master's woods, on the night of 22 November, for the purpose of protecting the game, and whilst in the act of preventing some pheasants from settling on the trees,

10   Richard Vachell *Esq* of the Priory in Essex.

11   Richard Wedd was replaced by John Charlton—the owner of the Woods where the offences took place.

the prisoner Blundell came up and struck him. A violent scuffle ensued, and the prosecutor received several blows from a gun, which the prisoner had in his hand, the butt-end of which broke off. There was another man in the prisoner's company, who could not be identified. The prisoner and his companion, after the scuffle, ran off, leaving the prosecutor senseless on the ground. An assistant of the prosecutor had left him when the affray commenced for the purpose of procuring assistance. When the prosecutor came to himself, he found he was desperately wounded in his left thigh with a knife, or some other sharp instrument. The wound penetrated to the bone. On the scene of action were left a clasp knife, and the fragments of a gun, the latter of which formed part of a gun which the prisoner Knight had got repaired at Maidstone on 23 November. Positive evidence was given of Blundell's identity, but the case against Knight rested only upon circumstances of strong suspicion. A surgeon, who had examined the prosecutor's wounds, proved that the wound on his thigh must have been inflicted with a sharp instrument. He had sustained other bodily injuries.

'The prisoners denied their guilt, but the Jury, under the learned Judge's directions, found Knight not guilty, and Blundell guilty, against whom a sentence of death was recorded.'

It seems obvious from the above reports that Joseph was considered the main perpetrator by both Judge and Jury.

The Maidstone Gazette of 10 January 1826 reported:

'Joseph Blundell, 27, and Sam Knight, both labourers, were tried at the Kent Winter Assizes on Tuesday 3 January 1826 for cutting and maiming George Pearson. Particulars of this case were stated at the time in our paper. Guilt of Blundell fully proved. Identity of Knight not established. Principal evidence against him—a gun having been in his possession a week before affray and he told a man he'd been in a row. Mr Wedd, surgeon, deposed that the wound in Pearson's thigh was a puncture, edges not jagged. A knife found on the ground nearby was produced. It was shut and had no blood on it.

'Mr Hullock, summing up, directed the Jury to bear in mind that they should distinguish in the verdict whether the wound was given for the purpose of causing the prosecutor's death or to avoid apprehension. "Verdict—Death".'

In the *Fatal Shore* (*op cit*) Robert Hughes writes:

'The number of poachers transported was very small, those who were had usually been convicted of assaulting the gamekeeper. Few countrymen thought poaching wrong, for poaching laws were among the most corrupt of English Statutes.'

The Kentish agricultural labourer at this time typically suffered a life of grinding labour and unremitting poverty, with wages between £10 and £15 *per annum*. During the 1820s and 1830s those with the intestinal fortitude to rebel against this cruel lot, including many of the followers of 'Captain Swing' (*ie* the rick-burners and machine breakers) were tried and shipped off to Australia.[12]

The Maidstone Convict Book notes that Joseph was transported for life, reflecting the commutation of his 5 January 1826 death sentence.

Joseph was taken in chains with James Clackett (who was also sentenced to 'Life') as part of the Kent Special Gaol Delivery on 25 January 1826[13] to Woolwich where he was held on the prison hulk *Retribution* in the Thames River, about three miles from Greenwich where his ancestors hailed from. The irony of the hulk being called *Retribution* will not have escaped the reader.

The police wagon depicted on the next page which conveyed them from Maidstone to Woolwich—some 26 miles in the depths of winter— would have taken a whole day of up to ten hours. The picture, which was taken in Sessions Square at Maidstone with the Prison in the background, also shows people dressed in the garb of the day in 1811.

Detained on the *Retribution* Pending Transportation [14]

The Spanish built 74-gun Third-rate HMS *Edgar*—launched in 1779—was converted into a prison hulk in 1813, renamed HMS *Retribution* and moored at Woolwich and Sheerness until she was broken up in 1856.

---

12   Nobby Blundell *op cit*.

13   UK Prison Hulk Registers and Letter Books 1802-1849.

14   Royal Arsenal History and Port Cities London websites.

Police wagon in Sessions Square at Maidstone with the Prison in the background

The *Retribution* was the most dreaded hulk of all of them by the prisoners, its death rate being double that of the other hulks, *ie* an incredible 60%. It was one of the largest and longest-serving hulks with up to 450 men kept shackled on the three lower decks. Despite numerous reports of murder, robbery, suicide and 'unnatural crimes' no officers dared to descend among them after dark.

No special accommodation was available for gentlemen to rent, so they were forced to sleep on straw with the other convicts and share the barley and putrid meat provided. This 'gave them such serious bowel problems that they were sure it would soon terminate their miserable existence.'

'In Spring and Summer, the *Retribution* was a popular destination for tourists who were curious to view its awful bulk and famously depraved inmates from the safety of a small boat. From there they could also observe the multitude of convicts in chains working on the Warren' (*ie* the Woolwich Arsenal).[15]

James Hardy Vaux described conditions on the *Retribution* during the early 1800s while awaiting transportation for a second time:

> 'There were confined in this floating dungeon nearly 600 men, most of them double ironed; and the reader may conceive the horrible effects arising from the continual rattling of chains, the filth and

---

15   This and the previous two paragraphs from 'transported convicts to Australia' *via* google.

Hulk at Woolwich, similar to the Retribution.[16]

vermin naturally produced by such a crowd of miserable inhabitants, the oaths and execrations constantly heard amongst them ...

'On arriving on board, we were all immediately stripped and washed in two large tubs of water, then, after putting on each a suit of coarse slop clothing, we were ironed and sent below; our own clothes being taken from us ...

'I soon met many of my old Botany Bay acquaintances, who were all eager to offer me their friendship and services, that is, with a view to rob me of what little I had; for in this place there is no other motive or subject for ingenuity. All former friendships are dissolved, and a man here will rob his best benefactor, or even messmate, of an article worth one halfpenny.

'Every morning at seven o'clock, all the convicts capable of work, or, in fact, all who are capable of getting into the boats, are taken ashore to the Warren, in which the Royal Arsenal and other public buildings are situated, and there employed at various kinds of labour, some of them very fatiguing; and while so employed, each gang of sixteen or twenty men is watched and directed by a fellow called a guard.

'These guards are commonly of the lowest class of human beings; wretches devoid of feeling; ignorant in the extreme, brutal by nature, and rendered tyrannical and cruel by the consciousness of the power they possess.'

16   http://www.frankmurray.com.au/wp-content/uploads/2010/04/Hulk-Woolwich-1.jpg

The day-to-day life of a convict on a hulk was also described by William Day, a prisoner on the *Justitia*, moored at Woolwich, towards the end of 1838:

> 'Before going on board, we were stripped to the skin and scrubbed with a hard-scrubbing brush, something like a stiff birch broom, and plenty of soap, while the hair was clipped from our ears as close as scissors could go ... We were then supplied with new 'magpie' suits—one side black or blue, and the other side yellow. Our next experience was being marched off to the blacksmith who riveted on our ankles rings of iron connected by eight links to a ring in the centre, to which was fastened an up and down strap or cord reaching to the waist belt. This last supported the links and kept them from dragging on the ground.

> 'In this rig-out we were transferred to the hulk where we were given our numbers for no names were used ... There were prayers conducted by the chaplain night and morning and compulsory schooling from 5 o'clock to 7 o'clock every evening. The prisoners were marched on shore each day, under the supervision of guards with whips, to work on the docks and at Woolwich arsenal ... (where it was moored).

> 'During all this time, I was never for a moment without the leg irons, weighing about 12 pounds. Though our work was constant we did not fare badly as regards victuals. Our mid-day meal often consisted of broth, beef and potatoes, sometimes of bread or biscuit and cheese and half a pint of ale ...'

These descriptions paint a picture of the appalling conditions endured by the convicts. The deck where they were held was barely high enough to let them stand up. Bad living quarters, cramped conditions, having to sleep in fetters, poorly dressed and often unhealthy, the quality and monotonous daily meals were kept as low as possible. And the men who controlled the ships often pocketed the money provided by the Government rather than using it for the purposes for which it was allocated.

Rations provided by the Contractors were inadequate in terms of the energy and nutrition required to perform the arduous hard labour. Convicts frequently went hungry and suffered malnutrition.[17] This was done on purpose. Indeed, ' ... the Parliamentary Act authorising the use of Hulks

---

17   This and the next two paragraphs sourced from 'Convict Hulks/The Digital Panopticon.'

stipulated that convicts were to be fed little other than bread, any coarse or inferior food, water and small beer.'

The punishing regime meant that the men became weak, demoralised and susceptible to disease. Hygiene was so poor that disease spread quickly, the sick received little medical attention and were not separated from the healthy. Dysentery was widespread caused by drinking brackish water from the Thames. Sanitation and cramped living conditions meant that infections and diseases such as Cholera and Typhus spread quickly.

Discipline was severe, and any attempt to remove chains around their waists and ankles led to flogging with a cat of nine tails, extra irons and solitary confinement in tiny cells with names like the 'Black Hole.'

The *Retribution's* records show that Joseph 'was disposed of on 5 May' and the *Marquis of Huntley* manifest has him on board at Sheerness on 10 May 1826, the day before the ship sailed for Australia. How he got to Sheerness from Woolwich is not clear, but it was likely on an escorted ship down the Thames.

By 1830, some four years after Joseph was transported, there were still ten hulks in operation, holding 4400 inmates.

The *Marquis of Huntley*

The picture of the ship *Ann* overleaf is believed to be of the same size and type as the *Marquis of Huntley* for which there are no known images.[18]

Constructed in Aberdeen in 1804, as a purpose-built convict wooden Tall Ship sheathed with copper over boards with iron bolts 560 tons in weight and owned by Latham and Co in London, the *Marquis of Huntley* undertook its maiden journey in 1826 to NSW, followed by voyages in 1827, 1830 and 1835.

The Master was Captain Ascough an old visitor to the Port. The Surgeon General, Dr Rae RN, recorded three deaths during the journey to NSW. The Guard formed part of the 39th under Major McPherson.

---

18   Courtesy of the Rights and Images Sales Executive of the Royal Museums Greenwich.

English ship, Ann, *similar to the* Marquis of Huntley.

William Ascough was the Master and Captain of five different convict ships and eight journeys to Port Jackson:

- *Malabar*, 1819;
- *Ann and Amelia*, 1825;
- *Marquis of Huntley*, 1826, 1828 and 1830;
- *Portland*, 1832, 1833; and
- *Mary* 1835.

Major Donald McPherson (1790-1852) was Commanding Officer of the detachment of the 39th Regiment (*aka* the Dorsetshire Regiment of the Foot) on the *Marquis of Huntley*. He was subsequently posted in 1828 as Officer Commanding to Bathurst and was in charge there when serious disturbances arose among the convicts in the District in August 1830, necessitating the deployment of large reinforcements of the Regiment from Sydney to quell the uprising. McPherson was then redeployed to Madras in India in 1832.

The *Marquis of Huntley* with 200 male prisoners sailed from Sheerness on 11 May. Ten of these were from the Kent Special Gaol Delivery, but only Joseph Blundell and James Clackett seem to have been held on the hulk *Retribution*.

Typically, in a ship this size, Prisoners were restrained in the hold, battens being fixed fore and aft for hammocks, which were hung 17 inches apart from each other; but being encumbered with their irons, together with the want of fresh air soon rendered their situation truly deplorable. They were, however, permitted to walk the decks of the ship in turns ten at a time. Humane Masters released the prisoners from their irons so that they could strip their clothes off at night and during the day wash and keep themselves clean.[19]

Dr William Rae, Surgeon and Superintendent, recorded details of the cases he treated on the *Marquis of Huntley* and other observations in his Journal from 29 March until 21 September, departing for England on the Brig[20] *Fairfield* on 11 October 1826 and arriving home about 25 February 1827.

There are, however, no entries before 11 May and the list of medical treatments starts on 27 May and concludes on 13 September.[21]

The route, which took 120 days (about average for those days) was recorded by Dr Rae in his Journal as follows:[22]

- 11 May—5 West Longitude, 49 North Latitude, departed Sheerness to the mouth of the River Thames to turn south between England and France;
- 14 May—off the Bay of Biscay between France and Spain—stormy;
- 16 May—16 West Longitude, 21 North Latitude off the coast of Spain;
- 28 May—squally;
- 1 June—22.5 West Longitude, 15 North Latitude, off the coast of Africa in the Atlantic Ocean—opthalmia;[23]

---

19   Charles White *op cit.*

20   A two-masted sailing ship.

21   UK Government Archives, Admiralty Records reference ADM 101/50/7.

22   Longitude lines start from zero at Greenwich and go vertically 180 degrees East and West whereas Latitude is represented horizontally by lines which go 90 degrees north or south of the Equator.

23   Inflammation of the eye.

- 15 June—27 West Longitude, about to cross the Equator;
- 17 June—clear;
- 1 July—rain;
- 3 July—38 West Longitude, 31 South Latitude, half way down the east coast of South America, turning left towards Africa to catch the roaring 40s westerly winds;
- 9 July—catarrh;[24]
- 11 July—8 West Longitude, 35 South Latitude, about half way between South America and the horn of Africa in the Southern Ocean;
- 13 July—opthalmia;
- 13 July—1 West Longitude about to cross the Greenwich line to East longitude, still around 35 degrees South Latitude;
- 19 July—20 East Longitude, 40 South Latitude off the southern tip of the Cape of Good Hope, Africa—strong gales, rain;
- 21 July—terrible gale;
- 25 July—stormy, hail, catarrh;
- 29 July—rain;
- 2 August—71 East Longitude, 40 South Latitude in the middle of the Southern Ocean between Africa and New Holland;
- 3 August—hazy;
- 6 August—clear, diarrhoea;
- 8 August—clear;
- 10 August—clear, sunny, fever;
- 12 August—dark, rainy, dysentry;
- 14 August—clear, sunny;
- 16 August—119 East Longitude, 40 South Latitude off the southern tip of New Holland—rain, scurvy;
- 20 August—132 East Longitude, 41 South Latitude, (south of Port Lincoln in South Australia)—clear;

---

24   Mucus in the eye/throat.

- 26 August—142 East Longitude, 40 South Latitude off the coast of Victoria turning right down the west coast of Van Diemen's Land (VDL *ie* Tasmania from 1856);
- 30 August—143.75 East Longitude, 42.6 South Latitude off the west coast of VDL—clear;
- 3 September—147 East Longitude, 45.5 South Latitude off the southern tip of VDL—cloudy, fever;
- 5 September—off the north-east tip of VDL—clear, winds variable; and
- 12 September—Sydney.

I'm grateful to Graham Humphries—the Principal of Cox Architecture—for assembling the Map on the next page which charts the *Marquis of Huntley's* journey from Sheerness to Port Jackson. The avid reader can compare the dates on the Map with Dr Rae's remarks on the previous pages.

By the time of Joseph's departure from Sheerness, the voyage to Australia was far less unpleasant and dangerous than it had been ten to twenty years earlier, when many prisoners died of dysentery or fell ill with scurvy and when there was little attempt to keep the ship clean or the men properly fed.

Nevertheless, the conditions below decks on the relatively small sailing ships of those days were cramped and stuffy-smelly, especially when traversing the tropics. There were still, as in the earlier transports, long rows of berths, one above the other 18 inches apart, in the locked prison between the decks. Four men occupied each berth with an 18-inch wide space for each person to lie in.

The Medical and Surgical Journal

William Rae was born in 1786 in Dumfries, educated at Loch Maben and Dumfries, before graduating with an MD at Edinburgh University. Aged just 18, he joined the medical service of the East India Company in 1804, transferring to the Royal Navy the next year as a surgeon and becoming a member of the Royal College of Surgeons in 1811.

He served as Surgeon Superintendent on the convict ships *Eliza* in 1822, *Isabella* in 1823, *Marquis of Huntley* in 1826, *Prince Regent* in 1827 and finally on the *Marquis of Hastings* in 1828.

Other senior level appointments followed, and he was knighted at St James Palace in 1858. He died at Newton in Devon in 1879 aged 87, his second wife Margaret being his sole heir.

In his *Journal of the Voyage to NSW of the Marquis of Huntly* (*sic*), Rae records treating a series of cases of Ophthalmia (inflammation of the eye, probably conjunctivitis) among the accompanying troops of the 39th Regiment, catching a slight case of it himself as did the Prisoner employed in the Hospital:

> 'This complaint it appears has been prevalent in the Regiment for some time past and there now seems a strong disposition towards its recurrence amongst the troops on board though they all appeared free from it on embarkation.'

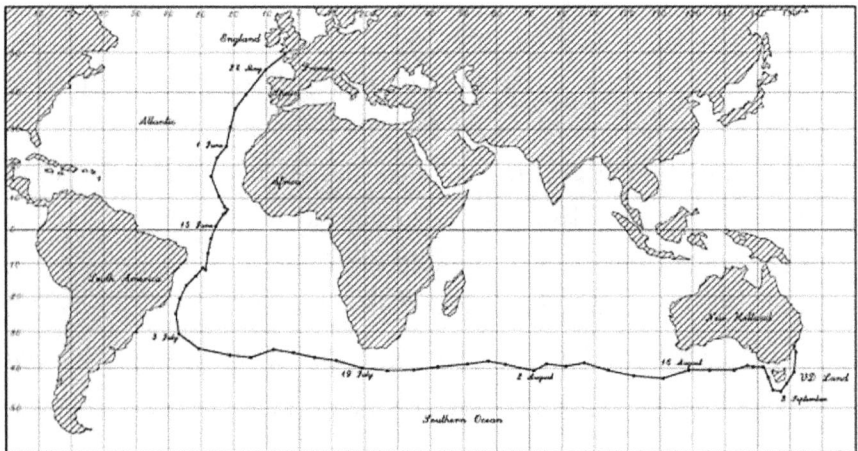

From Sheerness to Port Jackson—Map of the Voyage

The Master Roll of the *Marquis of Huntley* includes Joseph as one of 200 convicts who left Sheerness on 11 May, 197 of whom completed the journey on 12 September, three convicts having died *en route*.

While that is right, there were four deaths on the journey:

- John Harvey, convict, aged 18, a weak sickly and rickety looking boy, convicted of burglary and sentenced to 14 year's transportation, who was first treated on 30 May and died from Scorbutics (Scurvy) on 28 July;
- John Amyess, convict, aged 60, a weak and infirm man of feeble intellect, sentenced to seven years, first treated for Diarrhoea on 17 August and died on 19 August;
- an unnamed infant who died from Marasmus;[25] and
- William Weller, convict, aged 19, convicted of Highway Robbery and transported for life, who died from typhus on 11 September off the NSW Coast.

No mention of Joseph Blundell appears in the Surgeon's Journal.

Arrival in Port Jackson

An extract from the Master Roll of the *Marquis of Huntley* shows that:

'Joseph Blundell, a Farmer's Man, born about 1798 in Kent England, married with no children, was tried at Kent on 2 January 1826 for 'Afsault' at Maidstone and given a life sentence, this being his second conviction or having had two prior convictions. He was transported to Sydney Cove under Master Wm Ascough being one of 200 convicts who left Sheerness on 16 May 1826, 198 of whom arrived in Port Jackson on 13 September 1826. He was 28 years of age, had no education, was of the Protestant faith and was married with a wife only. Joseph was 5 feet 6 and a half inches in height, ruddy complexion, light brown hair and blue eyes. He had a scar on the corner of the right eye brow and his left leg was bowed above the ankle.'[26]

I have been unable to find out anything about the reference above to Joseph's

'... second conviction or having had two prior convictions.'

---

25 Severe malnutrition caused by a scarcity of food and a diet which is deficient in calories, protein and carbohydrates.

26 NSW Archives Reel No: 397. It will be noted in the quote that 198 arrived in Port Jackson, but we know from earlier on that three convicts died on the journey meaning 197 arrived.

The Transportation Record also says that Joseph was 'married with a wife only' when he was sent out to Australia for life, making it highly likely that he was indeed married before transportation. It would, however, have been very unlikely for wives to accompany husbands transported to Australia for the term of their natural life. Not only was it hard to get passage out here, the price of tickets was far beyond the means of a worker's wife.

The *Marquis of Huntley's* manifest doesn't show Joseph's wife as a passenger.

A convict's family could be brought out to join them at Government expense if they were thought worthy of this indulgence and the family given a small grant of land, but again there's no record that Joseph or his putative wife followed this course of action.

A Marriage Index for the ancient County of Kent maintained by Michael Gandy in England and which covers the period 1813-1837 contains only one Joseph Blundell marriage—to Anne Sargent at Bromley on 2 August 1818.

This Joseph was a son of George Blundell and Anne Johnson, George being the third son of Thomas of Chelsfield, brother of our Joseph's Father.

Our Joseph would not have been married before 1813 when Gandy's marriage index started, being only 15 years old then. If and who he was married to at the time of his transportation to Australia seems destined to remain a mystery.

The Colonial Secretary, accompanied by the Principal Superintendent of Convicts, were occupied for the whole of Thursday 14 September 1826 in mustering the prisoners on board the *Marquis of Huntley* prior to the convicts' embarkation in Sydney Cove the following Tuesday 19 September.

Joseph's Assignment to Dr Robert Townson on Arrival

The Shipping Record shows that Joseph was assigned on arrival to Dr Townson of Bunbury Curran, who owned 1000 acres of land in the Parish of Minto, County Cumberland—through which Bunbury Curran Creek, a small western tributary of the George's River ran.[27]

---

27   *Australian Dictionary of Biography*. This area was referred to as the birthplace of the NSW pastoral industry.

It is useful to include a brief biography where possible of the people that our early ancestors worked for to give a better picture of their lives at the time.

Dr Robert Townson, who was born in 1762 at Richmond in Surrey, went on to become a scholar, scientist and settler from Shropshire.

A friend of Sir Joseph Banks, Robert's brother Captain John Townson returned from the Colony to England in 1800. Discussions with them and other contacts, together with John's decision to return to Australia, led Robert to approach the British Government in 1806 about going to the Settlement. He was warmly received and informed that he was exactly the sort of person most urgently needed in the Colony accompanied by a promise of land and other indulgences.

Townson thus arrived in Sydney on the *Young William* on 7 July 1807 as a polymath and the most eminent scholar in the young Colony, being proficient in all branches of natural science as well as French, German, Greek and Latin.

Townson and his brother John, who had arrived earlier with the promise of similar privileges, were affronted by Governor Bligh's lack of appreciation of their talents and refusal to honour the undertakings given to them in London.

To Townson's consternation, the pugnacious Bligh stood on his dignity and referred the matter back to the Government in England for further instructions which left him in no doubt that he was to issue the promised land grants.

Deeply chagrined, Townson became a vocal opponent of William Bligh[28] and he was cited as one of the principal six people who influenced Major George Johnston's views and actions outlined in Chapter Five.

Indeed, Robert Townson was at the dinner in the Officer's Mess on the eve of John McArthur's trial which precipitated what came to be known as

---

28   The following six paragraphs are sourced from the NSW State Library, the *Australian Dictionary of Biography* and the NSW Office of the Environment and Heritage publication 'Varroville'.

the Rum Rebellion. Townson signed the requisition to depose Bligh on 26 January 1808 and took part in the formal deposition at Government House, where Bligh was arrested, and the Colony placed under military rule, the only time in Australian history that a Government has been overthrown by a Military Coup.

The military stayed in power until Governor Lachlan Macquarie assumed office at the beginning of 1810. By then, Townson had fallen out with the rebel administration over land that he wanted. Macquarie responded to the insurrection by cancelling all grants of land to Townson and the rest of the rebels, until he could personally reconsider them.

Having done so, Macquarie re-granted Townson 1680 acres at Botany Bay in 1811 and later the 1000 acres that he had previously owned in Minto.

The latter holding where Townson lived, having withdrawn from society, became the famous Varro Ville farm, named after the Roman writer Marcus Terentius Varro (116-37 BC). This celebrated Estate became a significant contributor to agriculture, fine-wool sheep and cattle, food production, horticulture and viticulture. His contemporaries opined that no man had accomplished more than Townson in stock rearing. The house and its show place surrounds are still preserved in a Campbelltown suburb called Varroville.

It was only after Macquarie's departure on 12 February 1822, that Townson took his proper place in society, becoming a Magistrate in 1826 whereupon he developed a reputation for supporting worthy causes and initiatives to help the poor. In the meantime, he became aggrieved at his treatment, eccentric to the point of being a borderline psychopath and renowned for his parsimonious and rigid economic application to Varro Ville farm.

A bachelor, Townson died on 27 June 1827 at Varro Ville, was buried at Parramatta and left his fortune to his brother John of van Diemen's Land, two nieces in England and his nephew Captain John Witts RM (Royal Marines).

Re-assignment to Richard 'China' Jones

Extracts of the November 1828 Census of NSW records reveal:

Name	Age	F/B	Ship	Date	S	R	Occupation
Blundell John (*sic*)	28	GS	*M Huntley*	1826	L	P	Servant
Bellis John	23	GS	*John*	1827	L	P	Labourer
Jenna James	24	GS	*M Huntley*	1826	14	P	Labourer
Morton James	22	TL	*Ocean 3*	1822	7	P	Labourer
Phillips William	27	CF	*Prince Regent*	1824		P	Superintendent
Sullivan Michael	26	FS	*Dick*	1821	7	C	Labourer
Sweeney Patrick	40	GS	*Brampton*	1823	L	P	Labourer

Key: F/B = Free or Bond; GS = Government Servant or Assigned Servant; TL = Ticket of Leave, CF = Came Free, FS = Free by Servitude; S = Sentence—Life, 14 or 7 years; Religion—P = Protestant, C = Catholic.

The references to 'Blunden' in some of the official records and elsewhere shows transcription errors as being quite frequent at a time when many people couldn't read or write, clerks recorded what they thought they heard (different dialects being common) and spelling was idiosyncratic.

The November 1828 NSW Census records Joseph Blundell as having been reassigned as a Servant to Richard Jones at Cabramatta. The other people in the table above were all employed by Richard Jones[29] on his Black Creek, Luskintyre property (on the Hunter River adjoining Windermere). It will have been noted that James Jenna, one of the other men employed by Jones, also came to Australia on the *Marquis of Huntley*.

Some 17 months after his reassignment following Townson's death, Blundell had been relocated to the Cassilis District to work on Jones' Hunter River properties. It may be that Jones became aware of Blundell's previous occupation as a farmer's man and thought that that would be a better and more profitable use of his skills than as a servant.

The great majority of assigned convicts were employed as agricultural labourers or shepherds in conditions of considerable hardship, the shepherds enduring a solitary life exposed to more dangers than any other class. As

---

29   *Australian Dictionary of Biography.*

pioneers of the country they worked they were either very good or very bad men, some using their lot as a stepping stone to something better while others were reduced to the lowest levels of degradation. The measure of their comfort really depended on the character of their Master, the number of men employed and whether they had an Overseer. The latter were generally Ticket-of-Leave men or Emancipists who were unable to succeed elsewhere and generally unfit to regulate others.[30]

In 1824, Jones and Walter Stevenson Davidson were partners in a 5000-acre sheep property at Collaroi on the Krui River near Cassilis. By 1828 Jones owned 9360 acres of land with 12 horses, 938 cattle and 1101 sheep.[31] In 1834, he got another 2560 acres adjoining the Krui River property, the Breeza station on the Liverpool Plains, the 2030-acre Bolwarra Estate on the Hunter River near Maitland and other land totalling over 10000 acres.

As an interesting aside here, a former owner of Bulwarra, John Brown, who had spent a large fortune on the Estate and in the Colony suffered a severe setback in his pecuniary affairs to the extent that he lost everything. This:

> '... induced him to fly to the rum bottle and steep his senses in forgetfulness. To excess in this baneful antidote his death was evidently attributable, and the Jury returned a verdict of Died by the Visitation of God.'[32]

Cassilis was an incorporated District in the County of Bligh containing an area of 1481051 acres. The Police District of Cassilis embraced the western portion of the County of Brisbane and the greater portion of the County of Bligh, bounded on the North from Mt Terell by the Liverpool Range, West to the source of the Coolaburragundi River down to Balaroo then to Cobbora and Wialdra Creek to the Goulburn River source in the Great Dividing Range.[33]

---

30   Charles White *op cit*.

31   The sources for this Section are *Early Merchant Families of Sydney* Janette Holcomb Anthem Press London 2014 and D Shineberg's *Australian Dictionary of Biography* synopsis.

32   *Sydney Gazette* 31 March 1825.

33   Bailliere's *NSW Gazette* 1866.

Richard Jones (1786-1852) arrived in Sydney on 14 August 1809 on the *Mary Ann* becoming Chief Clerk to Captain James Birnie of Alexander Birnie and Company in O'Connell Street Sydney. By May 1815, he was in partnership with Alexander Riley and a successful mercantilist in his own right, sailing to China[34] on business in October 1818 and then on to England.

In 1819, Governor Lachlan Macquarie complained to London that the order prohibiting convict ships from carrying merchandise made the Colony unduly dependent on the goods imported by Jones and his partner Riley who owned the solitary mercantile firm, that this 'sordid Rapacious House' controlled market prices and had consequently raised their prices by 100%. He went on to suggest that Jones had proposed and succeeded in establishing the prohibition while in England. Macquarie also resented the Jones-Riley close association with Walter Stevenson Davidson who with his friend John Macarthur possessed large land grants at the Cowpastures.[35]

Jones and Alexander Riley developed trading relationships with his younger brother Edward Riley in Calcutta and Walter Davidson in Canton.[36] Davidson was later involved with Robert 'Merchant' Campbell of Duntroon fame.

Jones cemented his relationships with the Colony's financial, political and religious elite through membership of various causes and as a founding Director and then President of the first bank in 1816—the Bank of New South Wales—and later as a Founder and one of ten Directors for the new Bank of Australia with John Macarthur in 1825, both of which suffered from the 1826 American and British banking crises.

In December 1822, Jones (37 years of age) married 20-year old Mary Louisa Peterson and 'retired' from the Sydney firm, while still acting as their agent in England and simultaneously collecting a 700 strong flock of the pure-bred Saxony line of Merino sheep in preparation for his

---

34 Thus, his title as 'China Jones' for his eminent role as a tea merchant.

35 Near Camden.

36 A sprawling port city on the Pearl River, north-west of Hong Kong, now known as Guangzhou.

undeclared intention to return to the Colony.

Jones came back to Australia on 4 April 1825 on the *Hugh Crawford* with his wife, infant son and the first shipment of his sheep and cattle. His brother Edward and sister Elizabeth arrived a few weeks later with more of his Saxony sheep. Jones' avowed intention was to become a pastoralist on a considerable scale with Davidson who owned a half share in the stock.

Jones introduced the pure-bred Saxony sheep strain from England and added to his stock by buying merinos[37] and cattle in the Colony.

Having already been granted 2000 acres, Jones bought 4000 more during Brisbane's Governorship. In 1829, he received an additional grant of 10000 acres on the Hunter River in recognition of the great expense associated with bringing the Saxony sheep to Australia (omitting to mention Davidson's share in the venture) and other services to the Colony. As well as another property on the Condamine River, he held the Fleurs Estate near Penrith on which he kept a dairy herd, pigs, poultry and a six-acre vineyard.

By the late1820s, Jones had become a Magistrate and leading public figure in Sydney, well known for his conservative views and objection to Governor Bourke's reforms and restoration of civil rights to Emancipists, which sat oddly with his ardent opposition of convict transportation.

Jones was appointed to the Legislative Council in 1829, serving there until 1843. A committed Church of England member, Jones was responsible for Bourke's resignation by successfully manoeuvring to have a Church of England Opposition colleague elected to Chair the Quarter Sessions rather than Bourke's Roman Catholic candidate.

Ill health forced his retirement from the mercantile business in 1837 and then he was severely hit by the onset of the 1842-44 Depression and declared insolvent in November 1843.

In 1841, Jones and Stuart Alexander Donaldson as Executors of Edward Riley Junior's Estate finalised purchase of the 1920-acre Cavan Estate on

---

37   Probably 184 Rambouillet ewes of French origin.

the Murrumbidgee River now owned by the meddling media magnate Rupert Murdoch.

As an aside, Rupert's media outlets were to the fore in the 2019 Federal election ensuring his candidate got the prize.

Australia has been wandering in the wilderness since December 2006 when Prime Minister Howard's Chief of Staff—Arthur Sinodinos[38]—left his office.

As Donald Horne observed:

> 'Australia is a lucky country run by mainly second-rate people who share in its luck.'

We've had seven Prime Ministers in the last 13 years. Our world record run of economic growth has continued despite political ineptitude and lacklustre leadership and there's still no obvious candidate to redress that situation.

We're still bedevilled by anti-intellectualism, bouts of racism and xenophobia,[39] suppression of our indigenous heritage, the Rum Corps mentality and practices and more recently the sarcastic 'Canberra Bubble' appellation to describe what happens in Parliament House. There's very little recognition of the politicisation of the public service or the implications of that for the nation and body politic.

Having lost the unlosable election Labor is still in denial about the causes of that outcome. Scott Morrison's Prime Ministership may turn out to be a critical term of Government for Australia's future as the chickens come home to roost in a developing storm of seemingly irreconcilable political, social, economic, diplomatic and national security issues.

Although 'China' Jones was renowned as a trustworthy man and respectable merchant of extreme caution and great wealth, his obsession with land ownership led him to be tardy in settling creditor's accounts and diverting money entrusted to him in pursuit of his own interests. He comingled different business accounts with a dodgy accounting system that he used to 'rob Peter to pay Paul.'

---

38   The best Chief of Staff I ever saw in action.

39   Despite our success as a multi-cultural society.

Overextension of his personal and business activities led to his undoing but like so many do, he was able to divert many of his assets to his wife, children and wider family before he came unstuck.[40]

Tickets of Leave

Well behaved convicts were eligible to be granted Tickets of Leave a few years before their sentences were up. In the case of 'lifers', this usually meant after having served ten to 12 years.

A Ticket-of-Leave allowed convicts to hire themselves out to any Master for wages and to acquire property on condition of residing within the District specified. The holder was not allowed to move to another District without permission and the Ticket could be rescinded at any time at the pleasure of the Governor, in which case the holder reverted to being a prisoner of the Crown.

Petitions for Tickets of Leave and Pardons could only be presented once per year and were required to be lodged on the first Monday in each month. The prescribed form had to be countersigned by the convict's Master or Overseer as well as the Clergyman and Principal Magistrate of the District wherein the applicant resided, certifying, that in their opinion the petitioner was deserving of the indulgence so solicited. The application form had to be presented personally by the applicant to the Petty Sessions in the District that they resided and they had to attend the Court to answer questions about their conduct if required.

Clergymen and Magistrates were enjoined not to sign such certificates for anyone whose real character they were not well acquainted with and must specifically certify the applicant as sober, industrious and honest.[41]

Many Kentish Blundells were farmers and agricultural labourers, with useful skills for early pioneering work in Australia. Joseph may also have picked up blacksmithing skills from his Father. He certainly qualified as a

---

40   Reference 31 *op cit.*
41   The certification representing an interesting sequence of criteria.

model convict who got remission for his good behaviour and application to whatever the task at hand was.

Tickets of Leave were not considered until the person had been employed by the Government or private individuals for the full space of three years. The Colony had run out of Tickets of Leave in 1834, so Certificates of Freedom were issued in their stead although there was no real difference between them.

Joseph was granted 'Certificate of Freedom' (No:34/1365) on 9 December 1834, slightly early for a 'lifer' and more akin to a convict serving a 14-year sentence, being allowed to remain in the Cassilis District, County of Brisbane.[42]

Joseph had to present himself twice a year at the Police Office for the General Muster and could not change his residential address without informing the police. Breach of these conditions risked rescission of the Certificate of Freedom and/or delay in granting a Conditional Pardon.

The 'C P' (Conditional Pardon) on the Certificate of Freedom was added when that was awarded, as the practice at the time was to go back and amend the records in the light of developments. The Shipping Record was similarly amended to record Joseph's Certificate of Freedom Number.

The 1837 General Return of Convicts in NSW records Joseph Blundell aged 39 *Marquis of Huntley* Ticket of Leave for the Cassilis District.

Pardons

Persons applying for Conditional Pardons or Emancipations who were under sentence of Transportation for Life were required to have resided at least ten years in the Colony before making such an application. The conditions for Absolute Pardons were even more stringent, requiring 15 year's residence and being strictly confined to the industrious, sober, honest and strictly meritorious who had unquestionable proofs of rectitude of conduct over many years.

---

42   NSW Archives Reel No: 2688.

A Conditional Pardon when approved by Her Majesty through the Secretary of State restored the rights of freedom from the date of the instrument within the Colony only. There was no right to leave the Colony and none beyond any limits incorporated in the instrument. When such a pardon was confirmed, it could not be revoked, and the holder was empowered to pursue his lawful occupation in any part of the country as if he had never been convicted.[43]

Convicts who moved on to Conditional or Absolute Pardons were called 'Emancipists' because they had been set free or emancipated by an Act of Grace. Those who served the full term of their sentence were called 'Expirees' because their time had expired or run out.

With a Pardon, convicts no longer reported to the police every six months and were free to go wherever they liked, but not back to England or Ireland until the sentence expired. For 'Lifers' this meant never returning 'home.'

Joseph's pardon denoted that he could then leave the Government Establishment for 'his own private advantage'—*ie* he could find a job of his own choosing and earn money for himself. Ticket of Leave convicts had to present themselves twice a year at the Police Office for the General Muster. If they broke the law, their Ticket of Leave could be rescinded, and/or Conditional Pardon delayed.

Joseph was granted Conditional Pardon No. 42/136 on 14 September 1842,[44] 16 years after his arrival.

The Australian of Friday 21 October 1842, page 4, includes:

'Conditional Pardons
Principal Superintendent of Convicts' Office
Sydney 12 October 1842.

'Conditional Pardons granted to the undermentioned prisoners are now lying at this office and will be delivered to the respective parties on payment of the fees due thereon to the public.

'Blundell Jos *Marquis of Huntley* 1826.'

---

43   Charles White *op cit.*
44   NSW Archives Reel No: 779.

Name:	Ship:	Year of Arrival:	Where Tried:	When Tried:	Sentence:
Joseph Blundell	M of Huntley	1826	Kent England	2 Jan 1826	Life

John Menadue wrote an article about what it means to be an Australian on 28 January 2013 with the theme 'redemption'—giving people another opportunity/chance—citing that as a core value of the Australian ethos.

Such was the case with Joseph Blundell, sentenced to death aged 27, transported for life at 28 and an assigned convict at that age, reassigned at 32 years of age, Certificate of Freedom at 37, Conditional Pardon and in Canberra at 45 and died 32 years later.

You have to think that Joseph Blundell did rather well for himself given all those circumstances and positioned his children to benefit from his travails.

The Start of a New Life

Joe continued to work in the Cassilis District from 1829-30 as a convict for Richard Jones on his properties up there. From 9 December 1834, when Joseph received his Certificate of Freedom and as reflected in the 1837 General Return of NSW Convicts, Joseph remained in the Cassilis District, probably still working for Jones, but not as a convict.

The next part of the story concerns the development of Joseph's relationship with 'Susan Osborne', the forthcoming birth of their first child in March 1842 and the necessity of a new start in life as free citizens in an area where Joseph and 'Susan' and their past was not known.

This subject is detailed in the next Chapter, but their planning to this end must have been well underway, including for Joseph to get his Conditional Pardon, which was granted on 14 September 1842—by which time Joseph and Susan had 'left' the Cassilis District and must have been nearing what is now Canberra. The 'C P' was critical to their future, as Joseph no longer had to present to the police and was free to change his place of residence without informing the authorities.

Joseph was said to have died in Canberra on 13 February 1874 at the age of 88, # having suffered from senile atrophy for 18 months. He was buried in St John's Section C Row 1 No:136. The grave has the name Joseph Blundell in the Blundell plot which consists of six grave sites surrounded by concrete kerbing.

Joseph was baptised on 7 October 1798, so he was probably 77 when he died.

CONDITIONAL PARDON.

No.

42/136

WHEREAS, HIS LATE MOST EXCELLENT MAJESTY KING GEORGE THE THIRD, by a Commission under the GREAT SEAL of GREAT BRITAIN, bearing date the Eighth Day of November, in the Thirty-first Year of His Majesty's Reign, was graciously pleased to Give and Grant, full Power and Authority to the Governor (or, in case of his Death or Absence, the Lieutenant-Governor) for the time-being of His Majesty's Territory of the Eastern Coast of New South Wales, and the Islands thereunto adjacent, by an Instrument or Instruments in Writing, under the Seal of the Government of the said Territory, or as me or they respectively should think fit and convenient for His Majesty's Service, to REMIT, either ABSOLUTELY or CONDITIONALLY, the Whole or any Part of the Term or Time for which Persons convicted of Felony, Misdemeanor, or other Offences, amenable to the Laws of Great Britain, should have been, or should thereafter be respectively Conveyed or Transported to New South Wales, or the Islands thereunto adjacent.

BY VIRTUE of such Power and Authority so vested as aforesaid, I _Sir George Gipps Knight_ ———— Captain-General and Governor-in-Chief of Her Majesty's said Territory of New South Wales and its Dependencies, and Vice Admiral of the same, taking into Consideration the Good Conduct of _Joseph Blundell_ ———— who arrived in this Colony in the Ship _Lloyd Huntley (1) Clough_ Master, in the Year One thousand eight hundred and _twenty six_ ————, under Sentence of Transportation for _Life_ ———— and whose Description is on the back hereof, DO hereby CONDITIONALLY REMIT the remainder of the Term or Time which is yet to come and unexpired of the Original Sentence or Order of Transportation passed on the aforesaid _Joseph Blundell_ ———— at _Court S. A. of G. A._ ———— on the _second_ ———— Day of _January_ ———— One thousand eight hundred and _twenty six_ ————

Provided always, and on Condition, that the said _Joseph Blundell_ ———— continue to reside within the Limits of this Government for and during the space of _his_ Original Sentence or Order of Transportation:—Otherwise the said _Joseph Blundell_ ———— shall be subject to all the Pains and Penalties of Re-appearing in Great Britain and Ireland, for and during the Term of _his_ Original Sentence or Order of Transportation; or, as if this Remission had never been granted.

GIVEN under my Hand and the Seal of the Territory, at Government House, Sydney, in New South Wales, this _fifth_ Day of _July_ ———— in the Year of Our Lord One thousand eight hundred and _forty one_ ————

(L.S.)   (Signed)

By His Excellency's Command.

(Signed.) _E. Deas Thomson_   _Geo. Gipps_

314

DESCRIPTION.

Standing Number	
Name	*Joseph Blundell*
Ship	*Regt Huntley (1)*
Master	*Ascough*
Year	*1826*
Native Place	*Neah*
Trade or Calling	*Farmer's Man*
Offence	*Assault*
Sentence	*Life*
Year of Birth	*1798*
Height	*5 feet 6½ inches*
Complexion	*Ruddy*
Hair	*Light Brown*
Eyes	*Blue*
General Remarks	*Scar corner of right eye brow — Left leg bowed above the ankle —*

I Certify that Her Majesty's Gracious Approbation and Allowance of the above CONDITIONAL PARDON, granted to *Joseph Blundell* —— has been signified to me by the Right Honourable the Secretary of State for the Colonies, in His Despatch, No. *93.* —dated *22°* *April 1842* ——————

GIVEN under my Hand, at Government House, Sydney, this *fourteenth* Day of *September* —— One thousand eight hundred and *forty two* ——————

(Signed.)   *Geo: Gipps*

ENTERED upon Record, at Pages *313* — and *314* — Register No. *10* ———— this *Sixteenth* Day of *September* —— One thousand eight hundred and *forty two*

E. Deas Thomson.

Susan Osborne[1]

1   Photograph courtesy of Stan Melville, who passed away earlier this year, not long after
    I completed the last draft of this Chapter. He is descended from Catherine ('Kate')
    Blundell, the 11th of Joe and Susan's children.

Seven
'Susan Osborne'—the Matriarch

Background

Information provided by the Matriarch under her alias 'Susan Osborne' such as dates, events and names were fabricated to conceal her real identity and the circumstances of her relationship with Joseph Blundell.

Joseph's transportation record and court documents say he was married before being sent out as a convict, but the details of that have proved elusive.

NSW Registration of Births, Deaths and Marriages began on 1 March 1856.

Joseph and Susan's first child born after this date was Rosanna, whose Birth Certificate (Susan being the informant) shows her Mother's maiden name as 'Osborne', born in New Romley Kent and that she and Joseph had married in the village of Thurnam in the County of Kent in 1830.

When Joseph died on 13 February 1874 in Canberra, his 'wife Susan' being the informant, the Death Certificate records Joseph as born in Maidstone Kent, married to Susan 'Horsburn' at the village of Boxley Heath, a mile or so away from Thurnham, when he was 54 years of age and that he was 88 years of age.

The two places where the marriage was said to have happened—Thurnham and Boxley—are neighbouring Parishes about four miles north of Maidstone in Kent. Thurnham was where Joseph Blundell was baptised in 1798. As we saw in Chapter Six, there is no trace whatsoever of Joseph Blundell's marriage in England—let alone to 'Susan Osborne.'

Susan Blundell died at Canberra on 8 April 1892. Her Death Certificate gives her age as 80, birthplace as Kent and Father's name as Abraham Osborne, the informant being her son-in-law Isaac Meech (her 10th child Rosanna's husband).

After her daughter Susan died, son-in-law John Robertson registered Susan senior as 'Horsburn'—as did the source for her son John's death. When son George married in 1874, his Mother's name was given as 'Osborn.'

As mentioned earlier, Kent marriage records for 1813-1837 contain only one Joseph Blundell marriage—to Anne Sargent at Bromley on 2 August 1818. This Joseph, being a son of our Joseph's Uncle George Blundell and Anne Johnson, was a first cousin of our Joseph. These same records contain no mention of any Susan Osborne before 1830. Nor does the Sussex Marriage Index reveal anything about a Susan Osborne.[2]

Bromley is now one of the 32 Boroughs of London, but historically was a market town and ancient Parish in the County of Kent.

Convicts could apply for their family to be brought out about four years after arrival if they had not been in any trouble. After a separation of seven years by sea, an absent spouse could be presumed dead. Remarriage could then occur with the remarrying spouse described as a widow/widower.

A search of Archives Office NSW Reel 699 which records 'Convict Applications for their Wives and Families to join them in Australia' shows no application from Joseph Blundell. Convict Marriage Banns from 1826 to 1841 revealed nothing and there is no record of a marriage between Joseph Blundell and Susan Osborne in the pre-1856 Register of Marriages for NSW. Moreover, there is no trace of a grant or refusal in the 'Convicts Applications to Marry' 1842-50 and no application for either party to marry someone else.

---

2   Personal correspondence with William Good

Who was Susan Osborne?

An extensive search of likely 'Osborne' candidates for the Matriarch of the Blundell line over a ten-year period through NSW Archives Office reels of records and other sources proved fruitless.

The first mention of our 'Susan Osborne' in Australia was on 7 October 1849 when five of her and Joseph's children were baptised together at St John's Anglican Church Canberra. A further four Blundell children were baptised at St John's between 1850 and 1855 and two later births/baptisms registered there after the NSW Registration of Births requirement came into effect in 1856.

Birth Certificates of the two youngest children—Rosanna born at Canberra on 13 July 1858 and Catherine born at Canberra on 18 December 1859—give their Mother's details as Susan, formerly Osborne (1858) or Ossenburn (1859) aged 46 (on both certificates) born at New Romley Kent. On Rosanna's Birth Certificate, the date and place of her parent's marriage is given as 1830 in Thurnham Kent. On Catherine's, the marriage was in 1842 at Boxley Kent. In both cases the informant was Susan Blundell herself.

In the three years given or calculated for the marriage—1830, 1840 and 1842—Joseph Blundell was a convict in NSW. This purported marriage in Kent could not have occurred at any time after Joseph's arrest in November 1825. But there is the lingering problem of Official records saying that he was married and the fact that the Constables captured him in Bearsted two miles east of Maidstone centre after he '... had been in bed with a young woman.' Perhaps, this was his wife, or they were in a common law marriage?

While the indent of the *Marquis of Huntley* records that Joseph had a wife living in 1826, Susan could not have been that wife as based on her stated age when she died from her Death Certificate, she would have been no more than 13 years old at the time of Joseph's arrest—she was actually born in in 1814 meaning she was about 11 at that time.

I have been unable to find any record of Joseph Blundell and Susan Osborne's marriage in England or Australia.

Susan claimed to have been born at New Romley around 1813.

The only place in Kent with a similar name to New Romley is New Romney.

A search of the Parish Registers of New Romney reveals only one child with the name Susan baptised there between 1811 and 1814—Susan, daughter of Robert and Jane Colegate baptised on 20 December 1812. At the time of the 1871 English Census, Susan Colegate born at New Romney aged 58 and unmarried lived in Beach Street Folkestone Kent.

No person named Susan Osborne (or Ossenborn/Horsbarn/Horsburn) or other variations) was born at New Romney in Kent in 1812, 1813 or 1814.

There is only one record of a Susan Osborne arriving in NSW prior to 1849. She sailed from England on 20 October 1838 on the *Juliana* which was wrecked off the Cape of Good Hope on 19 January 1839. Although some of those passengers, including that Susan Osborne, arrived in Sydney on the *Morayshire* on 20 April 1839, the associated papers give her age as five on 29 September 1838, so she would have been 8 in 1841— too young to marry or deliver a son in March 1842.

I have never found any evidence of a Susan Osborn(e) or Susan Blundell in either England or Australia before 7 October 1849—she seemed to appear out of nowhere. So where did 'Susan Blundell/Osborne' come from was one of the questions that continued to puzzle me from 1980 onwards.

Serendipity

In a fortuitous and extraordinary coincidence, I had been exchanging letters with Patricia Evans about Susan Blundell (Joseph's second child), her husband John Robertson and their family (to be covered in the second Blundell book).

Patricia—who was reviewing her Warby/Blanch line—was simultaneously aware that neither of us could find out anything about where Susan Osborne had come from—or in her case—what had happened to Mercy Balcomb who was married to Robert Blanch. She sent me the copy of the Notice (see reproduction on the next page).

NOTICE.

WHEREAS, my wife, Mercy Blanch, having absconded from my protection, with an infant, and leaving four helpless ones behind her, without any cause or provocation whatsoever, with an emancipated convict of the name of Joseph Blunden, against whom a warrant has been issued by the Bench at Newcastle for robbing me, I hereby offer a reward of five pounds for his apprehension and conviction; and I caution the public not to give my wife any credit, as I will not hold myself responsible for any debts she may contract from this date.

his
ROBERT ⋈ BLANCH.
his   mark.
Witness—John ⋈ Machonochy.
mark.

N B.—The man served his time with R. Jones, Esq.; has J. B. on his arm. is of a light complexion, about 5¾ feet in height, rather bald forehead, and left Ash Island with a horse heavily laden.

Newcastle, August 6.   1831

William Good, who was the source of the *Sydney Morning Herald* clipping, also wrote an excellent article about the matter.[3] These two sources and the help they have freely provided in our correspondence underpins what follows, aided and abetted by my research and analysis.

This led to other hitherto unknown information, explaining the series of events behind Joseph Blundell and 'Susan Osborne' with their infant son John coming to Canberra—William's discovery makes this Chapter possible.

Moreover, Peter Procter[4] has confirmed my belief that there are no records of a 'Joseph Blunden' in all the official convict records.

Any residual doubt about Mercy Blanch (*née* Balcomb) being Susan Osborne/Blundell can be immediately resolved by comparing the photo attached to various Blanch/Balcomb Ancestry entries with the big Susan Blundell photo in Blundell's Cottage on the shores of Lake Burley Griffin in Canberra shown at the start of this Chapter. The photos are all replicas of one another.

3   See the December 2013 *Descent*, the Journal of the Australian Genealogists.

4   Personal correspondence

'New Romley'—supposedly 'Susan's' birthplace—may have been a small play on New Romney where she was baptised under her real name (Mercy Balcomb) on 8 May 1814 or a transcription error. Mercy grew up with her parents until the birth of her first child in August 1831 and marriage in October 1831 to Robert Blanch, some five years after Joseph had been transported to Australia for the Term of His Natural Life.

New Romney—a small harbour and market town at the mouth of the Rother River in Kent, 35 miles south east of Maidstone—which had a population of 938 at that time, was one of the Confederation of the Cinque (five) Ports grouped together for defence purposes by King Edward the Confessor.[5]

King Edward the Confessor saw the key to security of the realm from a Norse invasion was to control the English Channel, so he granted the five port towns the right to keep all legal fees arising from Court cases in their jurisdictions, a profitable enterprise for them. In return, the towns agreed to provide ships and sailors when required to do so by the Crown.

As the last Anglo-Saxon King of England, (ruling from 1042 to 1061), Edward's death incongruously led to the transformation of Medieval England through the reign of William the Conqueror from Normandy in France and his troop of descendants of an earlier Norse invasion and settlement.

Edward was a first cousin once removed and friend of William the Conqueror. Childless, Edward promised the throne to William, but on his deathbed reneged and named Harold Godwinson as his heir. Incensed by this betrayal, William invaded England, defeating King Harold who died at the famous Battle of Hastings on 14 October 1066. William, crowned in Westminster Abbey on Christmas Day, commissioned the Domesday Book which recorded all of England's landholders and their holdings

---

5   King Edward the Confessor, son of King Ethelred the Unready; the 'Confessor' post-nominal was added when he was Canonised in 1066 to distinguish him from King Edward the Martyr (962-979).

in 1086. After he died in 1087, it was 400 years before another English-speaking King took the throne.[6]

On 12 October 1831 at All Saints Church Biddenden Kent (half way between Maidstone and New Romney) Mercy Balcomb (aged 17 and who had had their first child Alfred[7] on 29 August 1831 at Rolvenden), meaning that she was just 16 when her son Alfred was conceived, married Robert Blanch of Rolvenden aged 23, a Farm Labourer and Shepherd.

Robert and Mercy, both illiterate paupers, used a cross to indicate their approval of the marriage, the witnesses being William Milsted and William Button.[8] A pauper was a destitute person in receipt of relief under the poor laws at the time, Robert's Father and grandfather had also received assistance from the Parish.

Biddenden and Rolvenden are 6.8 miles apart, while Burwash is 15 miles north of Hastings.

Mercy Balcomb's Line

Richard I 1655 ?–28.3.1685 Godstone, married Margaret Kidder 1660 Lewes–1696 Godstone[9] at St Nicholas Godstone Surrey on 8 November 1681, producing:

- **Richard II 1678 Burwash–15.4.1720 Burwash;**
- Mary ?.8.1682 Godstone–? ;
- Elizabeth ?.12.1683–? ; and
- John ?.8.1684 Godstone–?.1.1702 Godstone.

---

6   From BBC/iwonder 'How did William the Bastard become William the Conqueror?' https://www.bbc.com/timelines/zp88wmn

7   William Good notes that although Alfred's tomb has his birthdate as 29 August 1831, he was baptised on 16 September 1832 at Tenterden, suggesting the year of his birth was 1832. An alternative explanation is that he was of the Baptist faith and it was not unusual therefore for the baptism to be a year or so after the birth as we have seen elsewhere throughout this book.

8   Geoff Bell's Ancestry contribution is the source of the witnesses.

9   Daughter of Bishop Richard Kidder 9.2.1633 East Grinstead–26.11.1703 Wells Somerset and Anne Osbourne! 1635–1703.

Richard II, married Hester Henrietta Russell (c1680–9.10.1752 Burwash) at Burwash on 29 January 1701, producing:

- Anna 1703 Burwash–1716 ?;
- Thomas 25.12.1705 Burwash–1768 ;
- Abraham 1708 Burwash–1731 ?; and
- **Richard III baptised 15.6.1712 Burwash–1750 ?**

Richard III married Elizabeth Carter c1710 Burwash–?. at Burwash on 27 April 1732, producing:

- Elizabeth 1732 Burwash–?;
- Lydia 2.3.1734 Burwash–?
- Abraham 1738 Burwash–1778 Burwash;
- Richard 1737 – 1817;
- John 14.11.1740 Burwash–1801 Ticehurst;
- Mary 1742 Burwash–? ;
- Sarah 1744 Burwash–? ;
- Esther 1746 Burwash–1748 Burwash; and
- **Thomas baptised 9 April 1749 Burwash–13 April 1780 Burwash.**

Thomas, married Susanna Collins 1.11.1750 Heathfield Sussex–1823 Brightling Sussex at Brightling on 8.6.1772, producing:

- Thomas 1772–? ;
- Elizabeth 1776–? ;
- Francis 1778–? ;
- Daniel 1778–1837 ? ; and
- Abraham 7.1.1781 Burwash, a Labourer–1832 ?.

After Thomas died (before his son Abraham was born, probably in 1780), his wife Susanna Collins remarried William Kemp (1742–1.10.1811 Warbleton Sussex) on 27 April 1783 at Burwash, moved to Brightling in Sussex and had another four children (William, Richard, Henry and Sarah).

Geoff Bell has postulated that Susanna Collins was a daughter of ? Collins and **Susan Osborne** and that this was the source of her Mercy/ Susan and Balcomb/Blanch/Blundell/Osborne names and the surname she used with her Father's real Christian name in associated documents where she says he was Abraham Osborne. No corroborative evidence has been found that such is the case, most sources attributing Susanna's parents as Richard Collins and Mary Saunders.

Abraham Balcomb(e) married Mercy Webb (c1787–9.1.1832 Ticehurst), at New Romney on 13 October 1809, producing:

- James? c 1809?–died young;
- Ann 30.4.1810 (baptised 9.9.1810) New Romney–1847 ?;
- married John Thomas Pilgrim on 7.1.1829 at Dover;
- Sarah14.6.1812 (baptised 2.8.1812) New Romney–buried 4.4.1816 New Romney;
- **Mercy born 22 March 1814 (baptised 8 May 1814) New Romney[10]–8 April 1892 Canberra;**
- Mary Ann 2.10.1815 (baptised 26.11.1815) New Romney–;
- married James Blanch at Rolvenden on 12.8.1832;
- Sophia Sarah 5.5.1817 (baptised 22.6.1817) New Romney–10.5.1900 New York;
- Harriett 12.9.1818 (baptised 18.10.1818) New Romney–26.2.1832 Ticehurst;
- Hannah 25.3.1821 (baptised 5.4.1821) New Romney–? New York/USA;
- Abraham 3.2.1823 (baptised 9.2.1823) New Romney–1901 New York/USA;
- George 10.5.1825 (baptised 19.6.1825) New Romney–19.9.1825 New Romney; and
- Eliza 18.9.1826 (baptised 27.9.1826) New Romney–6.5.1827 New Romney.

It will be noted that four of the children above died while they were young *viz* James, Sarah, George and Eliza.

It's not known who Mercy Webb's parents were, but the Webb family were in New Romney from the middle of the 18th Century.

---

10   Biddenden Parish Registers, Kent Archives page P26.

Abraham Balcomb was a Labourer at New Romney and after the Napoleonic Wars[11] ended, the area was relatively prosperous.[12] Conditions elsewhere in Kent, particularly in the industrial areas were deteriorating and the Great Agricultural Depression started in 1822-1823.# New Romney experienced a decade of hard times from 1822 to 1832.#

By 1830, the plight of the Balcomb family had become desperate. Abraham had decamped, probably to London to avoid Debtor's Prison; his destitute wife and four underage children becoming the Parish's responsibility.#

Under the Poor Laws of the time, a woman adopted her husband's home Parish as her own when she married. Abraham Balcomb was baptised at Burwash, so—when his family needed relief—they were returned to the Workhouse that served his home Parish. Thus, on 24 April 1830, Mercy and her four youngest children (Sophia aged 12, Harriett 11, Hannah 9 and Abraham 7) were removed from New Romney to the Ticehurst Union Workhouse in Sussex, which covered eight Parishes.#

This was the 15th Century Lamberhurst Workhouse which accommodated 24 inmates up until 11 September 1835 when a new workhouse was erected for 300. A derivative of the Anglo-Saxon word for lamb, Lamberhurst is a small village near Royal Tunbridge Wells.

Mercy Balcomb senior's health deteriorated and she probably died there, being buried at Ticehurst on 9 January 1832 aged 45—one of her daughters (Harriett), who died the following month was buried on 26 February 1832, aged 14.

Being committed to a workhouse, meant back-breaking work, harsh treatment and the associated stigma felt by those who were obliged to live in them. These actions were purposely designed by the Government to act as a deterrent.[13]

---

11   After the French Revolution ended in 1799, Napoleon Bonaparte came to power and initiated a series of wars from 1803-1815 against various European powers, usually financed and led by Great Britain.

12   Sourced from William Good, plus the # items.

13   Helen Allinson, *Life in the Workhouse* and *Farewell to Kent*, Synjon Books UK. Helen is Dorothea Teague's daughter. (^ in the following paragraphs are based on those references.)

Passage of the Poor Law Amendment Act of 1834 required Parishes to group together to build joint workhouses for their destitute. Prior to this, each Parish had been responsible for its own poor; some were housed in small workhouses established in the 18th Century, while most were given out-relief.^

The 1834 Act aimed to stop all out-relief to the able-bodied on the principle that if they were fit they should be able to fend for themselves and if they could not they must enter a workhouse. The Gentry and Farmers saw these unfortunate people as the undeserving poor. ^

Workhouses provided a harsh, disciplined, grinding and back-breaking repeated routine in an endeavour to dissuade people from entering them in preference to struggling with poverty at home. The women cleaned the workhouse, did all the cooking, sewing and washing as well as making the inmates uniforms—the parallel with being in prison was not accidental.^

Children were given cursory education in such institutions.

The diet was plain and monotonous, mostly an allowance of six ounces of bread with one ounce of cheese for breakfast and supper and the same for the main meal four days of the week. ^

Poverty in the early 19th Century resulted from large scale unemployment and wages so low that Farm Workers could not support their families. Farm Workers became engaged by the job or day instead of by the year as had been previous practice. There was no sickness benefit or old age pension. ^

Soon after Abraham's third daughter Mary Ann married Robert Blanch's younger brother James on 12 August 1832 at St Mary the Virgin, Rolvenden, Abraham Balcomb (under the assumed name of 'Collins', Abraham's Mother's maiden name) migrated to New York on the *Sovereign* with other family members (*ie* his eldest daughter Ann [with her husband John Thomas Pilgrim and their daughter Sophia], Sophia Sarah, Hannah and Abraham) arriving in New York on 24 September 1832. #

This means that after the death of their Mother Mercy and sister Harriett—Sophia, Hannah and Abraham junior must have been reunited with their Father. Abraham's occupation was listed as 'Farmer' and John Pilgrim's as 'Fisherman' on the *Sovereign's* passenger list.

Some Parishes paid the passage money, but records prior to 1838 are difficult to come by, so how the Balcombs ('Collins') and Pilgrims sponsored their journey is unknown, although Abraham's brother John was already in the USA—most probably at Delaware.

Nothing much is known about what happened to Hannah and Abraham senior, the latter supposedly having died in New York. #

The Pilgrims settled in Steuben County New York. The 1840 Census shows Ann with five children. She died around 1847. By 1850, John Pilgrim was living at Barrington in Yates County New York married again to Jane ? who was only 24 years old. #

In 1850, Abraham junior was living at Cameron Steuben County New York and his sister Sophia Sarah Hargrave was living at Senia in Ontario County New York. In 1860, they were both living at Cameron.# All of the places in the last two paragraphs still have very small populations.

The remaining daughters Mercy Balcomb Blanch and Mary Balcomb Blanch and their families migrated to Australia in 1838—further details are provided later in this Chapter.

Robert Blanch's Line

George 1600—30.6.1690 Somerset Kent, married Catherine Atkins 1595 Hawkhurst Cranbrook—1680 Somerset, at St Mary's Redman Canterbury on 16 July 1622, producing:

- **Edward 8.2.1628 Rye Sussex—23.5.1692 Salehurst Cranley Hambledon Sussex.**

Edward married Elizabeth ? 1640 Smarden Ashford Kent—26.9.1689 Salehurst, at St Michael the Archangel Smarden on ? , producing:

- unnamed daughter stillborn 19.1.1659 Rye;
- Elizabeth 29.12.1664 Rye—24.3.1665 Rye;
- Katherine stillborn 15.5.1666 Smarden;

- George 1668 Smarden -1675 Salehurst;
- **John 30.10.1670 Salehurst—17.9.1737 Salehurst;**
- Edward ?.4.1674 Salehurst—?; and
- Thomas ?.2.1675 Salehurst—7.3.1675 Salehurst.

John married Mary Ballard 17.4.1640 Salehurst—8.10.1729 Salehurst, at St Mary the Virgin Salehurst on 6 June 1693, producing:

- Martha 9.4.1694 Smarden—?;
- **Edward 13.1.1695 Smarden—6.7.1773 Salehurst Sussex;**
- Elizabeth ?.5.1698 Salehurst—?;
- Mary 15.3.1706 Salehurst—?; and
- John?.5.1713 Cranleigh—?.

Edward married Hannah/Honour Heather 1707 Smarden—10.2.1784 Salehurst, at St Mary the Virgin Dallington Battle Sussex on 23 November 1731, producing:

- John 21.1.1731—?;
- Mary I ?.11.1733 Rye—?;
- Edward 23.2.1734 Rye—6.7.1773 Sussex;
- Mary II 1740 Smarden—?;
- Martha 1740 Smarden—?;
- Elizabeth 30.8.1741 Rye—1.10.1741 Sussex;
- Mary III 17.9.1742 Salehurst—?;
- George ?.3.1745 Smarden—1805 ?; and
- **Robert 1.2.1753 Hollington—1831 ?.**

Robert married Elizabeth Brann 1 or 8.10.1755 Sandhurst Kent—6.5.1795 Rolvenden (daughter of Benjamin Brann {1714- 15.4.1791 Sandhurst} and Ann Fitlow {1729-1795}), at Rolvenden on 27 December 1776 and produced:

- Martha 29.6.1777 Sandhurst—1839 ?;
- Elizabeth 14.3.1779 Sandhurst—1831 ?;
- Mary 24.9.1780 Rolvenden—?;
- Robert 1783–1860 ?;

- Ann 19.6.1785 Rolvenden—1830 ?;
- **Edward 27.5.1787 Rolvenden—7.1.1860 Williams River NSW;**
- Sarah 30.3.1789 Rolvenden—1851 ?;
- Philadelphia 9.1.1791 Rolvenden—1839 ?;
- John 18.3.1792 Rolvenden—7.2.1793 Rolvenden; and
- Mary Ann?—1795 ?.

Presumably, Robert's wife Elizabeth having died on 6 May 1791, Robert remarried (to whom?), leading to the two last children above.

Edward married Maria Ashdown 25.1.1879 Westfield Sussex—31.5.1837 Rolvenden (dau of Thomas Ashdown {1741-1841} and Mary Catt {1753 1791} at Ewhurst Sussex on 1 October 1807, producing:

- **Robert 19.4.1808 Rolvenden[14]—17.10.1885 Woodford Island Maclean NSW;**
- Thomas 4.12.1809 Rolvenden—3.7.1892 Buladelah;
- James 4.8.1811 Rolvenden—10.11.1895 Plattsburg;
- Edward 12.4.1814 Rolvenden—2.3.1881 Duckholes, Newcastle;
- George 31.12.1815 Rolvenden—14.9.1893 Ulmarra, Clarence River;
- John 17.1.1817 Rolvenden—5.1.1903 Raymond Terrace;
- Isaac 3.1.1819 Rolvenden—19.7.1899 Ulmarra, Clarence River;
- Stephen 20.1.1820 Rolvenden—23.9.1867 Woodford Island, Clarence River;
- Elizabeth 20.1.1823 Rolvenden—30.7.1910 Ulmarra, Clarence River;
- Philadelphia 30.5.1824 Rolvenden—29.3.1872 Newcastle;
- David 19.12.1825 Rolvenden—7.3.1826 Rolvenden;
- Samuel 10.9.1827 Rolvenden—27.5.1919 McLean;
- Mary[15] 28.10.1828 Rolvenden—23.10.1915 Manila, Dagett County, Utah, USA; and
- Ann 25.9.1831 Rolvenden—7.12.1896 Newcastle.

---

14   Biddenden Parish Registers, Kent Archives.
15   Mary married James Warby {15.11.1822 Hythe Kent–14.12.1906 Manila USA} in 1848 at Clarence Town Raymond Terrace and they had nine children.

Edward was in receipt of money from the Parish as had his Father (Robert) and grandfather (Edward) before him, just like the Balcombs.

Edward and Maria, together with their sons Isaac and his wife Sarah, and George with a wife and child, were named as assisted emigrants to Australia from Rolvenden—their home Parish in 1838.

Edward's wife Maria had died in May 1837 in Rolvenden, but Edward (a Labourer and Baptist) went to Australia on the *Maitland*, which sailed in June 1838 and was chartered for a single journey by the Admiralty to take Bounty Migrants to Australia, the Parish paying £5 for each family. Most of the emigrant families came from southern England in Kent and East Sussex.

The Charter organisers crammed 223 adults, 127 children and some livestock for fresh food on to the ship which departed on 24 June 1838 from Gravesend on the south bank of The Thames, just west of the River's mouth, and arriving in Sydney Cove on 6 November 1838. The Ship's Manifest records Edward was accompanied by Elizabeth (in the wife column) and children, suggesting Edward had married again very soon after his wife Maria's death in May 1837.

Edward Senior was accompanied by his eldest daughter Elizabeth and her siblings Philadelphia, Samuel, Mary and Ann.

Edward Junior (single), George (married) both Agricultural Labourers and brothers John (married, Farm Labourer) and Stephen (single, Labourer) were assisted migrants who arrived in Port Jackson on the *Cornwall* on 1 September 1839.

William Blundell (single, Sheep Shearer) and Thomas Blundell (Gardener) with a wife and one daughter from Bodiam in East Sussex, a small village in the valley of the River Rother near Sandhurst, were also on board.

Beset by crowded and unhygienic conditions on the *Maitland*—exacerbated by the effect of Typhus and Scarlet Fever—35 passengers (including 29 children) were fed to the sharks before they sighted Sydney Heads and another five died when they were quarantined at North Head provoking a Committee of Inquiry which handed down a damning indictment of a system under which 'herds of immigrants were transported to the Colony like cattle.' Shades of the Second Fleet experience.

Clearly, the family re-united with the older children who were already here as Edward Senior died at Caswell's Farm on the Williams River on 7 January 1860. Moreover, we can see from the table on page 200 that the entire family ended up in Australia except for David who died in Rolvenden at the tender age of three months.

Isaac and Sarah and George with a wife and child are named as assisted emigrants from their home Parish.

Robert was christened at what seems to have been the family's place of worship *etc*—the Church of Saint Mary the Virgin Rolvenden on 10 July 1809, almost a year after he was born—his Father Edward, who was a declared Baptist—being baptised two years after he was born.

We can only speculate that Mercy and Robert (and other family members) must have struggled to make ends meet between their marriage in October 1831 and departure from England in March 1838.

NSW Beckons

In any event, four of the Blanch brothers—Robert, Thomas, James and Isaac—together with their wives and children left Gravesend on 25 March 1838 on the *Westminster* which arrived in Sydney on 27 June 1838. The ship's manifest shows that all received assisted passage, but not from whom.

Robert and Mercy, with three children at that stage—Alfred 5 and Robert 2, lost their youngest son George (born July 1837 Rolvenden) eight months old on the voyage. George, who suffered from continuous sea sickness since setting sail from England, succumbed to Marasmus (severe malnutrition and dehydration) on 24 June, three days out of Sydney and was buried at sea.

The *Westminster* log says that Robert and his brothers—all of whom were said to read and write!—were engaged by James Brindley Bettington Esq of Sydney. We know that at least Robert and Isaac were illiterate from their marriage certificates.

Robert and Isaac were to be paid an annual salary of £25 as Farm Labourers while Thomas and James who were also Wheelwrights received £28—all were also to receive rations. Thomas was recorded as a Calvinist,[16] accompanied by a wife aged 28, three boys and two girls, the other brothers being of unstated parts of the Protestant faith. James' wife was 26 and they were accompanied by three girls, while Isaac's wife was 20 and they had one girl with them.

Although James Brindley Bettington's address was Sydney, he and his brother John Henshall Bettington had taken up the Brindley Park land at Gummun Plains Merriwa in 1824. In the 1830s, James Brindley and John Henshall Bettington were joined by their brothers William and Joseph Horton Bettington in acquiring the additional pastoral estates of Piercefield and Martindale in the Hunter Valley near Muswellbrook.

Thomas, James and Isaac Blanch and their families moved to Raymond Terrace Newcastle, followed by Robert after 1841 as he is the only one of the brothers who does not appear in the 1841 Hunter Valley Directory. Thomas was admitted to Newcastle gaol on 27 August 1842 as a debtor.

Mercy's sister Mary Ann who married James Blanch on 12 August 1832 at Rolvenden, died at Plattsburg (now Wallsend, a western suburb of Newcastle) in 1904, aged 89, having had 17 children, seven of whom survived her.

The clue to where Robert and Mercy went between 1838 and 1841 is the birth of their children, Maria and Abraham. While there is no record of the children's baptisms, their places of birth can be found from later documents, Maria being born at Piercefield NSW in 1839 and Abraham at the Williams River, north of Raymond Terrace in the District of Cassilis NSW in 1841.

Piercefield Station, a big property about 10Km west of Muswellbrook, west of the Great Dividing Range, on the Denman Road, belonged to the Bettington family.

---

16   A major branch of Protestantism which followed John Calvin's theological practices.

Following dissolution of the partnership in 1835, John Henshall Bettington retained Martindale, Joseph Horton Bettington held Piercefield and James Brindley Bettington retained Brindley Park, Merriwa.

As Robert Blanch was working for Joseph Horton Bettington by 1839, he must have been at Piercefield and was probably still there when the 2 March 1841 Census recorded Joseph Horton Bettington at Piercefield.

Among the residents on his property were five married couples, two boys aged under 14, two boys and one girl aged under seven, and one girl aged under two.

The infant girl was the only person on the Estate who had been born in the Colony. Robert and Mercy's children who were certainly alive when the Census was taken were Alfred and Robert, aged about eight and five, and Maria aged between one and two. The ages of the children at Piercefield recorded in the Census fit their ages and Maria seems likely to be the infant girl born in the Colony.

Cassilis District, where Abraham Blanch was born, is centred on the town of Cassilis, about 115Km west of Piercefield, but only 40Km west of James Brindley Bettington's Merriwa property Brindley Park. Cassilis and Merriwa were adjoining Districts so at the time of Abraham's birth in 1841, Robert Blanch may well have been working at Brindley Park.

Robert Blanch's wife Mercy's decampment is canvassed below.

The only further reference to her in the Blanch family occurs on death and marriage certificates. To all intents and purposes, Mercy Blanch was expunged from the pages of history after she absconded from Robert Blanch's 'protection', not long before 6 August 1842.

To return to the *Sydney Morning Herald* advertisement, Joseph Blunden (*sic*), the man with whom Mercy Blanch scarpered 'served his time with Richard Jones Esq' and was an Emancipated Convict—identifying him as our Joseph Blundell.

The NSW 1828 Census records Joseph Blundell as arriving per the *Marquis of Huntley* (which docked at Sydney Cove on 13 September 1826) aged 28 living at Cabramatta and assigned to Richard Jones. The 1837 Convict Muster has him as 39, holding a Ticket of Leave, living at Cassilis, probably still in the employ of Jones as he was listed after two other convicts also assigned to Jones.

In 1829 Jones applied for and was granted an additional 10000 acres on the Hunter River which came to be known as Collaroi, a property on the Krui River, about 10Km south-east of Cassilis. He also bought the 2030 acres Crown Grant to John Brown on 8 March 1822 which came to be known as Bolwarra, the circumstances of that sale and Brown's unfortunate fate, having been covered in Chapter Six. Bounded by McDougall's land to the south between Maitland and East Maitland and Goulburn Grove near Lorn to the north, the property extended to the Hunter River on its East and West boundaries.

We also saw in Chapter Six that the *Marquis of Huntley* indent described Joseph as 5 foot 6 and a half inches tall, ruddy complexion, light brown hair, blue eyes.

This description matches 'Joseph Blunden's portrayal in the *Sydney Morning Herald* Notice—light complexion, about 5 feet and three-quarter inches in height.' By 1842, his light brown hair had receded to baldness on his forehead and 'J B' had been tattooed on his arm.

Robert Blanch was working on Ash Island at the time in the Hunter River estuary near Newcastle—linked to Hexham[17] by a wooden bridge.

Joseph Blundell was also working there for Richard Jones, thus the reference in the *Sydney Morning Herald* about Blundell leaving 'Ash Island[18] just before 6 August (1842) with a horse heavily laden' and Mercy Blanch. Was it destiny or happenstance that brought them together?

Joseph received his Certificate of Freedom on 9 December 1834 for the Cassilis District. His Conditional Pardon was recommended on 1 July

---

17   12 Kilometres west of the Pacific Highway.

18   Ash Island was one of a group of Hunter River estuarine islands which about 1952 became part of an Industrial Estate called Kooragang Island.

1841, approved on 13 April 1842 and granted on 14 September 1842. He died at Canberra on 13 February 1874—his Death Certificate has his wife as Susan.

After fleeing from her husband Robert Blanch 'without any cause or provocation whatsoever', Mercy adopted the 'Susan Osborne' alias to avoid detection and popped up in Canberra with Joseph and the infant John.

Parsing the 9 August 1842 *Sydney Morning Herald* Notice included earlier as William Good does in more detail in his marvellous Descent article corroborates the story.

'... leaving four helpless ones behind her ... '

Following Mercy's departure, Robert Blanch lived in Newcastle's Raymond Terrace area with his 'four helpless ones', *viz*:

- Alfred Blanch, born on 29 August 1831 at Rolvenden, [NB: before his parents' marriage—a not unusual occurrence at the time and likely explanation for their marriage.] Alfred, who was baptised on 16 September 1832 at Tenterden, married Margaret Lamont on 4 October 1863 at Ulmarra (north of Grafton) and died on 11 December 1898 at Greenridge near Casino leaving 12 children;

- Robert Blanch, born in Rolvenden about 1835, who was accidentally killed at the Williams River (a perennial stream of the Hunter River now known as the Paterson River) on 20 May 1844;

- Maria Blanch, born at Piercefield in March 1839 married Jacob Pearson Newton on 2 March 1861 at St John's Church of England Springfield near Gosford and died at Bulahdelah while living with her daughter Jane on 9 November 1928 aged 87 having had eight children, one of whom predeceased her; and

- Abraham Blanch born at Cassilis in 1841 married Ann Elizabeth Andrews *née* Robertson on 21 August 1862 at Scot's Church Grafton and died at Yakaloo Woodford Island Maclean on 10 June 1920 aged 79 having sired eight children, one of whom died as a child.

Some six years after Mercy absconded, Robert Blanch was said to have married Ann Callaghan (a native of Cork in Ireland and daughter of Timothy Callaghan, a Butcher, and his wife Catherine O'Keefe) at Morpeth in 1848, but no record of this marriage has ever been found. He had another two children with Ann—Robert Charles was born at Raymond Terrace in 1850. Mary Ann was born on 16 May 1852 at Nelson's Plains, baptised there on 1 August and she probably died and was buried there soon after.

Around this time, Robert (accompanied by his children Alfred, Maria and Abraham—Robert Junior having died) was farming at Nelson's Plains on the western side of the Williams River, possibly for Jacob Newton. In the 1850s, Robert moved to Myall Lakes where Newton also had a property.

Newton became Robert's son-in-law when he married Maria on 2 March 1861 at Stroud (a small country town about an hour north of Newcastle). Jacob Newton died on 1 June 1881 at Boolambayte Creek near Bulahdelah, west of Myall Lakes. Robert worked there until the late 1870's where he raised his second family and saw Robert Charles marry Elizabeth Malone in 1877.

Ann Callaghan-Blanch died from dropsy (an old term for swelling of the soft interstitial tissues due to accumulation of excess water, today described as edema due to congestive heart failure) at Villa on the Myall River on 22 June 1870 and was buried on 24 June 1870 in Neranie Head Cemetery (aka the old Bungwahl Cemetery at Bungwahl, Myall Lakes).

After Robert Charles' marriage, Robert Senior moved to the Clarence River where his sons Alfred and Abraham had been farming for some years. By 1881, he had established himself as a Farmer at Woodford Island (some 37 square Km) where the Clarence River splits into the south and north arms at the small village of Bushgrove and which re-forms at the town of Maclean near where Abraham's property was.

Robert Senior died at Abraham's residence—Woodford Leigh, a part of Woodford Island—on 17 October 1885 and was buried the next day in the Presbyterian section of the Maclean Cemetery. His Death Certificate records Mercy Balcomb as his only wife and ignores his second wife Ann and son Robert Charles who was still farming on the Myall River. Robert's brother Samuel Blanch, who was the informant, clearly did not regard his brother's union with Ann Callaghan as legitimate.

The Myall Lakes and Myall River near Newcastle shouldn't be confused with Myall Creek which is up near Inverell and the scene of the infamous 1838 murder of 28 Aboriginal men, women and children who were camped on the Creek by a group of 11 assigned convicts and ex-convicts led and spurred on by John Henry Fleming, a free settler.

Mercy Blanch Absconds

The youngest children of Robert and Mercy Blanch were Maria aged three born in March 1839 and Abraham aged one born in 1841. Both children stayed with their Father as two of the 'four helpless ones' Mercy left behind when she absconded in July 1842 with an infant, the others being Alfred ten and Robert seven. With a birth in 1841, it is unlikely that Mercy's next child could have been born before the beginning of 1842 and so the infant Mercy took with her must have been a babe in arms (John).

As with his Mother, different versions of John Blundell's birth date and place were concocted to conceal the truth.

According to John's Marriage Certificate and the Birth Certificate of his eldest daughter Mary Ann, John was born at Liverpool, a western suburb of Sydney. In both cases, John was the informant. On the Birth Certificates of his two eldest sons Alexander and John, his place of birth was given as Parramatta. In these cases, John's wife Sarah Ann (*née* MacKenzie) was the informant.

Dorothy Blundell (*née* Middleton) says her Uncle John was born under a bullock waggon on 29 March 1843 at Liverpool Sydney. Joseph was supposedly in the process of driving his dray to Canberra (a trip which took three weary weeks in those days) for a Ship's Officer who intended to settle in Canberra.

The balance of the evidence is that John was born at Liverpool Plains—another eerie coincidence or deliberate falsehood where the outer Sydney suburb of Liverpool conveniently appears in different versions of the story.

As mentioned earlier, Liverpool Plains was the name of a pastoral district in the North East part of the Colony, the chief towns being Murrurrundi, Wee-Waa, Narrabri, Nundle, Tamworth, Breeza, Gulligal, Walgett and Bendemeer.

John Blundell's Obituary in *The Queanbeyan Age* says that John was born at Liverpool Plains in 1838 (rather than 1843) and that he went with his parents to Canberra at the age of eight months.

In 1927, John said that:

> 'When he was eight months old his Father and Mother brought him from Liverpool Plains to Springbank Canberra.'

John's Death Certificate also records him as being born at Liverpool Plains. If these claims were true, he would have been born before Joseph and Mercy absconded—if that was so, who was the Mother and what happened to her? Second, Joseph and Susan waited until 1849 to baptise their first five children.

The Anglican Church of St John the Baptist in Canberra was consecrated in 1845, so it would be expected that the first two children, John and Susan, would have been baptised then and the other children baptised as they were born.

Why then did Joseph and Susan wait so long to baptise their children when they were living so close by?

St John's Baptismal Register records Joseph and Susan Blundell's first child, John Blundell as born on 29 March 1843. That would mean John was most likely conceived around the end of June 1842, suggesting the relationship between Joseph Blundell and 'Susan Osborne was underway just before Joseph Blunden (*sic*) absconded with Mercy Blanch in July 1842.

All of these peculiarities are readily explained if John was actually born in March 1842—not March 1843—and was the infant that Mercy ('Susan') and Joe took with them from Ash Island, probably around June-July 1842.

That resolves the uncertainty over John's place and date of birth consistent with his Mother's adoption of the Susan Osborne alias to escape detection by her husband Robert or those looking to collect the £5 reward for

'Joseph Blunden's' apprehension and conviction.

Their 'disappearance' would have been assisted by the associated move to the far southern reaches of the NSW Colony, circumstantial evidence indicating that they arrived in Canberra in October-November 1842.

The inescapable conclusion is that the infant Mercy and Joe took with them from Ash Island was John Blundell. Delaying John's baptism until 1849 with his four siblings made it easy to 'adjust' John's age from seven to six. On the Birth Certificates of John Junior in 1864 and Mary Ann in 1866, John's age is recorded as 22 and 24, consistent with a birth in 1842.

By 1927, Canberra had become Australia's National Capital and John Blundell had become a relic of the earliest days of the area. Any possible need to conceal his place of birth had long since passed. Therefore, John's own reminiscences provide collateral evidence that he was the infant that Mercy and Joe took with them from Ash Island in 1842.

It does, of course, raise the obvious question: was John Blundell's Father Robert Blanch or Joseph Blundell? That binary proposition has also been resolved courtesy of William Good[19] who has found DNA matches between his sample and Blundell descendants.

As Joseph was the Father, then Mercy must have formed a relationship with him at the latest around the middle of 1841.

The mystery of Mercy Blanch and Susan Blundell is also solved—they were one and the same woman: Mercy (daughter of Abraham Balcomb and Mercy Webb) born at New Romney in Kent in 1814 was a strong woman, leaving poverty in England with her husband Robert Blanch with whom she bore five children, then fleeing him for John Blundell by whom she had another 11 children before dying in Canberra at the then ripe old age of 78.

19   Personal correspondence.

From the 1920s onwards, economic growth was based increasingly upon the production of wool and other rural commodities for markets in Britain and Europe. This growth was interrupted by two major Depressions—during the ten years of the 1840s and from 1890 to 1894. There is little doubt that the Blanch family would have suffered hardship and deprivations during these times, although whether this was a factor in Mercy's subsequent flight cannot be known with certainty.

While Joseph was in the Cassilis District, he continued to work for Richard Jones who had property there. Joseph left the area not long after the decade long Depression started in 1840—it will be recalled from the previous Chapter that Jones went bankrupt in November 1843.

The Great Eastern Australian drought which started in 1838 and lasted until 1844, coupled with a disastrous downturn in the price of Australian wool on the London market, culminated in the worst economic Depression in the NSW Colony's nascent history.

The price of sheep dropped to as low as one shilling per head and many squattage[20] runs were relinquished. The Depression caused much hardship for many of the Colony's population, widespread unemployment and financial ruin to businesses, as well as the unfortunate investors in the pastoral industry.

The relationship with 'Susan Osborne' and the forthcoming birth of their first child in March 1842, together with the onset of hard times, may have triggered the desire to have a new start as free citizens in an area where Joseph and 'Susan' and their backgrounds were unknown.

They took over three months to get to 'Canberra' from Ash Island which they must have left around July 1842 with the 'horse heavily laden.'

It wasn't until 12 March 1903 that Lady Denman, wife of the Governor General, bestowed Canberra with its official name in a ceremony on Kurrajong Hill. Now Capital Hill, where the Federal Parliament is situated, Canberra was chosen as the future National Capital site in 1908.

---

20   'Squattage' runs were Crown land typically occupied by free settlers or ex-convicts under a Government lease or licence to graze livestock. Wikipedia.

One piece of evidence might explain how Joseph knew about this area. His first employer—Dr Robert Townson—established a head station at Tirrana, on the Yarr (Yass) River and sent his men to occupy outstations at Breadalbane Plains, Gunderue (Gundaroo) Murran-Bateman (Murrumbateman) and Wallagorong in 1822, well before Blundell's arrival on the *Marquis of Huntley* and his assignment to Townson as a servant on 19 September 1826.

In a letter to the Colonial Secretary that same month on the 26th instant (AO NSW Reel 2/7991), Townson complained about the 'overbearing insulting conduct of parvenus—up-start lads (who) want to take away my sheep stations' and being subject to 'vexation, loss of time, cattle *etc* in forming distant stations across swampy ravines, Rivers, in fear of Bush Rangers and Blacks, and even of our own Convict Servants.' Townson continued to fight off attempts to dispossess him of these assets until his death in June 1827.[21]

Blundell's association with Townson and Jones and their assigned men may have led to his (Blundell's) knowledge about the area where he absconded to on the outer limits of settlement at the time.

Robert Blanch being illiterate would not have known that his advertisement called Joseph—'Blunden.' The associated Newcastle Bench Warrant for robbery, together with Blanch's promise of a £5 reward, is all well and good, but satisfying that depended on someone identifying Joseph Blundell as 'Blunden' and apprehending him.

Joseph's Conditional Pardon was granted on 14 September 1842 and advertised as approved in 'The Australian' on 24 October 1842, by which time he, Susan and baby John would have already been at/or approaching the Limestone Plains settlement. This meant that Joseph no longer had to report to police every six months or seek permission for a change of residential address.

---

21   These extracts are sourced from *Gundaroo* by Errol Lea-Scarlett. An interesting piece of associated trivia is that Townson's station now forms part of 'Bowylie' (on the outskirts of Gundaroo) owned by Dick Smith, the famous aviator and entrepreneur, who is a mate of mine.

That set of circumstances provided a clear set of incentives for Joseph and Mercy to flee when they did.

The other unsolvable mystery is why Mercy Blanch absconded? Did she flee an unhappy marriage or follow her heart with the man she loved? Only Joe and 'Susan' knew the answer to that and—remarkably—they took the secrets above to their grave without sharing them with anyone.

Susan died on 8 April 1892 in Canberra at the age of 78 from haematemesis and was buried in the St John's Churchyard in the family plot at Section C Row 1 No: 32. The concrete surrounding the plot includes 'Susan Blundell' to denote where she is buried. It's also worth noting that the NSW Birth, Death and Marriage Records cite Susan as Brundell.

The other Blundell aspect is what must now be an extraordinary number of Blanch descendants and relatives.

Mercy's sister Mary (died 23 December 1904 Plattsburg) married James Blanch (died 10 November 1895 Plattsburg) on 12 August 1832–17 children.

Thomas Blanch (died 3 July 1892 Buladelah) married Hannah Austin (1809—8.7.1879 Newcastle) on 24 April 1830 Rolvenden—18 children.

Isaac Blanch (died 19 July 1899 Ulmarra, Clarence River) married Sarah Longley (1816–14.6.1873 Newcastle) on 5 March 1838 Rolvenden—nine children.

Mary Blanch married James Warby at Morpeth on 10 March 1846—they migrated to Utah USA on the *Julia Ann* on 22 March 1854–17 children.

Mercy's four children left behind with Robert Blanch produced 28 offspring.

And to all of that must be added the children and further issue of the other eight Blanch family members who came to Australia in 1838—Edward Junior, George, John, Stephen, Elizabeth, Philadelphia, Samuel and Ann.

Eight
Early Limestone Plains Settlement

For some 25 years after Captain Arthur Phillip landed in Port Jackson, knowledge of the surrounding country was restricted to a radius of 30 miles, constituting about 1500 square miles, because of seemingly impassable natural barriers except to the south where Moss Vale was reached around 1798.

Around 1820, drought in the Sydney basin forced explorers to search for good country beyond the then known lands; the two outstanding figures in the discovery of what became the Federal Capital Territory being Charles Throsby and Joseph Wild[1]—typical examples of the virile pioneers.

Joshua John Moore[2]—wanting to establish an outstation of his Goulburn 'Baw Baw' property—sent overseer John McLaughlin with James Clarke and John Tennant[3] to establish a presence in the south

---

1   Australian Bureau of Statistics Year Book Australia 1931.

2   A retired Army Lieutenant who arrived in Sydney on the *Elizabeth* on 5 October 1816, he fought in the Napoleonic Wars, completing his service at the Battle of Waterloo in 1824. He was Clerk to his brother-in-law Sir John Wylde, the Judge Advocate in Sydney, before becoming the first Prothonotary of the Supreme Court. Moore died at his Baw Baw property near Goulburn on 27 July 1864. Pre-1830, land grants were mainly bestowed on ex-Government officials and opportunists and within a few years of Moore's selection nearly all of the Limestone Plains land and the neighbouring area had been allotted to private holders.

3   An assigned convict who became a notorious bushranger.

towards the end of 1824. With their cattle, they occupied the land between Black Mountain and the Molonglo River, building slab huts on the ridge where the National Museum now stands.

That original 2000 acres—temporarily granted by the Colonial Secretary on 21 October 1824—became the first Limestone Plains land grant—extended by 1000 acres on 30 April 1827 eastwards to adjoin Robert Campbell's grant.

More about Campbell who was Sydney's first merchant[4] and played a critical role in the Blundell family's fortunes will be covered in Book Two.

Although an absentee landlord who never visited the property, Moore variously used Canberry/Canbury and Kamberry/Kamberra to refer to its location,[5] probably because McLaughlin mentioned the name to him.

From 1845, the Anglican St John's Registers referred to Canbury until 1858 when it became Canberry. The first reference to Canberra was when the Reverend Pierce Galliard Smith baptised his daughter Mary in 1862.

Timothy Beard came to Sydney on the *Fortune* as a convict Lifer on 12 July 1806. Conditionally Pardoned on 15 December 1817, Beard drove a herd of cattle around 1820 from Liverpool to near the confluence of the Molonglo and Queanbeyan Rivers. About one and a quarter-miles downstream from the junction, he built bark huts, outbuildings and sheds on 'Quinbean', named after the native name for the place.[6]

Beard returned to his Liverpool Inn, leaving three convict stockmen in charge—William Carter, Sambel Hall and Simeon Mills—who were still

---

4   Hence the soubriquet 'Merchant Campbell'. 'Early Merchant families of Sydney' Janette Holcomb Anthem Press London 2014. He was the second son of the last Laird of Ashfield in Scotland.

5   Other European variations included Caanberra, Camberry, Chamberry Gnabra, Karnberra, Kaamburry, Kembery, Kemberry and Ngambra. There is an inherent difficulty in Europeanising Aboriginal names, but it is likely that Canberra is derived from the Aboriginal name for that landscape.

6   This was between the River and the old Abattoirs in Oaks Estate and is now an Industrial Area named after Beard. Karen Williams cites Queenbeeann and Queenbeearm spellings in *Oaks Estate—No Man's Land*.

working this illegal squattage of 200 acres with 10 horses and 230 horned cattle in 1828.

Robert Campbell[7] received a land grant and sheep to the value of £2000 as compensation for the loss of his ship *Sydney* in 1806 off the coast of New Guinea which was under charter to the Government.[8]

James Ainslie[9] was employed as overseer to take delivery of a consignment of 700 sheep from Government flocks at Bathurst on 29 October 1825 and guide them to the area that Campbell had pre-selected on Mount Pleasant's south-eastern slopes. A few years later Campbell was given an additional 1000 acres compensation and permission to purchase 5000 acres on the south bank of the Molonglo River—becoming the District's largest land proprietor.

Campbell[10] built his homestead on the Pialligo land before 1833, naming it 'Duntroon' as a reminder of his Scottish heritage. In 1835, Campbell dismissed Ainslie due to 'irregularities and insubordination caused by liquor', leaving the property in the hands of his third son Charles as Superintendent.

Campbell senior informed his nephew George Thomas Palmer[11] of fertile grazing land on the Gininderra Creek and by 1826 Palmer was squatting there. Following exchanges of correspondence with the Colonial Secretary, Palmer was officially granted the land.

George Palmer's Father John established Jerrabomberra—on the western side of Mount Jerrabomberra two miles from Queanbeyan.

---

7   Sydney's first free merchant, who came to the Colony in 1798 to break the NSW Corps' trading monopoly—he 'retired' to Duntroon in 1843, died there on 15 April 1846 and was buried at Parramatta. During his life he was regarded as the most trusted colonist and greatest philanthropist in the community. Footnote 4 *op cit.*

8   Footnote 4 *op cit.*

9   Most of what is written about Ainslie is a farrago of lies.

10   Campbell gave evidence in Britain against the NSW Corps during Colonel Johnston's trial for his forcible incarceration of Governor Bligh.

11   A retired Lieutenant who served in Egypt during the Battle of the Nile.

In September 1828, he moved 2000 sheep there and added 640 acres in 1832, including Quinbeane.'[12]

The 1828 Census recorded 21 white inhabitants in the area—including five convict shepherds, a Superintendent and a Stockman employed by John Palmer—with another 15 in the Gininderra Creek vicinity.

1828 also saw a town reserve marked out not far from Beard's Quinbean. A small community was developing there near good water and a ford across the Molonglo River at the end of what is now River Street in Oaks Estate.

Returning to the chronology:

- on 27 January 1830, the first European children were born in the area—Helen Jane and John Alexander[13]—to John Macpherson and his wife Helen (*née* Watson) who were the initial resident landholders on a 640-acre grant called Springbank on the slopes of Black Hill as a reward for his part in the capture of a bushranger. The property is now under Lake Burley Griffin except for Springbank Island;

- James Wright and his friend John Hamilton Mortimer Lanyon settled on 'Lanyon' as squatters towards the end of 1833, having arrived from England earlier in the year, then purchasing 2340 acres between them in 1835. Lanyon returned to England leaving Wright as the owner of the property which had first been occupied by Timothy Beard;

- the County of Murray 1833 Census Return showed 500 white people living in the area, 351 of whom were convicts, on 12 stations;

- Edward John Eyre who had a block of land in the Upper Molonglo kept a very detailed diary on Aboriginal names and practices;[14]

---

12   John Palmer, who was Robert Campbell's brother-in-law, arrived on the First Fleet as Purser of Governor Phillip's Flagship *Sirius* and became Commissary of the Colony. He was most unfairly treated by the British authorities on the back of the Rum Rebellion for having the temerity to do the right thing and stand up to Macarthur and his cronies.

13   Who became Premier of Victoria 1869-1870.

14   Courtesy of Peter Procter who may well be the authority on Aboriginal aspects of our Region.

- in 1836, while staying at Yarrolumla, Charles Sturt was rewarded with a 5000-acre land grant, selecting the area between the Murrumbidgee and Molonglo Rivers and Gininderra Creek which he named Belconnel and later sold to Robert Campbell's son Charles;

- in 1837, the need for law enforcement led to Captain Alured Tasker Faunce's appointment as Police Magistrate with Patrick Kinsella as his first Constable leading to social control in the District.[15] Dr William Foxton Hayley settled in Queanbeyan and a Post Office was established there;

- Terence Aubrey Murray[16] acquired 2500 acres as the nucleus of his Yarrolumla Estate where he erected his homestead[17] and took on the 14-year old Stewart Marjoribanks Mowle as his understudy in 1836. By 1838, Mowle was responsible for managing the Yarralumla property with 50 people. Mowle learnt the Aboriginal language and recorded significant happenings;[18]

- on 28 September 1838, Queanbeyan was proclaimed a village;

- about 1838, William Klensendorlffe[19] was living at his stone residence on Elizabeth Farm, west of where the Albert Hall is and now under the man-made Lake Burley Griffin. The basement was used to house his assigned convicts. In the 1841 Census,

---

15   Prior to this, amateur Magistrates Palmer at Gininderra and Murray at Yarrolumla dispensed summary justice according to their views about social class, religion, free men, those in servitude and places of origin.

16   Murray came out in 1827 with his Father who was a Captain in the 48th Regiment of the Foot. He became the first elected member of the District in 1843 and was subsequently knighted for his services to the Colony.

17   Merchant Campbell's grandson Frederick bought Yarralumla in 1882, which was in turn purchased by the Government in 1913 and refurbished in 1925-26 to become the Governor General's residence in concert with relocation of the seat of Government to Canberra in 1927.

18   Peter Procter *op cit*.

19   Klensendorlffe who came free to Australia on the *Ocean* in 1818 acquired significant land holdings in Camden, Picton, the southern Monaro, Bombala District and the Limestone Plains.

11 males and three females (nine free, five bond) were living in stone and wood houses there. John and Margaret Shumack and their two children Joseph (four) and Elizabeth (one) together with brothers Peter and Joseph and John and Mary Gillespie and their two children who all came out on the 'Lascar', arrived in Sydney on 11 November 1841. John was immediately employed by Klensendorlffe of Limestone Plains at £20 per year with rations and the cost of their removal from Sydney to Canberra;

- 1838 also saw the beginning of a severe drought which lasted until 1842, the creeks drying up, the Molonglo reduced to a few waterholes and the Murrumbidgee ceased to run for two years. The crops failed, and a financial crisis ensued in 1843. Sheep became unsaleable and shepherd's wages on Duntroon were reduced by £6 to £18 a year. Moore was forced to sell his 1742-acre Canberry Estate to Arthur Jeffreys RN;

- transportation to NSW stopped in May 1840, followed by cessation of the convict assignment system in July 1841, meaning that cheap convict labour *via* Government servitude was no longer available to the landed gentry;

- the 1841 Census recorded Yarralumla with 100 males and 8 females (56 free, 52 convicts) Duntroon 61 males and 24 females (63 free and 22 convicts), Palmersville[20] 47 males and 21 females (47 free and 21 convicts) and Lanyon with 49 males and 10 females (28 free and 31 convicts);

- the Foundation Stone having been laid in 1841, St John the Baptist Church was consecrated on 12 March 1845 and the school house opened later the same year—both being used by the workers on Duntroon which had developed like English villages did at the large estates upon which they depended. This era coincided with Scottish tenants being turfed out of their

---

20   Later renamed Gininderra.

traditional highland estates and sent to London, Canada, USA or Australia;

- in October-November 1842 Joseph and Susan Blundell with their first child John arrived on the scene, settling at what came to be named Cathedral Hill near present day Regatta Point;

- discovery of gold in 1851 led to financial recovery;

- the 1851 Census recorded 2562 people in the Queanbeyan Police District—(1511 men and 1051 women) becoming a Municipality in 1852 with 16 pubs and seven flour mills;

- rubble stone cottages were constructed for the workers on Duntroon Estate, including Blundell's Cottage which was built in 1857-58 for the head ploughman William Ginn and his wife and four children. They were succeeded by the newlyweds George[21] and Flora Blundell in May 1874 who lived in the Cottage for over 60 years;

- around this time, the fencing of properties began to replace the need for shepherds, bullock teams were succeeded by draught horses, spring carts by buggies and sulkies and tools by machines;

- on 1 January 1863, the Canberra Post Office opened near Blundell's Cottage with local school teacher Andrew Wotherspoon as the first Postmaster, supplementing those at Gininderra (1860) and Lanyon (1861). The District was conferred with the status of a Postal Town and called Canberra[22] ;

- James Abernethy became the Schoolmaster at St John's, teaching there from 1863-1880, including many Blundells;

- Joseph Blundell's oldest son John was at Campbell's 'Honeysuckle' holding opposite Quinbean on the northern side of the Molonglo in 1867. He was 23 years old—married with three children— probably living in the shepherd's hut and tending the sheep being

---

21   Joseph's second son and third child.

22   Courtesy of Allen Mawer.

pastured in that area,[23] at a wage of about £24 *per annum*, plus rations. [24] Duntroon employed some 50-60 shepherds at that time;

- William James Farrer (3.4.1845 Kendal England—16.4.1906 Lambrigg where he is buried) came to Canberra as a Tutor to George Campbell's children at Duntroon around 1870, becoming a Contract Surveyor with the Department of Lands in 1875. He married Henrietta Sarah Nina de Salis in 1882 (no issue) and settled at 'Lambrigg'[25] near Tharwa in 1886 where he carried out experiments to produce wheat varieties resistant to drought and rust, laying the foundation for the Australian wheat industry. Farrer is commemorated with a bronze bust in Farrer Place opposite the Queanbeyan Police Station in Monaro Street, with the epitaph:

  'I wanted to think that when the end comes then my life had not been wasted';

  and,

- in 1886, the railway service from Sydney to Queanbeyan commenced, causing a massive change in the economy which must have impacted significantly on the Blundell's carrier business.

John Gale's important contribution requires highlighting. Born in Cornwall on 17 April 1831, he completed an apprenticeship as a printer in Wales before becoming a Probationary Wesleyan Minister and arriving in Gunning on 24 May 1854, preaching around the wider District.

He became Editor and Proprietor of the *Golden Age, Queanbeyan and Monaro Districts Advertiser*—the first edition was published on 15 September 1860. At that time there were over 500 people in Queanbeyan, 3000 in the immediate vicinity and a further 4000 in the Monaro.

---

23 Courtesy of Karen Williams' 1997 book *Oak's Estate—No Man's Land*. John had married Sarah Ann McLaughlin (their parents had to give permission because they were both under 21 being 19 at the time) on 23 October 1862 at St John's: Alexander was born on 15.11.1862 (!), John on 11.7.1864 and Mary on 23.9.1866.

24 Australian Bureau of Statistics 1931 *Year Book of Australia*.

25 Near Cuppacumbalong where the Gudgenby and Murrumbidgee Rivers meet, adjacent to Tharwa, owned by the de Salis family and named after his Mother's birthplace in England.

After Dalgety was rescinded as the proposed site because the border would have touched Victoria, Gale's advocacy led to declaration of The Federal Capital Territory on 1 January 1911,[26] followed by laying of the Commemoration Stone and naming of Canberra as the National Capital on Capital Hill on 12 March 1913—now Canberra Day.

The Prince of Wales laid the Foundation Stone for the temporary Parliament House on 21 June 1920.

Up until 1911, most of the land which now constitutes the Australian Capital Territory was occupied by nine large sheep stations: Canberry, Duntroon, Gungahlin, Uriarra and Yarralumla in the north; Booroomba, Cuppacumbalong, Tidbinbilla and Tuggeranong in the south.

Gale and his wife[27] were taken by a Commonwealth car to the opening of the temporary Parliament House in Canberra by the Duke and Duchess of York on 9 May 1927. Reports of the opening studiously avoided the Duke's stammer which later featured in *The King's Speech* after his brother King Edward VIII[28] left Britain to be with the American divorcee Wallis Simpson.

Prior to the opening, the Government sponsored an extensive propaganda campaign in the newspapers which misfired—the Press being indifferent and hostile rather than enthusiastic. Shades of modern-day Canberra bashing! The upshot was that far less people turned up than expected. 'Official muddling was rampant making a day which pre-eminently should have been a day for all Australians, just a day for the socially glorified ... The people who did gather in front of Parliament House ... were roped off so far from the centre of activity that they barely saw more than a coloured blur.'[29]

Peter Corlett's bronze statue of John Gale—'The Father of Canberra'—stands on the corner of Lowe and Monaro Streets in Queanbeyan.

---

26   Renamed the Australian Capital Territory in 1938.

27   Elizabeth Ann Foster, who he married in 1922 after Loanna died on 19 July 1919.

28   The Prince of Wales who succeeded his Father King George V before abdicating during his first year on the Throne in favour of his younger brother Albert—the Duke of York—who became King George VI.

29   *The Hallowed High Adventure* Alexander J McGilvray Devonshire Press 1910.

The early settlers faced great difficulties. Most good land had been allocated in large parcels to those entitled to Government grants. There were no roads or services, no mail, no police and no resident landowners. Establishing and running the stations was left to Emancipist overseers with convict labour until the 1840s when transportation and convict assignment ceased.

A general air of lawlessness was accompanied by bushrangers from around 1790 to the 1860s. Initially, they were escaped convicts called 'bolters'.

Around Queanbeyan these included the Tennant Gang—William Tennant, 'Dublin' Jack (Jack Jones), John Ricks, Thomas Kain and James Murphy Campbell. The whole group was caught by Ainslie and Cowan,[30] tried in Sydney in February 1828, sentenced to hang and sent to Norfolk Island. Tennant survived and was repatriated to the mainland, offended again, found guilty of a capital crime and executed in Darlinghurst Gaol.[31]

William Westwood ('Jackey Jackey')—dubbed the Gentleman Bushranger—was assigned to a property near Goulburn in 1837. He absconded a few times, was recaptured, flogged and returned to his employer. In 1840 he stole a firearm, bailed up his employer and embarked on his notorious career. The Police captured him frequently, but he escaped on at least seven occasions before being secured in 1841, sent to Norfolk Island and hanged in 1846.

Although not associated, Ben Hall and the Clarke brothers (Thomas and John) were notorious around the Queanbeyan District during the Gold Rush days in the late 1850s and 1860s.

The Clarkes committed some 50 robberies around Braidwood, including (with Pat Connell) holding up the entire village of Michelago. They assassinated four special constables sent to capture them but were eventually captured and hanged on 25 June 1867.

---

30   Moore's Overseer. Tennant had worked for Moore on Canberry.

31   John Gale's *Canberra—History and Legends* 1977. His book was dedicated to the memory of the Honourable Sir Austin Chapman MHR for his 'powerful political championship of Canberra as the best site for the Commonwealth of Australia's seat of government' materially aiding Gale's efforts.

Bush-ranging in the district ceased thereafter.

I had intended to include a final Chapter dealing with the traditional Aboriginal owners of the Australian Capital Territory and the name 'Canberra' based on a hearsay report of an interview with John Blundell which triggered a series of exchanges in the Letters to the Editor pages of the *Sydney Morning Herald* in 1927. The issues surrounding all this are complicated and contentious.

Primary sources show that the Ngunawal people—who lived around Gunning, Goulburn and Yass—were not the Limestone Plains' Aboriginal inhabitants.

The ACT Government's 10 September 2001 Cabinet Decision to enter
'... an historic agreement with the Ngun(n)awal people in relation to the management of Namadgi'

is curious writ large.

It seems clear to me that Onyong[32]—who was presented with his Breastplate[33] as 'Chief of the Namidge Tribe'—by Mr Robert Campbell on 17 January 1831, holds the key to who the traditional owners of the ACT really are.[34]

I intend to pursue this matter over the next few years in connection with a second book about Joseph and Susan's 11 children—including their progeny and exploits. This will include details of where the last full-blooded Aboriginals are buried in the District.

In this context, page 1 of the introduction to the *Australian Bureau of Statistics 1931 Year Book Australia* says:
'Canberra is the capital city of a continent, notable amongst other things as being the first in history committed to a policy of exclusive occupation by white people.'

---

32   *Aka* Hong Kong, Hong Gong, Honyong.

33   Also called breastplates and gorgets, these plates were presented by white authorities to recognise those who they perceived to be local Aboriginal leaders. Aboriginal clans did not traditionally have kings or chiefs, relying on older men—'Elders'- who consulted with each other on decisions affecting the group.

34   Reproduced on the next page courtesy of the breastplate's owner.

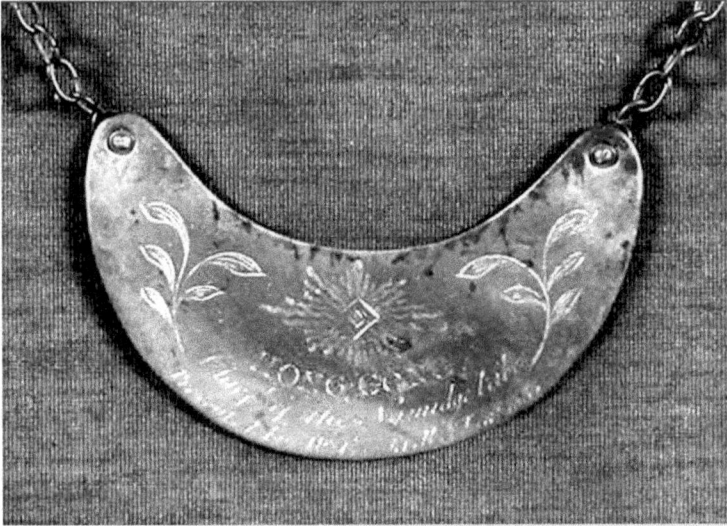

Breastplate presented to Onyong, chief of the Namidge by Robert Campbell on 17 January 1831.

Nine
Joseph, Susan and their children

Joseph, Susan and their infant son John arrived in Canberra around October-November 1842.

Family folklore says they settled at Regatta Point and 'Joe' built a small slab hut with a 'bathroom' on what came to be called 'Blundell's Hill'—where the Canadian Flagpole now sits on the eastern side of the Exhibition Centre at Regatta Point and established a farm which extended to where the Civic Olympic Pool is now. Like many stories about Joe and Susan and their antecedents, this story includes elements of the truth.

The farm house was actually built on the north-western slope of Cathedral Hill not far from Regatta Point on the site where the Catholic Archbishop's House now stands off Commonwealth Avenue.

A Journey from Sydney to the Australian Alps by John Lhotsky in 1834 includes the following description:

> 'The Old Bark Hut
> 'As the building of huts on Maneroo (and probably at all Australian outstations) is always upon the same principal (*sic*), I will give a short description of it. Such huts are built of stringy or iron-bark trees, the stems of which being straight, require little shaping and adjusting. The bark of both these trees being besides separable from the stem easily and in long sheets, is one of the principal materials of our forest architecture, as the latter is equally used by our natives. Such

sheets are nailed on the uprights and form the walls and of the same materials as the roof, all which produce of course a rather sylvan appearance. Such huts are composed, firstly, of the main room, in which a large fireplace is always fed with the robust branches of the adjacent forest. About this place, pieces of salted meat are hanging, ready, as it were, to glide into the equally large kettle which is constantly boiling or simmering.

'Next to the fireplace is the table, and a place like an armchair, the exclusive lounge of the overseer or stockman, which of course was always ceded to the honoured guest. One of the sides of this room opens into another place, where the beds of the men, also made on the long sheets of bark are visible. This place serves sometimes as a store for casks or beef, flour etc and above this is a loft, where other articles are deposited.

'As such huts are commonly near waterholes, where a quantity of the best humus and alluvial soil abounds, spots are often cultivated as kitchen-gardens.'[1]

Where Joseph lobbed was known by the white settlers as Canberry[2]— including the site where the Royal Canberra Hospital was for so long and which is now home to the National Museum of Australia and the Australian Institute of Aboriginal and Torres Strait Islander Studies (AIATSIS).

Joe took up a 'selection' running from Cathedral Hill eastwards to where St John's Anglican Church is and down to the Molonglo River which formed its southern border.[3] Some stone foundations and other remnants of Joe's place were still there when the Presbytery was first occupied on 13 November 1931.

Walter and Marion Griffin's 1911 Canberra Plan included Cathedral sites for the two major religious denominations, based on the Roman Catholic workers being on the northern side of the Molonglo River and the Government Officers who were Church of England adherents on the southern side. That religious distinction was also to apply to those who populated the suburbs on each side of the Molonglo River.

1   *Canberry Tales an Informal History* by Granville Allen Mawer published by Arcadia 2012.

2   Derived from the Aboriginal name for that area.

3   *The Canberra Times* article of 19 December 1933 marking the passing of George Blundell.

Typically, Federal Capital Commission officials persuaded the Government to ignore the Griffin's intention[4] and approve alternative Cathedral sites.

Joe and Susan's further ten children were all born at the Cathedral Hill farm house, nearly a mile downstream from what came to be called Blundell's Cottage—named after their third child and second son George and which was part of Robert Campbell's Duntroon Estate.[5]

The 'selection' which Joseph rented formed part of the Canberry Estate owned in the 1820s by the absentee landlord Joshua John Moore and managed by his trustees. During the 1840s Depression and droughts, the trustees continued to rent portions of Canberry Estate to tenants, including Joseph Blundell.[6]

Moore was eventually forced to sell Canberry because of the drought from 1838 to 1842 and the associated financial crisis. Arthur Jeffreys RN, who married Robert Campbell's second daughter Sarah, purchased Canberry Estate in 1843. After Arthur died in 1861, his son and heir John changed the name to 'The Acton Estate' around 1878

> '... allegedly because Canberry was a disreputable haunt near Limehouse in London.'

It was actually renamed after the ancestral home at Denbeighshire.[7]

After sacking Ainslie in 1835, Robert Campbell appointed his son Charles as Superintendent of the 30000-acre Duntroon Estate. Charles did much to improve that property and Ginninderra which he managed for his cousin George Thomas Palmer. He arranged to buy Ginninderra in 1837, paid the deposit and married George's daughter Catherine Irene. They lived at Ginninderra and had five children, but he lost everything in

---

4   *In Pursuit of a Catholic Cathedral for Canberra: A History of the Cathedral Hill Site* by David Flannery Journal of the Australian Catholic Historical Society.

5   From an interview with Susan Bedford (*née* Melville, daughter of Stan Melville and Catherine/'Kate' Blundell) by her nephew Stan Melville junior in 1975.

6   Reference 1 *op cit.*

7   Allen Mawer *op cit.*There's no supporting evidence for the Limehouse claim.

the 1837-1839 drought, causing his father-in-law to foreclose and take the property back. Charles then moved back to Duntroon and ran that until he returned to England in 1854, at which time the Estate of his Father— who had died in 1846—had still not been settled.

Robert bequeathed Duntroon to his youngest son George Palmer[8] Campbell who married his second cousin Marrianne Collinson Close in 1854. They lived at Wharf House in Campbell's Cove[9] until 1857 when they and their two children moved to Duntroon.[10]

Although it's not clear,[11] George Campbell seems to have managed the Acton Estate for the Jeffreys as well as Duntroon. Arthur Jeffreys had returned to England in 1854 with his wife for health reasons and they both died there.

George died in 1881 during a visit to England, while Marrianne, an accomplished artist, died at Duntroon in 1903, the property remaining in the family's hands until the Commonwealth resumed it in 1910, and which later became the Royal Military College.

The Reverend Pierce Galliard Smith of St John's wrote to Charles Campbell in England in 1888 to ask whether John Jeffreys would sell the Acton Estate to Arthur Brassey. Jeffreys refused but agreed instead to lease the station, which Brassey then held until the resumption by the Commonwealth and payment to John Jeffreys as the owner after he disputed the price—in 1912 for less than he had first been offered—this being the first compulsory acquisition.

By 1845, Joe was on the Duntroon workforce working for Campbell as a stock-handler, bullock team driver and farmer, as was his oldest son John who—as mentioned earlier—started out with the Campbell's as a shepherd.

---

8   His Mother's maiden name.

9   Near what is now The Rocks in Sydney.

10   Curiously, Charles continued to manage the Property after his return from a brief visit to England until George moved to Duntroon.

11   The records were destroyed in a fire at Duntroon in the 20th Century.

Robert Campbell of Duntroon in concert with William Grant Broughton (the Bishop of Australia) selected the site for St John the Baptist Church which was consecrated in 1845; the adjoining school opened later the same year.[12]

Following the great Molonglo River flood of 1852, William Sullivan took over Springbank from Joseph Kaye and after half a Century was so closely identified with the area that the locals referred to nearby Canberry Creek as Sullivan's thereby effecting the name change.[13]

In 1878, Surveyor Percy Hodgkinson was engaged to provide a status report and assessment of the Acton Estate. His accompanying sketch plan shows all of the river bank as having been rented out except for an access track to the ford across the river (Lennox Crossing—which went from the north-eastern side of where the National Museum is now to a couple of hundred yards north of the Albert Hall).

Richard/Dick Blundell (the fifth child and fourth son) 29 years of age occupied 104 acres—his eastern boundary abutting the western boundary of George Campbell's Duntroon property.

The 1878 sketch plan referred to above shows Joseph having moved to 42 acres on the western side of Canberry Creek[14] his western boundary being the property of Dr William Hayley and his other neighbours being Christopher Donnelly with 16 acres to his south and Cameron with 118 cares on the eastern and northern borders of his land. By this time only the two youngest children Rosanna and Kate would have still been living at home, prior to their marriages in 1885 and 1895 respectively.

Notably, Hodgkinson's name for the watercourse was the 'Queanbeyan River'.

The junction of the Queanbeyan and Molonglo Rivers is near Oaks Estate and later sources use the Molonglo terminology as the river through Canberra.

---

12   Reference 1 *op cit.*

13   Reference 1 *op cit.*

14   This land subsequently became part of The Australian National University where the Author studied for his degrees and later became Chancellor in 2006.

When John and Margaret Shumack[15] first came to Canberra in 1841 to work for William Klensendorllfe, they lived in one of the old stone buildings to the rear of the Albert Hall now covered by the Lake.[16] John Shumack's nephew Samuel wrote in his Memoirs that Klensendorlffe was a disgrace to humanity and his cruelty to his assigned servants was never to be forgotten.

In 1842, John Shumack was fortunate to lease about 100 acres of Glebe land where he erected a three-roomed slab house with a bark roof.[17] John was active in church affairs, helping to cart the stone used in building St John's school and church where he was one of the first Wardens. Although John died in 1849 and was buried at St John's, the family held the Glebe Farm until 1857.

A succession of tenants followed, Thomas Harrington Line reputed to have the best Wheat crop in County Murray. When rain fell in July 1859, Joseph Blundell and his son 'Jack' (John) planted 14 acres for Line and the yield was 800 bushells—a record for that Farm. Some years later 'Dick' Blundell had a yield of 1500 bushells from 32 acres on his neighbouring property.

In 1874, Ebenezer Booth was the occupant of the Glebe Farm house[18] and he built a replacement whitewashed brick house with a high shingled roof. The Blundell children played a trick on old Mr Booth one night by putting a light in a hollowed out pumpkin and lowering it down the chimney with fishing lines. After a while 'bang bang' he shot the pumpkin down.

Around 1895—when Kate and Bill Melville were living in Booth's Cottage at Glebe Park—there was nothing left of Joseph and Susan's original place not far from the Canadian Flag Pole except a chimney and some stone rubble.[19]

A single spur of Douglas Fir Tree from British Columbia 128 feet high and ten feet below ground, the Flag Pole was commemorated on

15   John was born c1812 near Kilfinane in Limerick to Peter and Eliza Shoemaker (his trade) who were unusually of the Anglican faith. John married Margaret Toole a Catholic who claimed to be a descendant of the Irish provincial King O'Toole—her Mother's maiden name. Margaret's surname was actually Hennessy.

16   From Elizabeth White's work about the Shumack family published in 1993.

17   Marked by a plaque near the original site in what is now Commonwealth Park.

18   Which came to be known as Booth's Cottage.

19   Reference 3 *op cit.*

20 November 1957 to symbolise the ties which unite the peoples of Australia and Canada.

The 1891 flood led Jack Scott and his wife Catherine (*née* Logue) to move from their Springbank farm to the western side of the River giving their name to Scott's Crossing (under King's Avenue Bridge)—still in use until the 1960s.

This causeway and its companion Lennox Crossing about a mile downstream were the only way to cross the River. The 'roads' were merely three-furrowed tracks, one for the horse and two for the wheels of the drays and wagons. One road went to Queanbeyan, another passed St John's on the way to Yass and the third went out towards the Cotter and Uriarra.[20]

The area occupied by the Scotts (later called Rattenberry/Rottenberry's Hill[21]) adjacent to St Mark's has long been earmarked as the site for an Anglican Cathedral. Like the Catholic Cathedral Site, church politics has prevented realisation of either dream to date. There's a small irony that the Anglican site sits on land first occupied by a Catholic and the Catholic site on land first occupied by our Joe Blundell of the Anglican persuasion.

On 1 January 1911, the Commonwealth of Australia took possession of the Federal Territory—freehold tenure was abolished and all land vested in the Commonwealth. This caused the cessation of transfer of properties from Father to son—a marked feature of the preceding epoch. Land resumptions followed, and this affected the Blundell family as will be seen in Book Two.

In May 1909, John Murray (1853-1933) and his family came from Cowra Creek near Bredbo to lease a 75-acre block of land which included Booth's Cottage. They erected a kitchen and weatherboard bake house to establish Canberra's first bakery and later added a small grocery store which was managed by his second wife Mary. The bread and groceries were initially

---

20   'The Hallowed High Adventure' Alexander J McGilvray Devonshire Press 1910.

21   Named after George—a carpenter-stonemason-bricklayer—who was brought out as an assisted migrant by Campbell of Duntroon. One of his George's sons—Frederick, a taxi driver in Queanbeyan, married my great aunt Violet Elsie Meech. They had no children and I lived with them as an 'adopted' son for some years.

delivered by horse and cart and later by the family car. In November 1923, a fire in the grocery store burnt it all down although remnants of the bakery remained until the 1960s. Murray had nine sons, six of whom served in WWI and one in WWII. The oldest—Ernest—is recorded as Canberra's first ANZAC.

In *More about the Old Pioneers*[22] Samuel Shumack mentions several names omitted from previous histories of Canberra—his:

> '... object being to draw attention to the inaccuracies that are put before the public as actual facts when they are the reverse. I was surprised when I saw no mention of the toilers that really laid the foundation of Canberra. Some authors mention Moore, Klensendorlffe and many others who had golden opportunities, but many of these failed. I consider the undermentioned persons to be among those who actually laid the foundation of our National Capital: Naylor, Edward Smith, John Shumack, Thomas Southwell, Mrs O'Keefe and Joseph Blundell. They proved that a living could be made where the elite of society's attempts had failed and this became an established fact when John Robertson's Free Selection Act became law.'

Sam Shumack's son—also Sam—says that Joe Blundell was known locally as 'The Heathen' because he continued to plough or gather his crops on Sundays on land that was quite close to St John's instead of attending church services.

Shumack also relates an interesting tale about convicts in September 1856, not long after he and his family arrived as free settlers from Ireland:

> 'A few days after father commenced his duties, he was with a few station hands who were discussing one of their party who was absent, and the absentee was referred to as an old 'lag'.
>
> 'What is a 'lag'? asked father. The party gazed at him in astonishment (and replied) A 'lag' is a man who has been 'sent out'—a convict ...
>
> 'A convict, said father, 'I am surprised at Mr Campbell having such a man on the station.' He was more surprised when a chorus came from around him, 'I'm a lag,' 'I'm a lag,' 'I'm a lag,' and he then learned that of the two dozen men employed there, about 18 were ex-convicts or Ticket-of-Leave men.'

---

22   'Tales and Legends of Canberra Pioneers' Samuel Shumack ANU Press 1967.

In Edgar George Williams' 1929 series of 'True Stories of Canberra' in *The Queanbeyan Age*, an article dealing with sport in the 1850s and 1860s says that:

> 'The old hands often spoke of the 109-pound cod, hauled out of Canberra River, just above the willows near the present bridge (Commonwealth Avenue Bridge), close to the Hostel, by Joe Blundell.'

Some family and other sources called these 'Blundell's Willows'—the poetic licence extending to the claim that Joseph had brought cuttings from the willows around Napoleon's tomb on St Helena which he visited on his journey from England to the NSW Colony.

We know this couldn't possibly be true as the convict ship *Marquis of Huntley* which brought Joseph to Australia didn't go anywhere near St Helena on its journey from England to Sydney Cove. Allen Mawer relates a similar story about Edwin Elijah Bambridge and goes on to attribute William Balcombe, the Colonial Treasurer, as the source of the willows which can still be found along the banks of Lake Burley Griffin.[23]

John Gale's 1977 *Canberra: Its History and Legends*[24] notes that:

> 'Another early Canberra settler was Joe Blundell forefather of the many Blundells still hereabouts. Joe had been an old soldier and one of his first jobs in Australia was that of hutkeeper. A bushranger was making a stir in the district at the time and had shot an employee on a station.

> 'There was a reward of 50 pounds for his capture, dead or alive.

> 'Joe had an army musket of flint-lock pattern and he was a dead shot with it. When he changed the sheep folding-grounds, which was daily, he always had his beloved musket with him feeling pretty sure that he had a fair chance of winning the 50 pounds. It was understood that the outlaw in question took a delight in murder and laughed at his victims' death agonies. Blundell like many others believed this and for some time lived in a state of terror on that account.

> 'There came a day when Blundell was in his hut kneading some dough preparatory to baking. A shadow darkened the door of the hut. He looked up. There was the outlaw, with a brace of the

---

23   Reference 1 *op cit*. But see the September 2019 *Historical Journal* article which considers the matter in more detail.

24   Published by the Library of Australian History 1977.

old-fashioned horse-pistols in his belt, and a carbine of the latest percussion-cap pattern in his hand.

'This weapon was the first of its kind Blundell had ever seen, his knowledge of firearms being confined to the flint-lock pattern. Blundell was at the far end of the table, near the door, and on a stool. The outlaw took in the situation at a glance, and stepping forward, took up the musket. Joe thought his last hour had come. But the first thing the outlaw did was to shake out the powder from the pan of the old flint-lock and remove the flint. Then Joe found his tongue. 'Would you like some dinner, mate?' he asked of his visitor. 'Yes' was the reply, 'and I am badly in want of the same'.

'After satisfying the cravings of hunger, he remained with Joe for about an hour. Joe was asked a few questions about the station bosses round about. In reply, Joe told him that his boss was a humane man and treated his men well and that he knew nothing about other bosses. On his departure, Joe gave the outlaw all the cooked food that was in the hut; and, so ended the harmless interview.

'Blundell heard later on that the man who was shot by this bushranger was a noted spy. There is every reason to believe this was the truth, as at that time spies were everywhere. They were mostly of the lowest criminal class, dead to all feelings of honour, self-interest being their only consideration, and they would spare no one to obtain that end.

'I later had a long conversation with Abraham Blundell, one of Joe's sons, about this bushranger; but he could not recollect his name. Abraham also told me that after the final disappearance of this daring outlaw, his father put aside his favourite musket and he considered that many of the yarns that were circulated about the fellow were without foundation.'

Gale also notes that the worst bush fire experienced in the District broke out on 31 December 1904 and continued until 1 January 1905:

'The greatest damage was wrought on the estates of E G Grace, Hatch Brothers, James Kilby and James McCarthy. George Blundell lost a bullock-waggon and bullock-yokes valued at about 100 pounds and E H Clark suffered severely.'

Queanbeyan Pioneers—First Study by Rex Cross and Bert Sheedy published in 1983, records Joseph as one of the 30 Senior Local Pioneers and Blundell as one of the 112 pioneer families.

Susan was very strict, but kindly and a good church goer. She named most of her children after Biblical personages.

Joseph was 43 and Susan 27 when their first child (John) was born and 61 and 45 when their last child was born:

1. John 29.3.1842 Liverpool Plains^—30.10.1927 Tumut;
2. Susan 4.12.1844 Canbury—24.5.1875 Canberra;
3. George 3.3.1846 Canbury—18.12.1933 Reid;
4. Abraham 3.4.1847 Canbury—5.6.1884 Wetangera;
5. Richard 6.12.1848 Canbury—28.11.1917 Queanbeyan;
6. William 21.7.1850 Canbury—4.5.1851 Canbury;
7. Isaac 5.11.1851 Canbury—9.5.1910 Yarralumla;
8. Jacob 9.3.1853 Canbury—1.8.1927 Jeir;[25]
9. Mary Jane 29.7.1855 Canbury—26.12.1873 Springbank;
10. Rosanna 13.7.1858 Canberra—5.4.1939 Queanbeyan; and
11. Catherine 18.12.1859 Canberry—25.5.1950 Queanbeyan.

^St John's Canberra records John Blundell's date of birth as 29 March 1843 in accordance with Joe and Susan's determination to disguise John's true birth date in the table above and the circumstances of their coming to Canberra.

The Liverpool Plains District, where John was born, was around the upper reaches of the Hunter River, the nearest Parishes at the time being at Maitland (established in 1834) and Stroud (established in 1836).

Five children were baptised at St John's on 7 October 1849 *viz* John, Susan, George, Abraham and Richard—seven years after Joe and Susan came to Canberra—another part of the subterfuge. The sponsors—William Appleyard and Edwin Elijah Bambridge—were two early Canberra identities who feature prominently in Samuel Shumack's 'Tales and Legends of Canberra Pioneers.'

The dates of the children's baptisms extracted from the St John's Registers are detailed in the table overleaf:

25   Jacob's burial date. The Jeir deceased index files have his death as 27 July 1927—courtesy of Pam Glover.

Child	Baptism	Surname	Occupation	Residence	Clergyman
John	7.10.1849	Blundel	Small Tenant	Canbury	Edward Smith
Susan	ditto	ditto	ditto	ditto	ditto
George	ditto	ditto	ditto	ditto	ditto
Abraham	ditto	ditto	ditto	ditto	ditto
Richard	ditto	ditto	ditto	ditto	ditto
William	25.8.1850	ditto	ditto	ditto	George Edward Gregory
Isaac	14.12.1851	ditto	Farmer	ditto	Thomas Hattam Wilkinson
Jacob	22.5.1853	ditto	Tenant Farmer	ditto	ditto
Mary Jane	14.10.1855	Blundell	Farmer	Canberry	Pierce Galliard Smith
Rosanna	22.8.1858	ditto	ditto	Canberra	ditto
Catherine	22.1.1860	ditto	ditto	Canberry	ditto

Annex B records the basic genealogical stem of Joseph and Susan's 11 children, their marriages and offspring.

The NSW Register of Births, Deaths and Marriages record the first eight of Joseph and Susan's children as Blundel with the last three as Blundell.

These 11 children produced 75 in the next generation, who in turn had over 300 in the one after, remarkable fecundity given the number who never married and strong streak of infertility which emerged in the female line. Work is still required on some descendants to ascertain details about their births, marriages, deaths and children *et seq* which it is hoped will be completed during 2021 for publication as the Second Volume of our Blundell family history.

Joseph was reputed to be a very jealous man—an outcome of the development of his own relationship with Susan/Mercy?

When the children were too young to help on the farm, he would sometimes employ workers to do particular jobs and forbade Susan to go down and milk the cows when there were any men around the stockyards.

Joe was also averse to letting his boys go to school because he wanted them home to work and was fearful that they might learn to forge a name. Although his son 'Dick' had no education, he could total up hundredweights and quarters and never made a mistake with money.

The girls all went to school—meaning the little school house in the St John's Church precinct—which is still there as a museum of Canberra's early days.

When it snowed, the children used to get stringy bark poles, roll them in the snow and then roll them down the hill towards Edwin Elijah Bambridge's place which was between them and Mr Arthur Brassey's Canberry Cottage.

Uncle 'Jack' had a place at Condor Creek.[26] His 'wife' Phoebe[27] was a great reader taking her children's names out of books she had read, that's why they had so many christian names.[28]

They would leave bands of stringy bark soaking in the river water and use them later to bind the hay.

All the Blundell boys were good Blacksmiths, building their own forge. They also had their own bullock teams and used to travel as far as Sydney—a trip that would take a few weeks—where they would unload and then load up with supplies and goods for the return journey.

No doubt they had to be wary of bushrangers near Geary's Gap[29] at the southern end of Lake George.

The reader will note the reference to 'about a dozen children' in the image on page 241.

The boys and girls used to reap the wheat with a reaping hook. A good reaper could do one acre a day from sunup to sunrise.

---

26   24 Km west of Canberra off the Brindabella Road, nestled between Mount Blundell and Blundell Hill.

27   Phoebe was his brother Abraham's wife, later becoming John's common law wife—covered in Book Two.

28   Reference 5 *op cit*.

29   Daniel Geary had a pub there from early 1830, close to where Weereewa Lookout is now at the Southern end of Lake George, a favourite spot for bush rangers as the coaches and travellers ascended the steep slope.

Joe separated the wheat out by beating it with a flail (which Stan Melville had) made of cherry wood stick and rawhide. Susan would then grind it with her flour mill. She had been known to reap a sheaf of wheat, thresh it, grind it and have it cooked for breakfast.

Other reaped crops were tied into sheaves and stored.

The corn fields on the Molonglo River banks were farmed by Uncles Richard and George from Regatta Point to Scott's Crossing. On the flats just out in front of Blundell's Cottage the yield was as high as 90 Bushells to the acre.

A story about how old Grannie Blundell in the early days, got to bake fresh bread before breakfast was recalled in Fred Robinson's book about 'Canberra's First 100 Years', which includes:

"Susan Blundell's *Tried and True Method for Producing Perfect Porridge*"

Susan Blundell (1812–1892) was the mother of
George Blundell (1846–1933)

"*Rise early, take a reaping hook to the wheat paddock and cut a good sheaf. Thrash out grain against a block, winnow, grind in a steel hand-mill, take the meal and proceed in the usual way.*

NOTE: If the family is large, cut two sheaves."

This, true in spirit if not in every detail, was Susan Blundell's recipe. She came to Canberra with her husband in the early (eighteen) forties, and has left in many minds the impress of a remarkably fine character. Susan had about a dozen children; she always cut two sheaves for breakfast.

St John's Church and Burial Ground

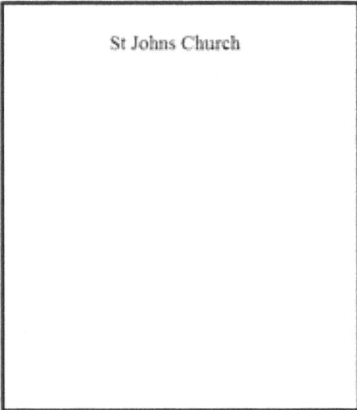

St Johns Church

Section A.

Emily   Susan Robertson
         Also E R ie Eliza

Section B.

Isaac

Section G.

George

Section C.
Row 1.

137 136 135 134 133 133 132   131 130

Key

130 Albert Henry Vincent (son of Richard and Mary Jane—*nee* Warner—from Jacob's line).

131 Hannah (John's son Joseph's wife) next to the family plot which has the following marked in the concrete surround:

132 Susan Blundell (the Matriarch) 8 April 1892 plus son William not identified.

133 CB—Caroline (daughter of Jacob) 24 March 1846.

134 MB—Margaret (daughter of Jacob) 9 March 1846.

135 AB—Abraham 5 June 1884.

136 Joseph Blundell (the Patriarch) 13 February 1874.

137 MB—Mary Jane Blundell 26 December 1873.

Known English Ancestry – Annex A[1]

1   **John Blundell** c1580–17 June 1642 St Mary Bletchingley
married[2] Katherine Benet 18 May 1600 Laurence Thanet Kent—30 April 1633 East Grinstead
at St George the Martyr Southwark on 27 November 1618.

2   **Thomas Blundell** 1626 Horne—3 July 1675 St Mary Bletchingley
married Joane Barber[3] 1636 ?–?
at St George the Martyr Southwark on 2 October 1655.

3   **John Blundell**[4] 1653 Horley?—30 January 1712 St Bartholomew Horley[5]
married Elizabeth Holmes 30 November 1653 Horley—4 May 1709 Horley
at St Peter and St Paul? Chaldon on 21 June 1675.

4   **Thomas Blundell** 1 April 1680 Horley—20 November 1740 Horley
married Mary Ede 26 May 1692 Horley—13 May 1753 Horley
at St Bartholomew Horley on 25 November 1713.

5   **Thomas Blundell** 15 March 1726 Horley[6]—10 February 1783 Horley[7]
married Elizabeth Comber 29 May 1730 Horley—c1799 Chelsfield
at St Mary Magdalene Reigate on 10 October 1752.

6   **Joseph Blundell** 7 August 1774 Chelsfield—8 May 1840 Maidstone[8]
married Elizabeth Presnall c1781 Maidstone—4 May 1845 Maidstone
at St Mary the Virgin Thurnham on 17 November 1797.

7   **Joseph** 7 October 1798 Thurnham—Patriarch of the Australian Blundells.

1 The dates represent baptisms and burials rather than births and deaths.

2 After Katherine Benet died John married again to Catherine Ede on 19 March 1636 at St Nicholas Deptford.

3 One Ancestry source has her born at Banstead Surrey.

4 One Ancestry source has a baptism date of 17 June 1655 at Burstow, although Pam Glover's search of the original Burstow Baptism Register didn't find that record. Both are buried in the grounds of St Bartholomew Horley, their tombstone being the earliest discernible of the many Blundells buried there.

5 Wherever Horley appears in the Annex above, the church is St Bartholomew.

6 From the original baptism register, but elsewhere wrongly transcribed as 18 March, courtesy of Pam Glover.

7 He died at Chelsfield and was carried back to Horley for burial.

8 Died on 2 May 1840 at Maidstone.

The First Two Generations of Joseph Blundell and Susan Osborne[1] – Annex B

JOSEPH BLUNDELL 7.10.1798 Thurnham Kent England (son of Joseph blacksmith and Elizabeth Presnall/Presnail) – 13.2.1874 Canberra
m? at Boxley/Thurnham?

x2 **SUSAN OSBORNE**[2] 8.5.1814 New Romney – 8.4.1892 Canberra
Both buried St John's Anglican Canberra in the family plot; Section C Row 1 No:s 136 and 132 respectively.

JOHN 29.3.1842 Liverpool Plains, farmer of Canberra – 30.10.1927 Tumut
m Sarah Ann MacKenzie 1.6.1843 Lanyon Murrumbidgee NSW (daughter of Alexander MacKenzie [a farmer] and Elizabeth Louisa Bass) spinster of Canberra – 16.12.1920 Ashfield
at St John's Anglican Canberra on 23.10.1862. Minister Pierce Galliard Smith; witnesses Walter Wotherspoon and Catharine MacKenzie. John buried Tumut General Cemetery; Sarah Ann at Anglican Section Rookwood Sydney.

Alexander 15.11.1862 Canberra, grazier of Tintaldra – 6.11.1940 Corryong
m Hannah Eliza Jarvis 22.5.1880 Towong Vic (daughter of William [a drover] and Caroline Jane Hadley) – 17.11.1974 Corryong
at All Saints Anglican Corryong on 6.5.1902. Minister Arthur Howard Wesley; witnesses Patrick Daly and Winifred C Wesley

John ('Jack') 11.7.1864 Canberra – 25.12.1945 Wee Jasper. Bachelor

Mary Ann 23.9.1866 Condo, Uriarra – ? 1917 Wagga
m1 James Bruce 1857 Sydney – 1895 Albury
at Queanbeyan on … 1886.
m2 George Portors 13.3.1853 Pinchbeck Lincolnshire England 1853 – ?.6.1920 Newtown
at Tumbarumba on … 1901.

Joseph 30.7.1868 Condo, Uriarra—6.6.1955 Yass

m1 Susannah (Hannah) Forrester 1869 Tumut—23.5.1902 Uriarra at ... on ... 1889.

Hannah[1] buried St John's Anglican, Canberra in the grave next to the family plot on the northern side; Joseph at Yass.

m2 Isabella Martin 4.8.1887 Nottingham Forrest Yass River (daughter of John and Alice Wells)—3.8.1921 Goulburn at All Saints Anglican Corryong on 29.6.1903. Minister Arthur Howard Wesley; witnesses Francis Harold Brunt and Alexander Blundell.

m3 Christina Pearsell (*née* Daly) 28.3.1880 Rye Park NSW—8.4.1942 Yass at Goulburn on 1928. No issue.

Henry ('**Brown**[2]') 27.6.1870 Condor Uriarra—5.6.1944 Biloela Qld

m Clara Harriett Jeffs 1881 Tumut—(daughter of James Jeffs and Mary A Higgins) 12.10.1925 West Wyalong at Weethalle/Talgogrin near West Wyalong according to the rites of the Catholic Church on 17.5.1899. Witnesses William Jeffs and Louisa Jeffs.

Eliza Jane 10.4.1872 Condor Uriarra—8.4.1915 Auburn

m Edward Henry Bruyeres ... 1870 Melbourne—... 1926 Goulburn (son of John Henry Fec Bruyeres and Sarah Rosanna Henry) at Wagga Wagga on ... 1895.

Catharine/Catherine ('**Kate**') 4.6.1874 Condor Uriarra—c1959 Parramatta or 1923 Braidwood

m Francis William Owens DCM 1886 Narromine—1955 Parramatta at Parramatta on ... 1915.

1   Details which still require verification are expected to be completed for Book Two about the 11 Blundell children, their offspring and exploits in 2021. In the meantime, any corrections/queries from descendants of Annex B might please be directed to allan.hawke@raiders.com.au

2   NB: Susan was actually Mercy Blanch (daughter of Abraham Blacomb/e and Mercy Webb) who married Robert Blanch on 12.10.1831 at All Saints Biddenden Kent.

Sarah Louisa 8.3.1876 Condo Uriarra— c1955 Newtown or West Wyalong
m Patrick John Collins c1881 -
at West Wyalong on ... 1901.

Margaret Anne ('**Maggie**') 5.1.1879 Condo, Uriarra— c1938 Wagga Wagga
m Ernest Henry Hedditch ... 1872/3, land agent of Wagga—5.10.1938 Wagga Wagga
(son of Edwin Henry Hedditch and Kate ?)
at St James' Anglican Croydon on 7.6.1910.

Eleanor ('**Leonora**') 27 Atwell ... 1882 Burwood, master baker of Sydney (son of Robert, financier deceased and Jane Elizabeth Bendell)—194?
m Alfred Sidney Atwell ... 11.1880 Condo, Uriarra—...5.1978 Ashfield
at St Stephen's Anglican Newtown on 19.1.1903.

Florence May ('**Florrie**') 2.8.1884 Condo Uriarra—1962 Newtown
m1 Andrew Douglas Lintern ... 1879 Paddington Sydney—28.11.1954 Prince Alfred Camperdown
at Waterloo Sydney on ... 1910.
m2 Arthur Edward Lynch ... 1872 ...—... 1954 Newtown
at Sydney on ... 1939.

x2 **Phoebe Anna Blundell (née Shumack**—his brother Abraham's wife)
Phoebe Anna died 1.4.1943 Tumut, buried Tumut General Cemetery.

Howard Norman 14.9.1886 Weetangerra—4.3.1920 Tumut. Died from exposure to mustard gas during the World War I.
Bachelor. Buried Tumut General Cemetery.

Muriel Pearl 1.9.1888 Weetangerra (illegitimate) home duties of Condor House—29.1.1963 Wamberal NSW
m1 Thomas Richard Lea ... 1886 Wilcannia (son of Thomas Francis [a brickmaker] and Jane Ann Surtees)—... 1932
Gosford; Surveyor's Assistant of Queanbeyan
at Condor House on 31.7.1911. Minister A H Champion; witnesses Howard Norman Blundell and Sylvia Blundell.
m2? James ('Jim') Ernest Waters ... 1885—... 1969
at Sydney on ... 1940.

Naomi Edith 'Sylvia' 25.1.1891 Weetangerra (illegitimate)—29.1.1963 Gosford domestic duties of Brindabella -
m John ('Jack') Smith ... 1882 Adelong (son of William [a labourer] and ?) labourer of Brindabella—... 1934 Tumut
at Christ Church Anglican Queanbeyan on 12.11.1913. Witnesses Edith Hirst and Carrie D Sheaffe, Minister Gordon H Hirst.

Everard Vivian Abraham 24.9.1895 Weetangerra(illegitimate)labourer of Uriarra—11.11.1964 Tumut
m Ethel Annie Martin 24.5.1898 Yass (daughter of William Henry [labourer]and Annie Hall) shop assistant
of Murrumbateman—25.7.1975 Tumut
at Christ Church Anglican Queanbeyan on 18.6.1919. Witnesses William Henry Martin, William John Martin
and Audrey Esmeralda Blundell, Minister Robert Elliot BD. Both buried Tumut Cemetery.

Bernice Sophia Hyacinth 29.1.1899 Condor House, Urayarra—21.4.1916 Condor.
*This is the only child of Phoebe and John for which John was registered as the Father. Bernice
buried St John's Anglican Canberra.

Audrey Esmeralda Phoebe Merle 31.7.1902 Condor Uriarra (illegitimate)—15.7.1996 Goulburn
m Donald Edward Bush 29.5.1900 Yass—10.12.1991 Goulburn
at 'Rocklow' Tomorromma on 15.6.1921 by Reverend Rix Anglican Minister.

SUSAN 4.12.1844 Canbury—24.5.1875 Acton Estate
m John Robertson 28.11.1844 at the convict female factory South Creek near St Mary's (son of unknown and Elizabeth Robertson later adopted by Duncan Robertson and Janet Kennedy—an unlikely coincidence?) farmer of Canberra—25.11.1911 Queanbeyan at Canberra on 29.5.1865 according to the rites of the Presbyterian Church. Reverend James Martin of St Stephen's Queanbeyan officiating; witnesses Allan Cameron and Elizabeth Williams. Susan buried at St John's Anglican Canberra (Section A Row 9 No 346); John at Presbyterian Riverside Queanbeyan.

Sarah Janet ('Jessica') 20.9.1865 Canberra—22.2.1926 Queanbeyan
m James Cartwright 12.4.1851 Landsborough/Loughborough Leicester England (son of John and Eliza King)—30.12.1917 Queanbeyan
at Christ Church Anglican Queanbeyan on 27.1.1909. Both buried Anglican Riverside Queanbeyan.

Katherine ('Kate') 1866 Acton—22.2.1926 Queanbeyan?
m William Ditchfield 16.10.1862 Vic—27.12.1915 Trigger Vale Lockhart (son of William Ditchfield and Margaret Farrell)
at St Leonards on ... 1886.

Mary 2.9.1868 Acton—18.12.1935 Queanbeyan
m George Frederick Percival 18.12.1866 Newcastle—2.2.1932 Queanbeyan (son of Samuel Percival and Henrietta Kelly)
at Wesleyan Parsonage Queanbeyan on 4.2.1889.

Margaret ('Maggie') 27.3.1870 Acton—28.1.1961 Royalla
m Thomas Edmund Bainbridge/Bambridge 16.3.1863 Canberra farmer of Queanbeyan—13.2.1915 Queanbeyan (son of Elijah Bambridge and Eliza Aldridge)
at St John's Anglican Canberra on 14.2.1899. Both buried St John's.

Anne ('Annie') ... 1872 Acton Estate -
m John White ... 1862 -
at Newcastle on ... 1888.

Eliza 10.6.1873 Acton—12.6.1873 Acton. Buried in the same grave as her Mother in St John's Anglican Canberra.

Rosanna ('**Rose**') 18.5.1874 Canberra—23.7.1963 Griffith

m1 John Mawson Lamb 10.1.1863 Deniliquin labourer of Wattamadra Cowra—15.2.1941 Goulburn (son of Decimus Lamb and Barbara Fincher)

at St John's Anglican Canberra on 27.4.1898.

m2 Albert Hogbin 1873 Armidale—1944 Goulburn (son of William Henry Hogbin and Harriet Shappard)

at Braidwood on ... 1942. No issue.

m3 John Bradley 1869 -

at Goulburn on ... 1945. No issue.

Son who died with his Mother during childbirth 24.5.1875 Canberra.

GEORGE HENRY 3.3.1846 Canbury, carrier—18.12.1933 Reid

m Flora McLennan 1845/8 Inverness, Scotland (daughter of John and Flora McKinnon) private life of

4.7.1917 Station Hill, Queanbeyan

at Wesleyan Parsonage, Queanbeyan on 6.5.1874. Witnesses Diana Rottonberry and Sarah A McMichael, Minister Rev Thomas R McMichael.

George buried St John's Anglican Canberra (Section G Row 3 No 567); Flora with her daughter Flora Susannah at Presbyterian Riverside Queanbeyan.

Flora Susannah 11.10.1875 Blundell's Cottage—12.8.1892 Blundell's Cottage (9211278).

John ('**Jack**') 31.1.1878 Blundell's Cottage—8.10.1972 Weethalle West Wyalong

m1 Edna Joyce Creech?

at ... on ...

m2 Alice?

Charles Frederick 17.4.1879 Blundell's Cottage, labourer of Canberra—28.4.1923 Queanbeyan m Sarah Ann McLaughlin 2.11.1883 Blundell's Farm, Uriarra (daughter of William, deceased, and Mary McCafferty, deceased—5.1.1942 Queanbeyan at Christ Church Anglican Queanbeyan on 24.4.1907. Witnesses Alice Maud Blundell and Joseph Lyle Blundell. Charles buried Presbyterian Riverside Queanbeyan section washed away in the 1925 flood Sarah in the Catholic Riverside Queanbeyan.

George Arthur 6.1.1881 Blundell's Cottage -

Herbert Frank 28.1.1882 Blundell's Cottage—26.6.1957 Queanbeyan m Ellen May Taylor 4.2.1887 Stoney Creek (daughter of James Samuel and Martha Cooper)—12.8.1971 Queanbeyan at St Stephen's Presbyterian Queanbeyan on 12.6.1907. Both buried Presbyterian Riverside Queanbeyan.

Ada Agnes 18.4.1883 Blundell's Cottage—28.1.1918 Queanbeyan m Francis J Tucker ... 1873 Sydney—... 1926 Liverpool at ... Sydney on ... 1908

Alice Maud 12.4.1885 Blundell's Cottage—10.11.1955 Queanbeyan m Edmund ('Ned') Johh Ryan (son of Timothy and Agnes Logue) 1876 Queanbeyan—11.8.1963 Queanbeyan at ... Queanbeyan on ... 1910. Both buried Catholic Riverside Queanbeyan.

Joseph Lyle 22.4.1888 Blundell's Cottage—3.12.1949 Gunnedah m1 Vera May Kitson 8.2.1892 Hillston—11.3.1928 Paddington Sydney at... Canberra on 5.6.1912 according to the rites of the Presbyterian Church. m2 Louise Maud McKay 27.8.1903 Maryborough—11.3.1974 Coffs Harbour at St David's Presbyterian Haberfield on 31.7.1929. Louise buried Gunnedah.

ABRAHAM 3.4.1847 Canbury, farmer of Wetangera—5.6.1884 (8413098) Wetangera
m Phoebe Anna Shumack 4.12.1857 Duntroon, (daughter of Richard, farmer, and Anna Shumack) spinster of Wetangera—1.4.1943 Tumut
at St John's Anglican Canberra on 22.8.1877. Witnesses Samuel Shumack and Kate Blundell, Minister Pierce Galliard Smith.
Abraham buried in the family plot at St John's Anglican Canberra (Section C Row 1 No 135); Phoebe at Tumut General Cemetery.

Clara Malvina Ann 22.1.1878 Weetangara, dressmaker of Uriarra—4.9.1951 Tumut
m John 'James' Goslett 29.8.1861 Gundaroo (son of William, farmer, and Mary Ann Turner) miner of Uriarra—15.8.1947 Tumut
at St John the Baptist Anglican Canberra on 28.9.1898. Witnesses Charles Wilson and Bridget Young, Minister Peter Preswell.

Dora Emily 18.9.1880 Weetangara—20.3.1941 Yass
m Michael ('Mick') Hollingsworth (son of Michael and Elizabeth Ann Butt) 23.8.1873 Murrumburrah—29.9.1939 Yass
at ... Quirindi on 5.1.1905. Dora buried at Murrumbateman.

Daisy Irene 12.5.1882 Queanbeyan—12.10.1964 Tumut
m Arthur George Buckley 2.5.1886 Tumut—23.7.1962 Tumut
at Condor House on 30.4.1913 according to the rites of the Methodist Church. Minister Alfred Brown officiating; witnesses Sylvia Blundell, Jean Shumack and Everard Blundell.

Lilian Jessie 'Stella' 7.12.1884 Weetangera—17.9.1965 Ainslie
m William Charles Tankey 23.10.1858 Newtown—26.3.1939 Queanbeyan
at St Gregory's Catholic Queanbeyan on 7.7.1906. Witnesses Patrick Buckley, Annie E Tankey; Father Birch officiating. Stella buried Woden; Bill at Catholic Riverside Queanbeyan

RICHARD 6.12.1848 Canbury—28.11.1917 Queanbeyan. Buried Anglican Tharwa Road Queanbeyan.

WILLIAM 21.7.1850 Canbury—4.5.1851 Canbury. Buried St John's Anglican Canberra in the family plot (No 132).

ISAAC 5.11.1851 Canbury, farmer of Yarralumla—9.5.1910 Yarralumla
m Emily Shumack 11.5.1860 Ginninderra (daughter of Richard farmer and Anna Shumack) spinster of Wetangera—25.3.1927 Queanbeyan
at St John's Anglican Canberra on 20.10.1882. Witnesses George Edward Shumack and Kate Blundell, Minister Pierce Galliard Smith.
Both buried St John's Anglican, Canberra (Section B Row 6 No 151 and Section A Row 9 No 347).

Charles Henry 17.7.1883 Bulga Creek, Yarralumla, labourer of Bywong—1.11.1955 Liverpool Hospital
m1 Pearl Jane Dungey 25.9.1871 Patrick's Plain NSW—1940 Sydney
at ... Sydney on ... 1900.
m2 Ethel Alice Hall 1891 Granville domestic duties of Hall—8.7.1925 Queanbeyan
at St John the Baptist Anglican Canberra on 31.5.1911.
Witnesses George F Hall and Susan Blundell, Minister A. H. Champion.

Edward 5.11.1885 Bulga Creek, Yarralumla—10.2.1950 Brisbane
m Grace Emily Wadley c1896 England—c1954 Qld
at ... Qld on 20.10.1915.

William 26.10.1888 Bulga Creek, Canberra, labourer of Queanbeyan—24.4.1960 Queanbeyan
m Dorothy Edith Middleton 12.4.1904 Fisher's Gate, Sussex, England (daughter of Clarence Sydney and
Annie Sophie Barnard domestic duties of Queanbeyan—31.12.2001 Queanbeyan
at Christ Church Anglican Queanbeyan on 14.7.1926.
Witnesses A Blundell and I Middleton. William buried Anglican Riverside, Queanbeyan.

Susan Mary 21.4.1891 Bulga Creek, Yarralumla—12.9.1978 Stanmore
m Joseph Augustine Cleary 20.1.1882 Woolloomooloo—7.12.1960 Bondi Junction
at St Francis' Catholic Paddington on 3.2.1918. Both buried Rookwood.

Beatrice Ann 5.4.1894 Bulga Creek, home duties of Queanbeyan—17.2.1972 Guildford
m Stuart Harry Janson 21.5.1889 Winnipeg, Canada, (son of Edward Armstrong and Rosaline King),
surveyor of Queanbeyan—14.9.1963 Burwood, Vic
at the residence of Mr McInnes according to the rites of the Anglican Church on 16.1.1913.
Witnesses A. H. Coppin and S. W. Kilby, Minister H. E. Lewin.

Sarah Rosaline ('Rosie') 22.8.1896 Bulga Creek, Yarralumla—3.2.1929 Queanbeyan
m John William Burn 5.9.1891 Queanbeyan—29.9.1959 Sydney
at St Gregory's Catholic Queanbeyan on 15.1.1920.

Emily 'Irene' 10.11.1899 Bulga Creek, Yarralumla, home duties of Queanbeyan—22.10.1984 Taree
m Clarence Albert Weller 2.7.1902 Albury, insurance representative of Queanbeyan—3.9.1964 Taree
at Christ Church Anglican Queanbeyan on 1.4.1929. Witnesses A J Blundell and D E Blundell.

Unnamed son 3.12.1902 Bulga Creek Yarralumla—3.12.1902 Bulga Creek. Buried Misty Corner Yarralumla.

Adrian# Isaac 1.5.1905 Yarralumla—15.7.1977 Carlingford (# Register of Births, Deaths and Marriages shows Adrain)
m Ivy Muriel Cooper 10.2.1904 Marulan—20.11.1963 Lewisham
at Christ Church Anglican Bungonia on 11.6.1932.

JACOB 9.3.1853 Canbury, farmer of Canberra—1.8.1927 Jeir
m Lucy Ann Plummer 2.4.1856 Burra (daughter of George carrier and Anne Bay now Licity) spinster of Burra—
15.1.1924 Queanbeyan
at St John's Anglican Canberra on 26.1.1876. Witnesses Henry Rottenberry and Kate Blundell, Minister Pierce Galliard Smith.
Jacob buried Hall Cemetery; Lucy at Anglican Riverside Queanbeyan.

Joseph (twin) 15.9.1877 'The Oaks', Oak's Estate—22.10.1944 Harden
m Ethel 'Maud' Hart 11.8.1893 Murrumburrah—23.4.1954 Harden
at St Paul's Anglican Murrumburrah on 14.11.1912.
Both buried Anglican Harden-Murrumburrah Cemetery.

Richard (twin) 15.9.1877 'The Oaks', Oak's Estate, farmer of Canberra—30.10.1966 Queanbeyan
m Mary Jane Warner 1867 Naas (daughter of Susan Warner), spinster of—4.3.1950 Queanbeyan
at St John's Anglican Canberra on 14.11.1900. Witnesses Joseph Blundell and Eleanor Blundell, Minister Pierce Galliard Smith.
Both buried Anglican Riverside Queanbeyan.

Margaret Anne 14.9.1879 Canberra—9.3.1886 (8613424) Wallaroo. Buried St John's Anglican Canberra in the family plot.

Caroline 4.11.1881 Canberra—24.3.1886 (8613428) Wallaroo. Buried St John's Anglican Canberra in the family plot.

Allan ('Ted') 19.6.1884 Wallaroo labourer of Gininderra—25.4.1963 Harden
m Ada Rottenberry 20.10.1890 Yass—2.8.1968 Harden
at St Clements Anglican Yass on 19.7.1911. Both buried Anglican Harden-Murrumburrah.

Lucy Anne 17.7.1887 Wallaroo Hall, home duties of Hall—5.5.1950 Wagga
m Albert Harold Williams 19.7.1885 Enmore (son of George Doulby, contractor, and Louisa Smith)
labourer of Hall—24.2.1968 Holbrook
at St John the Baptist Anglican Canberra on 27.2.1907. Witnesses Allan Blundell and Alice June Blundell,
Minister A. M. Hopcraft.

Alice Jane 14.9.1889 Wallaroo—2.6.1979 Queanbeyan
m Arthur Sydney Colverwell   Burbong—19.10.1949 Queanbeyan
at Christ Church Anglican Queanbeyan on ... 1922.

Arthur 5.10.1891 Wallaroo—29.7.1975 Harden
m Edith ('Edie') Madeline Mutch 25.10.1901 Cootamundra—5.2.1948 Murrumburrah
at Methodist Harden on 24.1.1921.

Emily 21.10.1893 Wallaroo Hall domestic duties of Hall—7.8.1978 Dubbo
m Samuel Coad (aka Dale) 28.8.1889 St Arnaud Victoria (son of Richard farmer and Elizabeth Dale) labourer of
Duntroon—16.9.1966 Dubbo
at Willow Farm Hall on 2.8.1913. Witnesses Maria Blundell and Arthur Blundell, Minister F G Ward.

Maria 24.9.1895 Wallaroo—5.10.1969 Harden
m Arthur Albert Searle 16.4.1882 Bruce SA—7.5.1976 Moss Vale
at ... Harden on 24.10.1921. Both buried Harden.

Margery ('Marge') Aymee 24.5.1898 Gininderra—19.9.1971 Goulburn
m William Clark 1895—
at ... Goulburn on ... 1924.

Charlotte ('Lottie') 30.1.1903 Jeir—1942 Mooroopna Vic
m Clarence Lindsay Gordon Thorn 1903 Shepparton Vic—1983 Echuca Vic
at ... Queanbeyan on ... 1926.

MARY JANE 29.7.1855 Canberry—26.12.1873 Springbank, Canberra. Buried St John's Anglican Canberra in the family plot (No 137). Baptised 14.10.1855 Where?

ROSANNA 13.7.1858 Canberra spinster of Canberra—5.4.1939 Queanbeyan
m Isaac Meech 23.9.1845 Fordington Dorchester Dorsetshire England (son of John overseer and Grace Bird/Burt) plummer of Queanbeyan—23.9.1920 Queanbeyan
at Christ Church Anglican Queanbeyan on 18.8.1885. Witnesses Joseph Lewis and Kate Blundell, Minister Charles Kingsmill. Isaac and Rosanna both buried Anglican Riverside Queanbeyan.

Sophia Jane Blundell (illegitimate) 16.11.1881 Canberra—1.5.1890 Queanbeyan. Register of Baptisms Queanbeyan Methodist records Thomas Meredith as the father. Sophia buried in the family plot at Anglican Riverside Queanbeyan.

Olive Mary 28.4.1886 Queanbeyan domestic duties of Queanbeyan—4.9.1947 Queanbeyan
m Thomas Rutledge O'Neill 29.5.1882 Queanbeyan (son of James Coach Driver and Mary Ann Affleck) Mail Driver of Queanbeyan—11.3.1944 Queanbeyan
at Christ Church Anglican Queanbeyan on 19.7.1905. Witnesses L. R. Poole and Grace S Meech, Minister H N White. Both buried Anglican Riverside Queanbeyan.

Richard Alfred 11.6.1887 Queanbeyan—7.8.1915 killed in action Lone Pine Gallipoli.

Grace Susan 23.11.1888 Queanbeyan—3.10.1954 Queanbeyan. Buried in the family plot at Anglican Riverside Queanbeyan.

Enid Caroline ('Pop') 4.1.1889 Queanbeyan Couturier of Paddington—3.4.1949 Lidcombe m John Stoker Clasper ?.4.1883 Stockton-on-Tees Durham England Boiler Maker of Lidcombe – 15.8.1956 Lidcombe

at Christ Church Anglican Queanbeyan on 4.11.1922. Witnesses Thomas Rutledge O'Neill and Isaac Meech junior. Enid cremated Rookwood Cemetery.

Louisa Jane 21.12.1891 Queanbeyan Dentist Assistant of Queanbeyan—9.1.1973 Queanbeyan m Edgar John William Thomas Blyton 26.11.1886 Ararat near Nimmitabel (son of George Contractor and Catherine March) Labourer of Queanbeyan—10.4.1957 Queanbeyan

at Christ Church Anglican Queanbeyan on 23.10.1913. Witnesses Charles Sagacio junior and Carrie Sagacio, Minister Gordon H Hirst. Both buried Anglican Riverside Queanbeyan.

Violet Elsie 21.4.1893 Queanbeyan Home Duties of Queanbeyan—10.5.1976 Queanbeyan m Frederick Henry Rottenberry 8.2.1886 Canberra, (son of George Henry and Eliza Jane Kaye), Taxi Driver of Queanbeyan—21.6.1960 Queanbeyan

at Christ Church Anglican Queanbeyan on 21.1.1931. Witnesses Claude Rottenberry and Jessie Wark. Fred buried Anglican Riverside Queanbeyan; Violet at Tharwa Road Lawn Cemetery Queanbeyan.

Isaac ('Ike') **Arnold** 21.8.1895 Queanbeyan, Shop Assistant of Queanbeyan—17.7.1964 Wagga Wagga m Charlotte Lilian (Lottie) Warren 3.12.1894 Orange (daughter of William Railway Employee and Frances Elizabeth Herbert) Domestic Duties of Queanbeyan—23.8.1984 Sydney

at Christ Church Anglican Queanbeyan on 26.8.1916. Witnesses Thomas R. O'Neill and Jessie Meech, Minister Gordon H Hirst. Ike buried Wagga Wagga Cemetery.

Jessie Elma 25.7.1897 Queanbeyan Waitress of Paddington—15.2.1983 Queanbeyan

m William Wark 2.3.1885 Molonglo (son of William and Elizabeth Beaumont/Bowman) Labourer of Newtown—30.3.1956 Queanbeyan

at St George's Anglican Paddington on 24.4.1920. Witnesses Violet Meech and Charles Victor Southwell. Both buried Anglican Riverside Queanbeyan.

Freda Roseline 9.4.1901 Queanbeyan—24.12.1902 Queanbeyan. Buried in the family plot at Anglican Riverside Queanbeyan.

CATHERINE ('KATE') 18.12.1859 Canberra spinster of Canberra—25.5.1950 Queanbeyan

m William Melville 25.10.1853 Smeaton Victoria (son of George farmer and Sibilla Ross) farmer of Canberra—6.12.1941 Canberra

at St John's Anglican Canberra on 25.9.1895. Witnesses William Henry Moore and Margaret Jane Young, Minister Pierce Galliard Smith. Both buried Anglican Riverside Queanbeyan.

Bertram Victor Blundell 25.12.1886 Canberra(illegitimate)—20.9.1959 Queanbeyan. Buried with his Uncle Richard in Anglican Tharwa Road Cemetery Queanbeyan.

Susan Sibella 4.3.1896 Canberra—19.2.1988 Nowra

m Rupert 'Harry' Bedford 20.3.1887 Randwick—10.6.1953 Revesby

at the ... Presbyterian Kogarah on 4.10.1924.

George William 15.9.1897 Canberra, labourer of Canberra—2.6.1974

m Elsie Sophia Rankin 18.5.1906 Sutton (daughter of Robert Francis Whittaker and Caroline Gamble)—14.11.1975 Canberra

at Christ Church Anglican Queanbeyan on 23.3.1940.

Laura 8.11.1898 Canberra—.2.1969 Katoomba. Buried Katoomba Anglican Cemetery.

Stanley 24.7.1900 Canberra labourer of Queanbeyan—22.11.1975 Canberra m Katie Shannon 14.4.1900 Condor Creek, Uriarra (daughter of Samuel and Maria/Martha Southwell) domestic duties of Queanbeyan—7.10.1987 Queanbeyan at Christ Church Anglican Queanbeyan on 16.4.1927. Witnesses A R Gregory, S Shannon, May Shannon; Minister Stanley Johnson West. Both buried Tharwa Road Lawn Cemetery Queanbeyan.

Reuben Robert 20.10.1901 Queanbeyan—17.9.1957 Royal Canberra. Buried with his parents at Anglican Riverside Queanbeyan.

Hilda May 13.1.1903 Canberra—4.7.1926 Queanbeyan. Buried Anglican Riverside Queanbeyan.

www.ingramcontent.com/pod-product-compliance
Lightning Source LLC
Chambersburg PA
CBHW060042100426
42742CB00014B/2673